THE VAULT EDITIONS GUIDE TO
MASTERING
THE ART OF
DRAWING

HOW TO DRAW FLOWERS

A HELPFUL MANUAL FOR ARTISTS AND DESIGNERS

STEP BY STEP

HAND DRAWN
UNIQUE **40** DESIGNS
BEST QUALITY

EDITIONS
Vault

INTRODUCTION

Flowers have always captivated artists and admirers alike, offering endless inspiration through their vibrant forms and deep symbolism. Whether you're new to drawing or looking to explore the nuances of botanical art, *How to Draw Flowers: A Step-By-Step Guide to Drawing Botanical Art for Beginners* is crafted to guide you through creating beautiful floral illustrations. This book is accessible to all skill levels, providing a straightforward, structured approach to mastering the details of each bloom.

With this guide, you'll uncover the unique meanings that have made flowers iconic in art and culture, from roses symbolising love to lilies representing purity. Each of the 40 flowers featured has been chosen for its distinctive form and history, and the book's step-by-step instructions ensure that you learn to draw each flower and appreciate its unique character.

Whether you aim to improve your drawing skills, create your own botanical illustrations, or simply connect with the elegance of nature's designs, How to Draw Flowers will be your creative companion. Embark on this journey to discover both the beauty and symbolism behind each flower as you build the skills to illustrate them with confidence and grace.

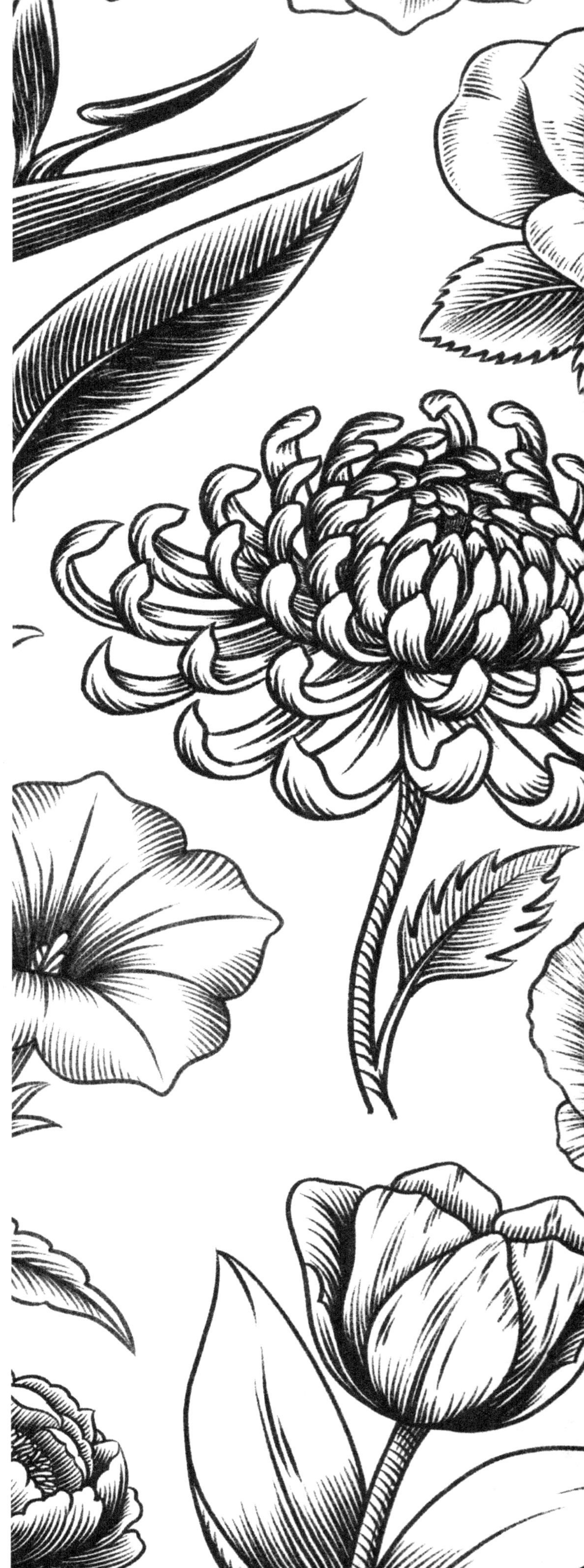

TABLE ◆OF◆ CONTENTS

DOWNLOAD YOUR FILES

Downloading your files is simple. To access your digital files, please go to the last page of this book and follow the instructions.

For technical assistance, please email: info@vaulteditions.com

Copyright
Copyright © Vault Editions Ltd 2024.

Bibliographical Note
This book is a new work created by Vault Editions Ltd.

ISBN: 978-1-922966-49-0

ANEMONE

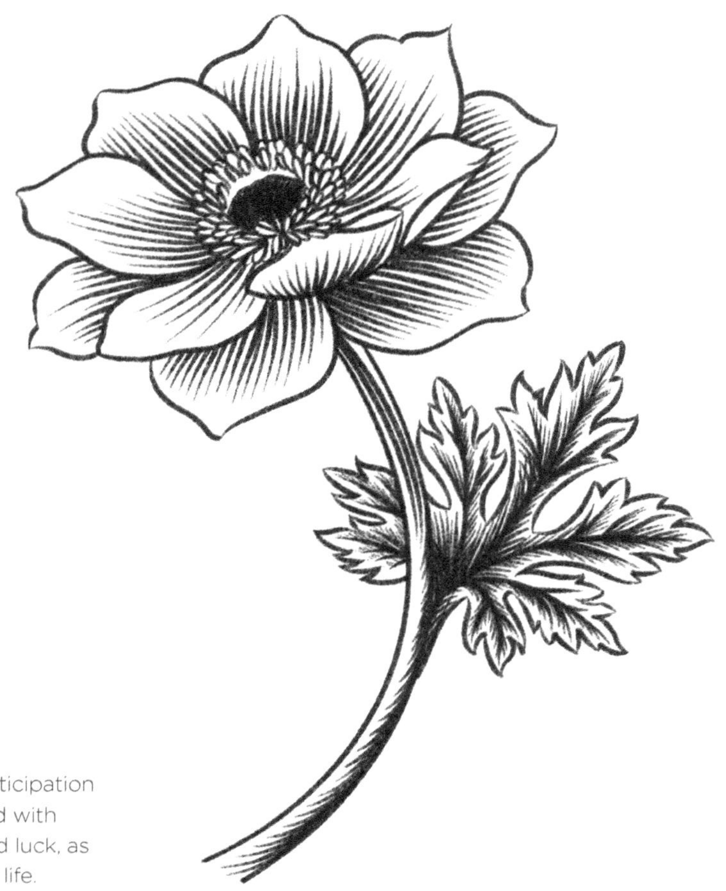

The anemone symbolises anticipation and fragility, often associated with protection against evil or bad luck, as well as the fleeting nature of life.

01

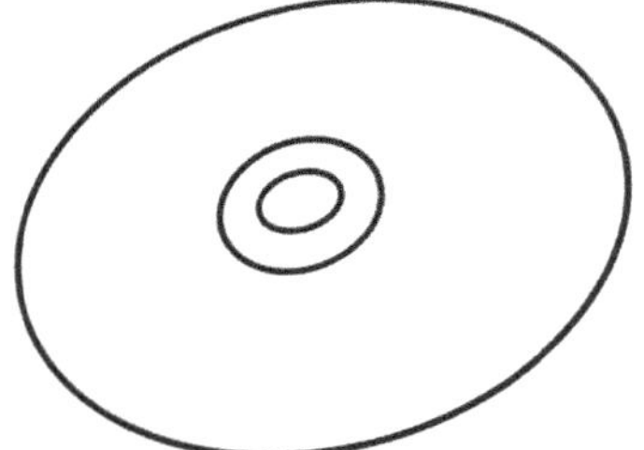

02

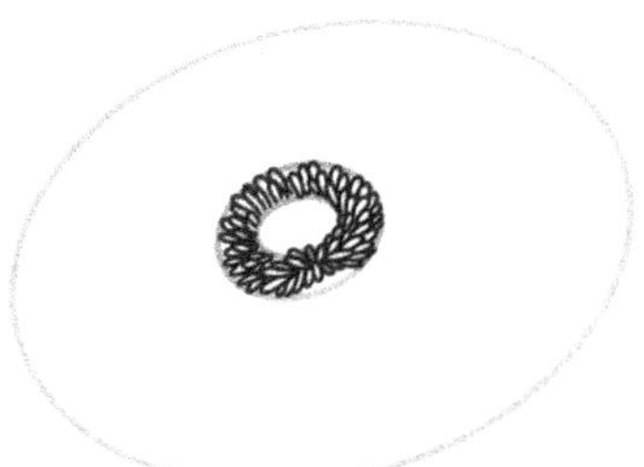

03

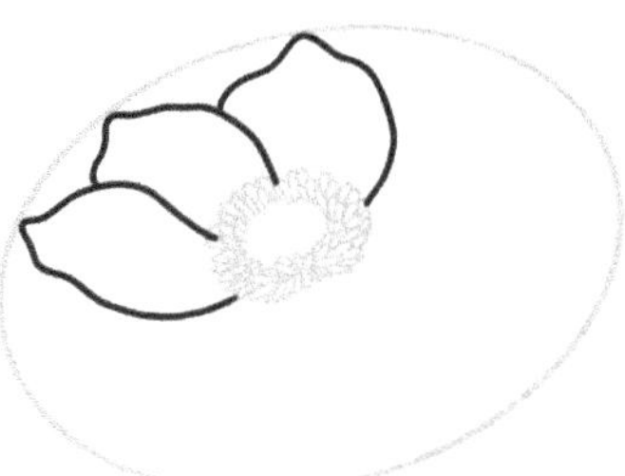

04

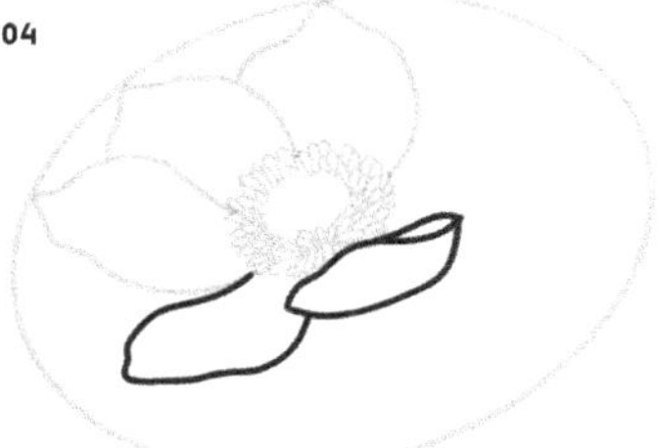

05

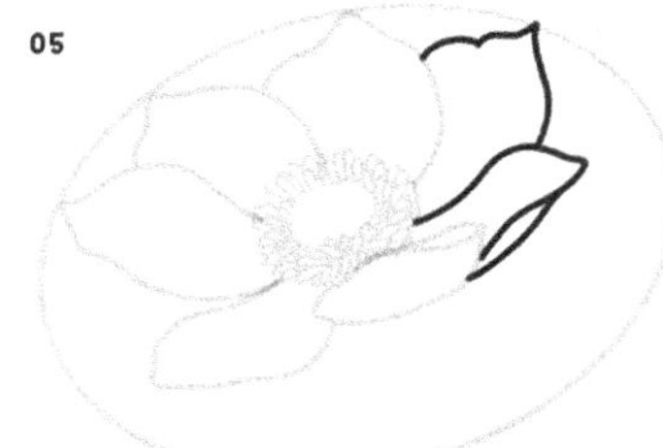

06

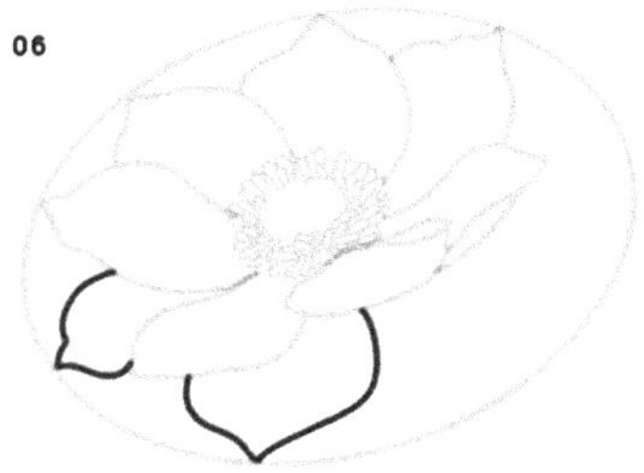

07

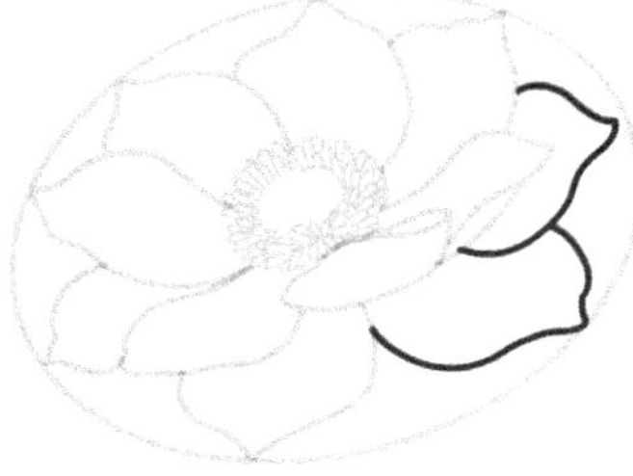

08

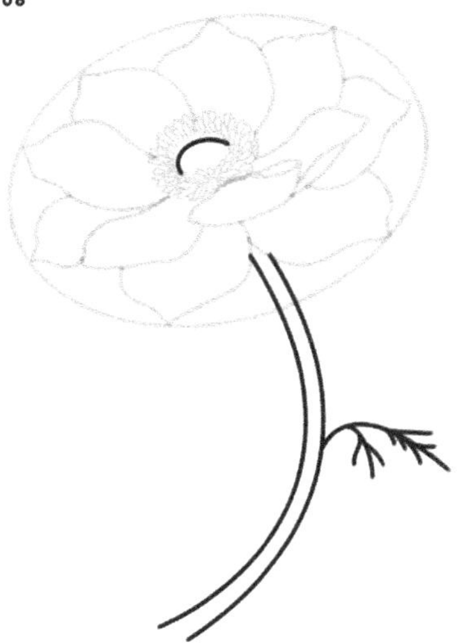

09

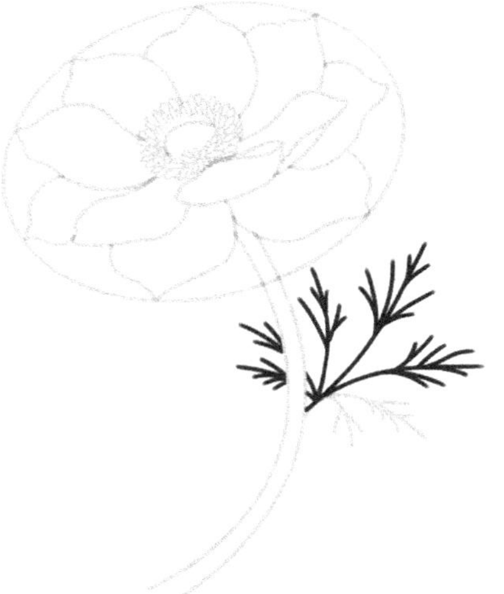

10

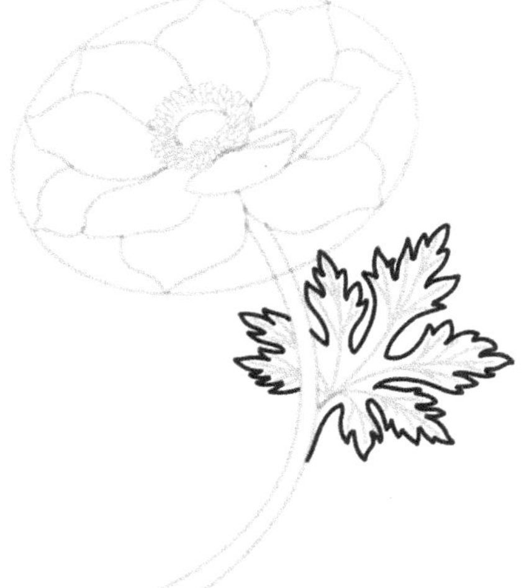

11

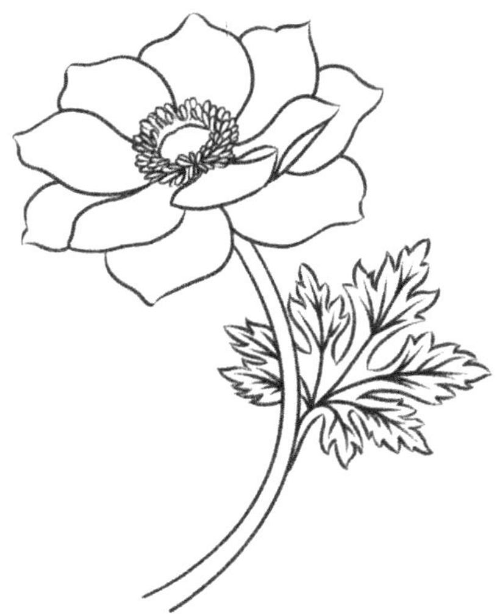

12

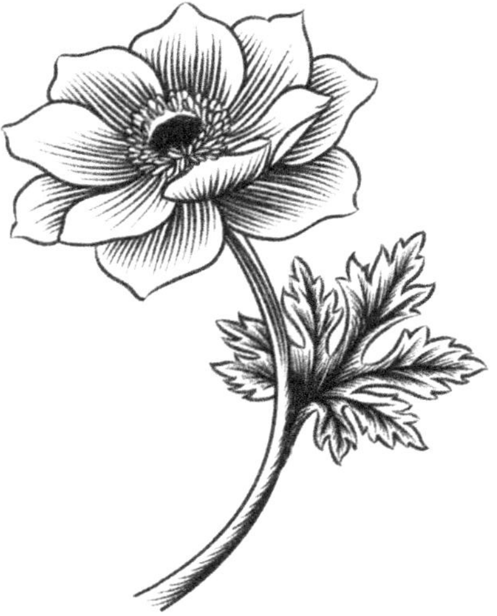

AZALEA

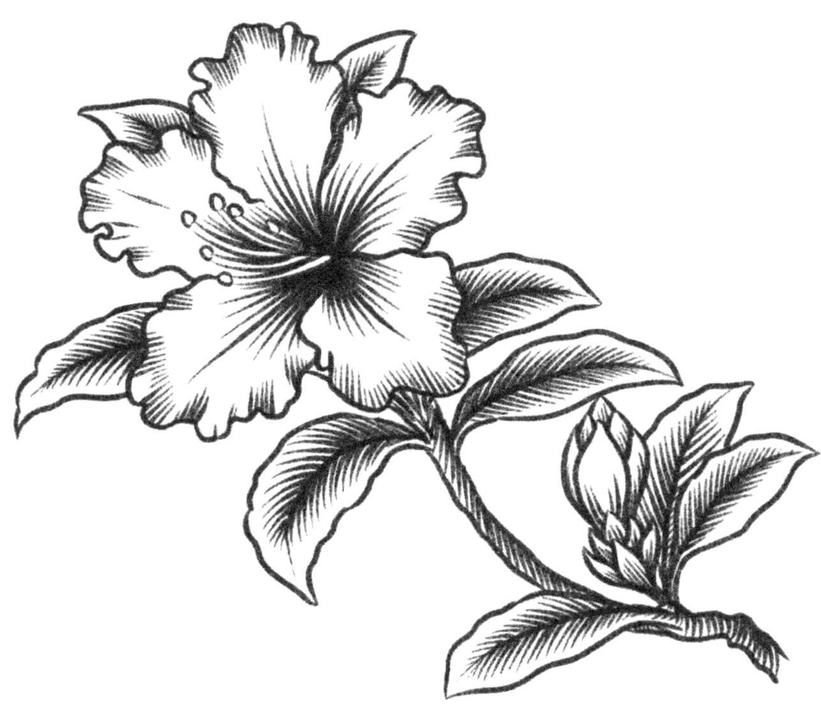

Azaleas symbolise temperance, femininity, and passion, often associated with beauty in fragile balance and sometimes with caution due to their toxicity.

01

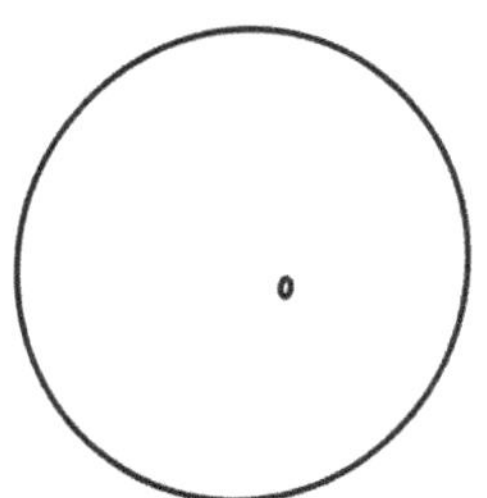

02

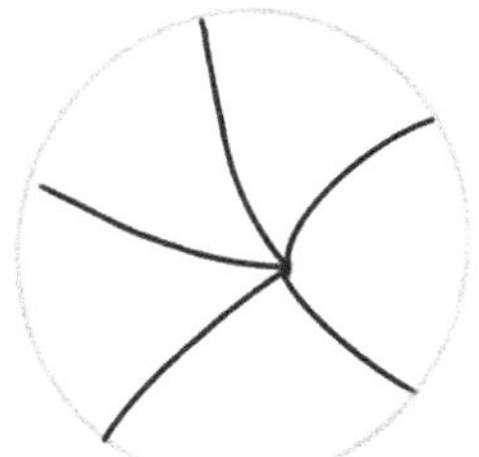

03

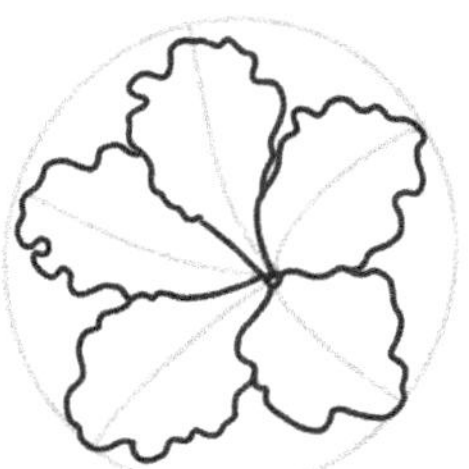

04

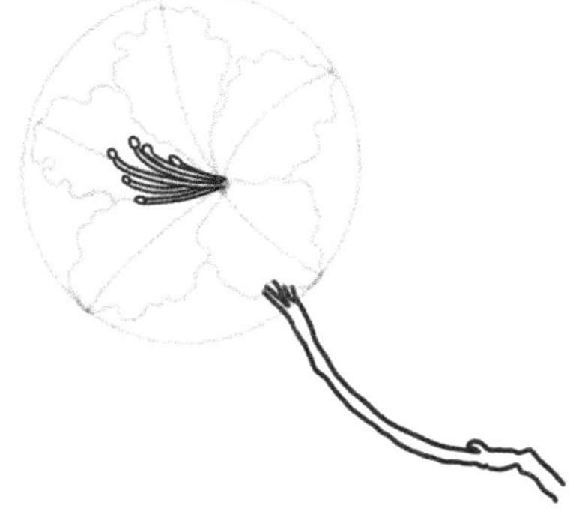

05

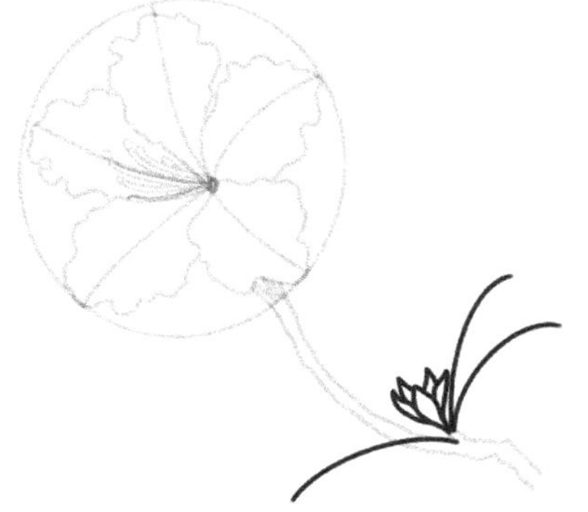

06

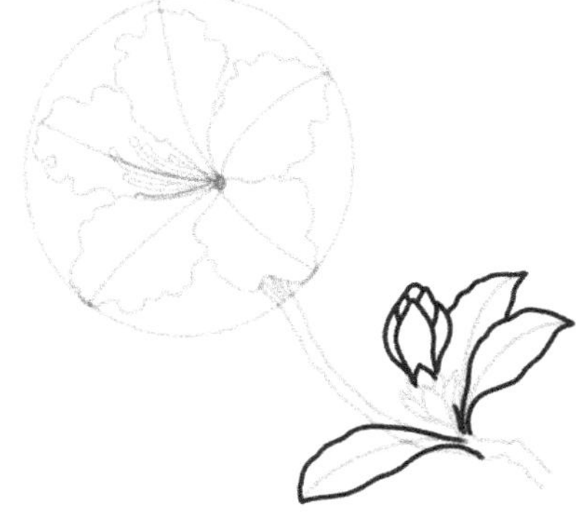

07

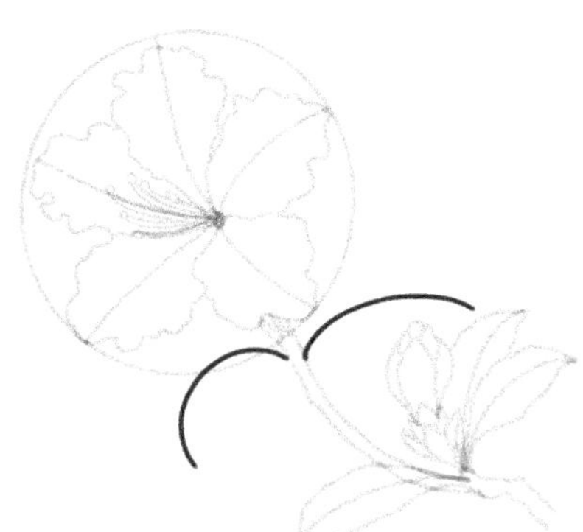

08

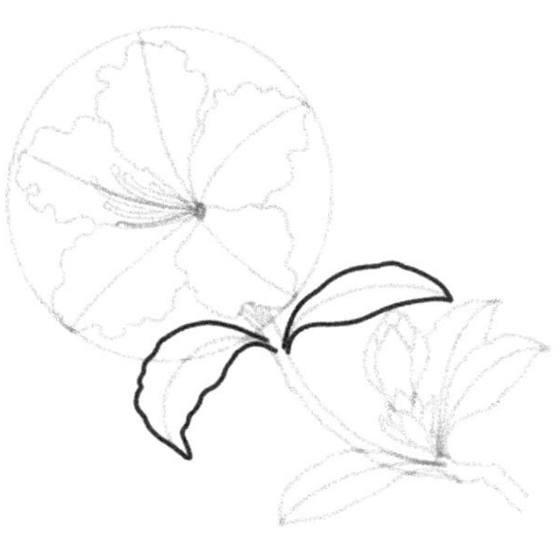

09

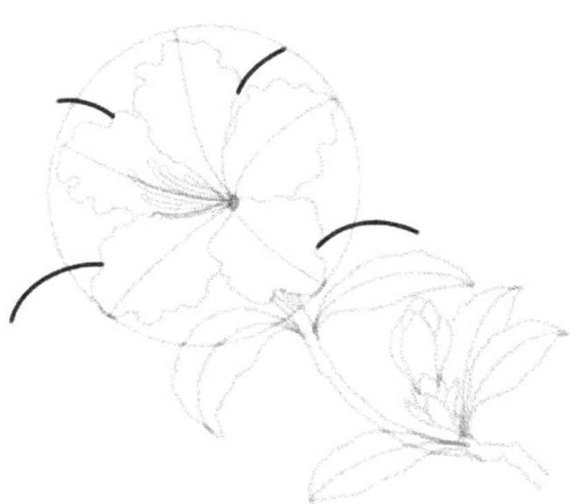

10

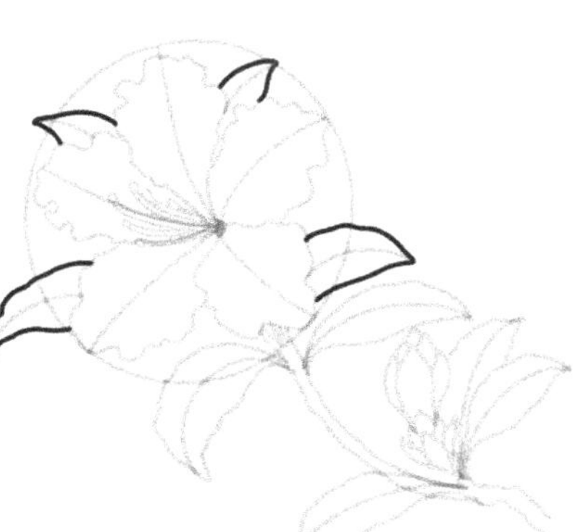

11

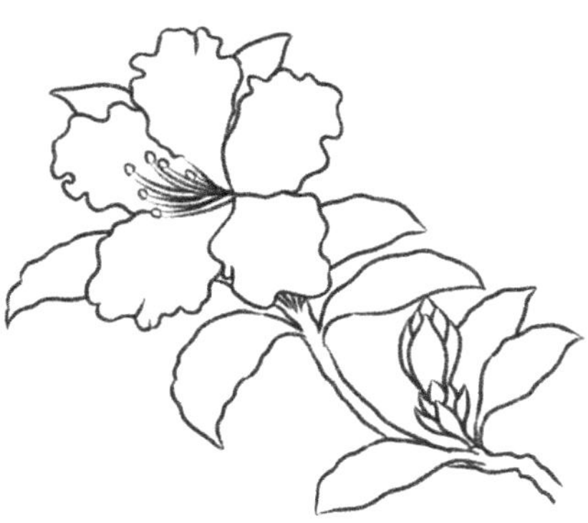

12

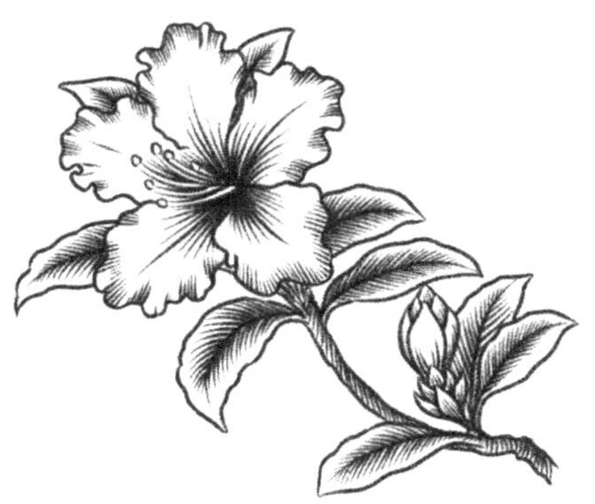

HOW TO DRAW FLOWERS

BEACH ROSE

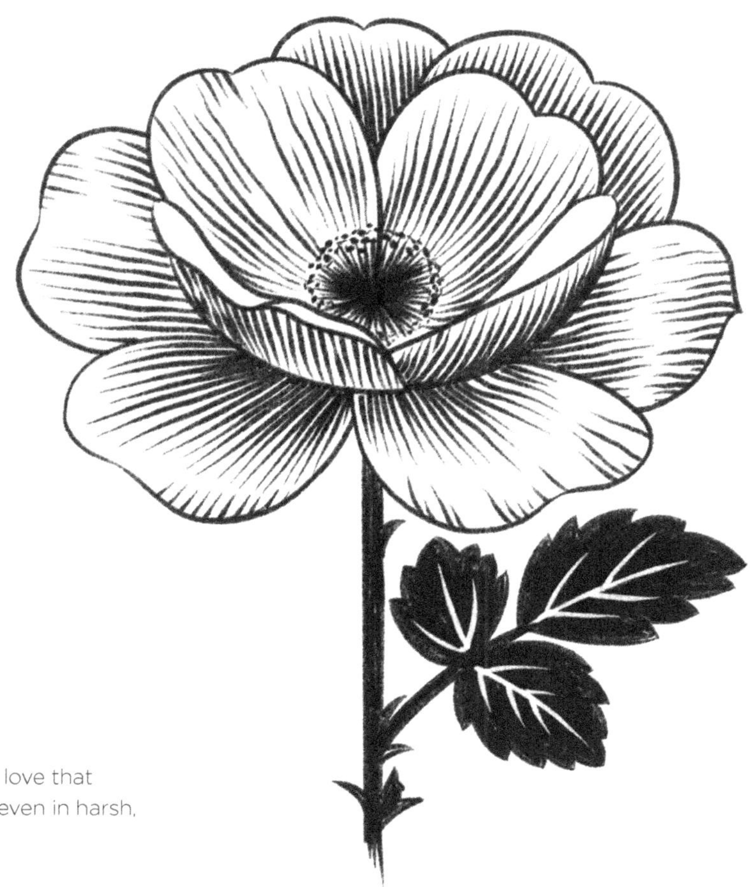

The beach rose represents love that endures hardship, thriving even in harsh, sandy coastal conditions.

01

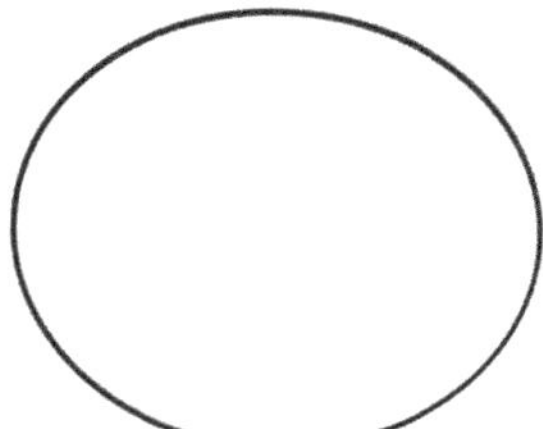

02

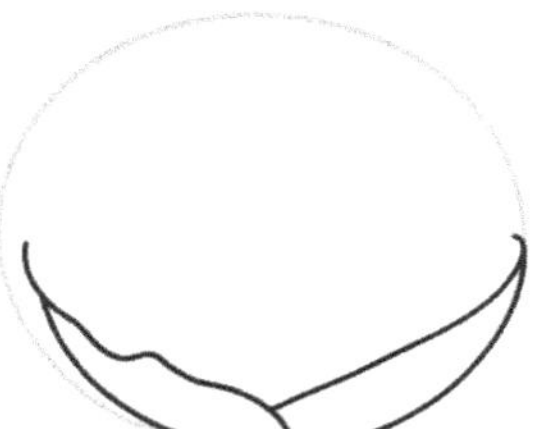

03

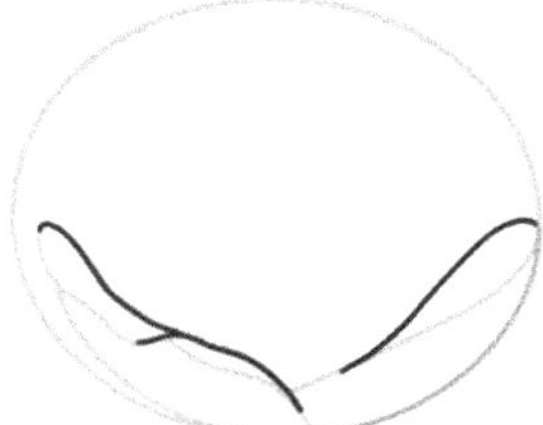

04

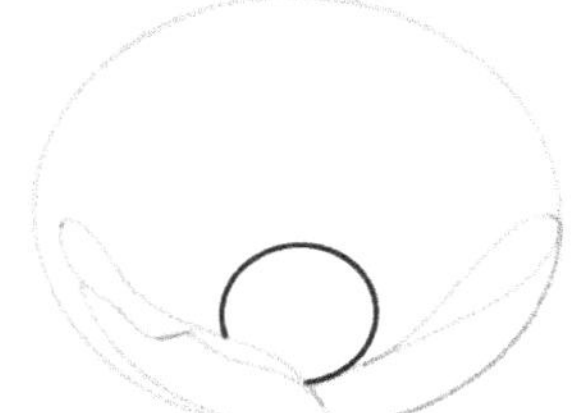

05

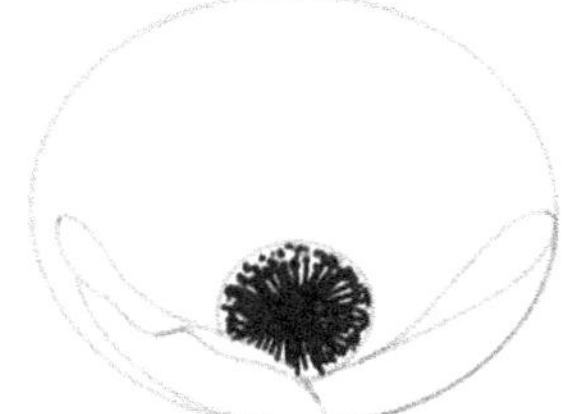

06

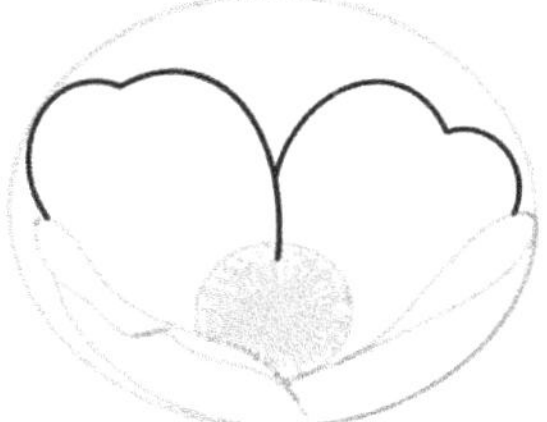

07

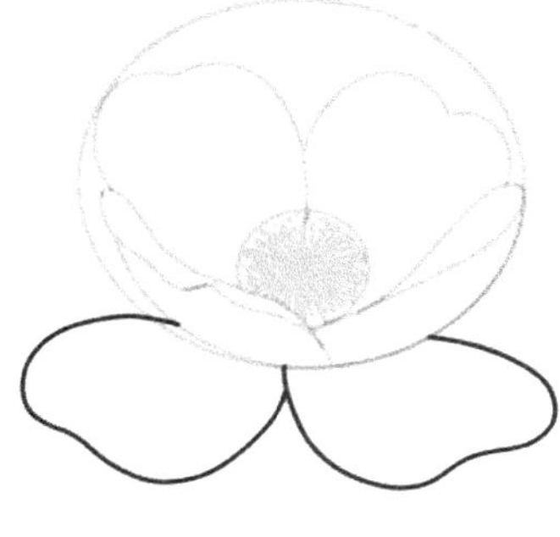

08

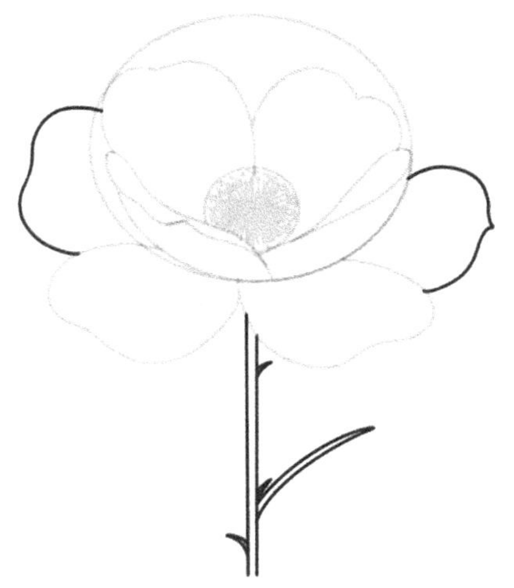

09

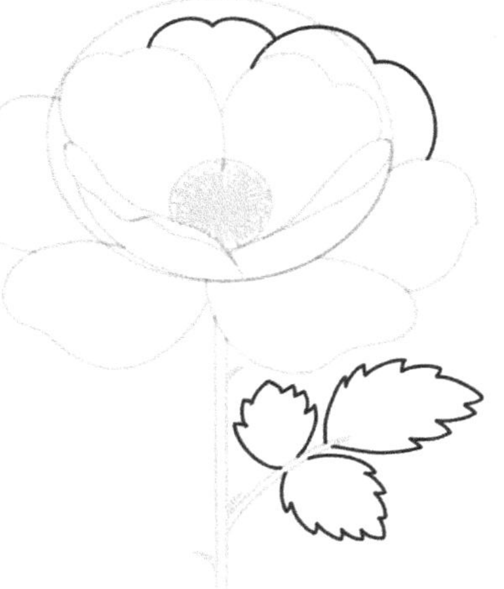

10

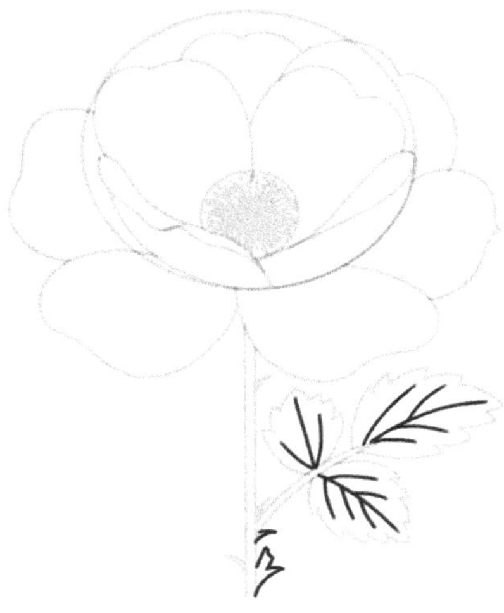

11

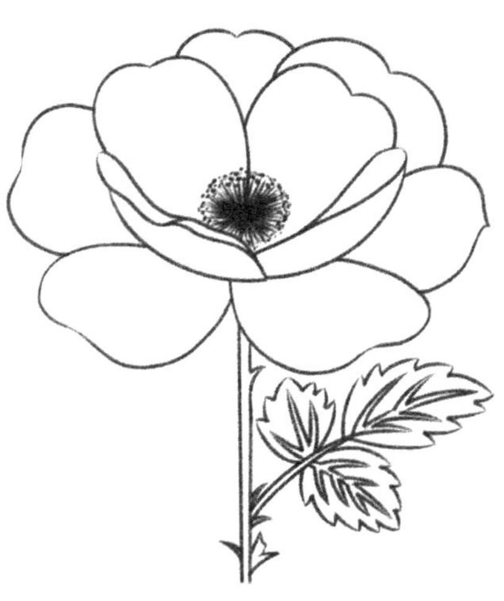

12

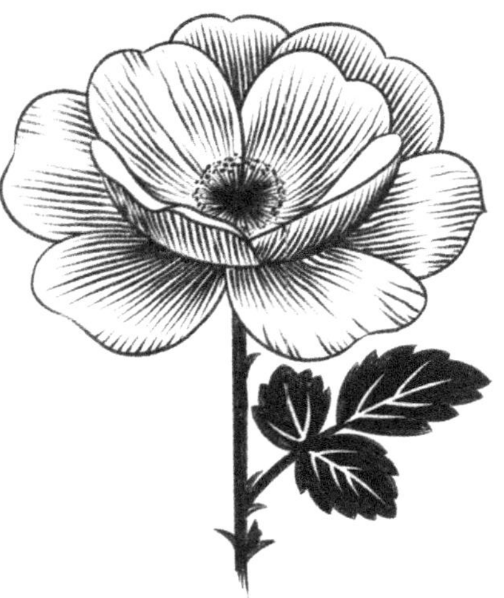

HOW TO DRAW FLOWERS

BEGONIA

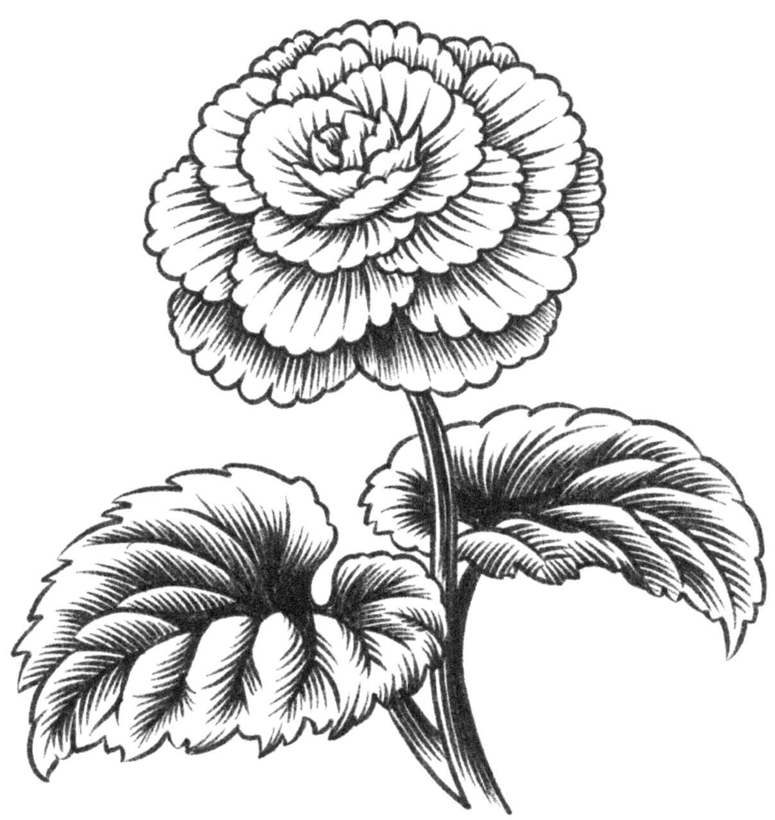

Begonias represent caution and introspection; they are associated with individuality and serve as a reminder to stay alert to hidden motives.

01

02

03

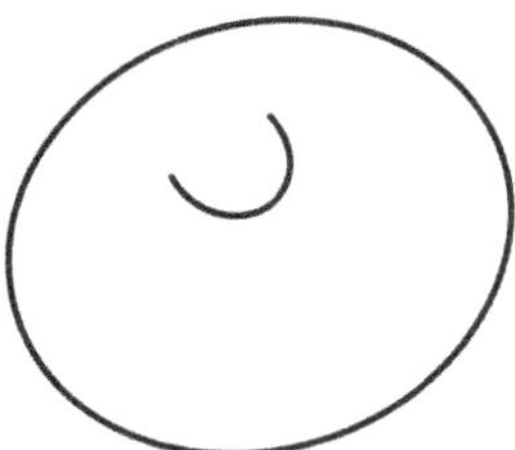

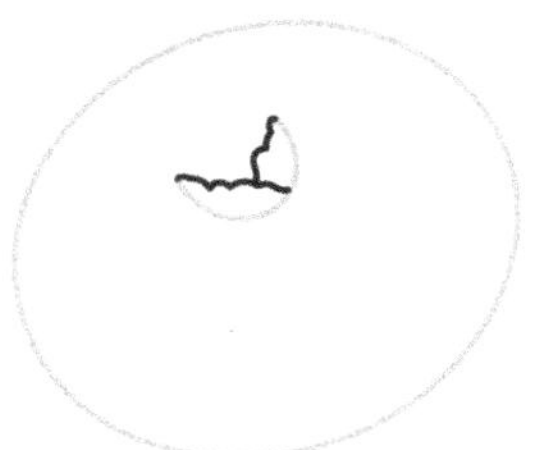

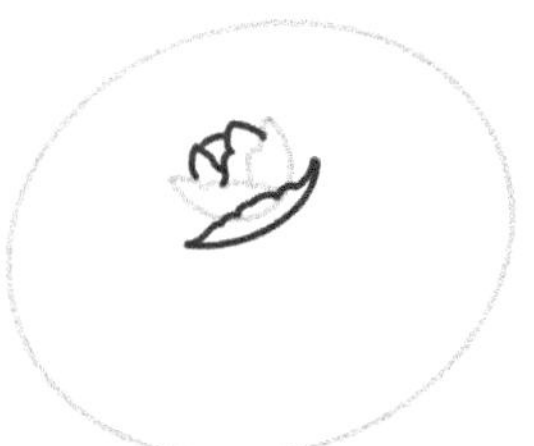

04

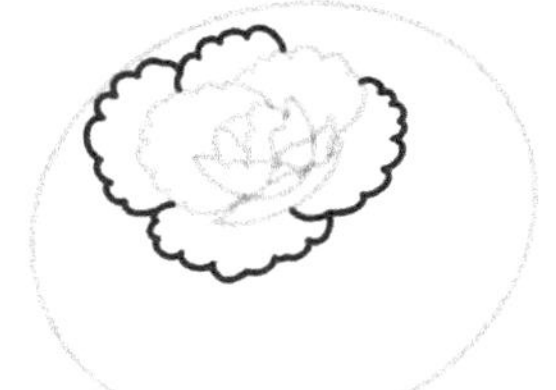

05

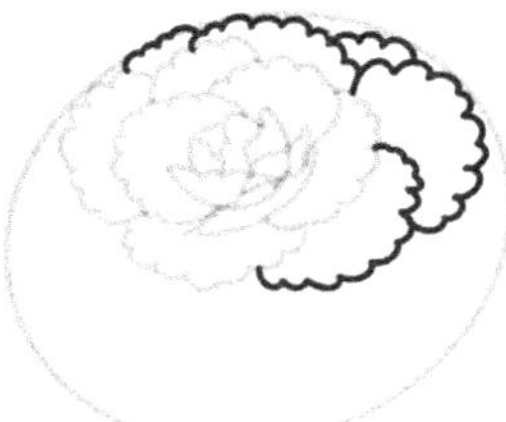

06

07

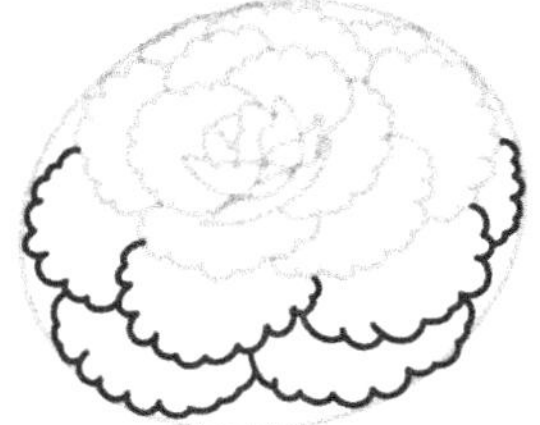

08

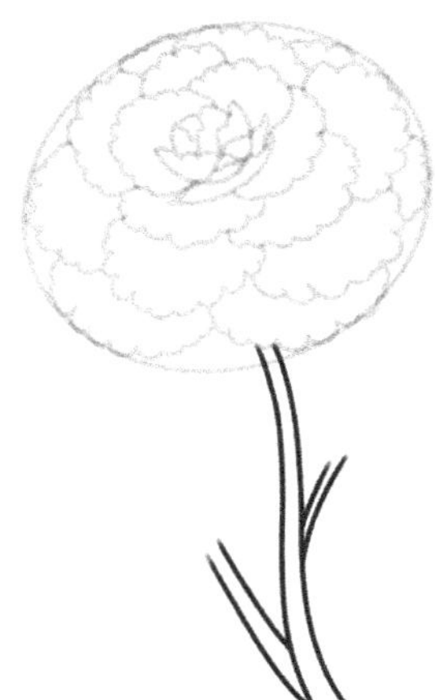

09

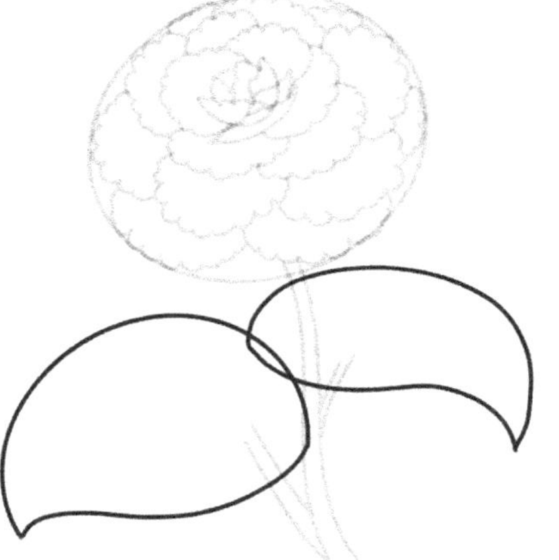

10

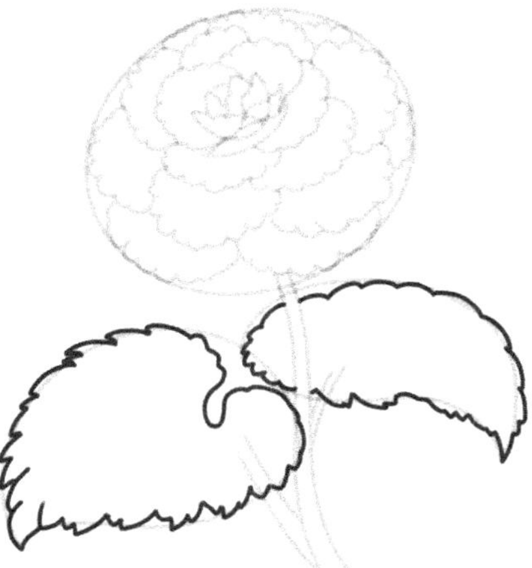

11

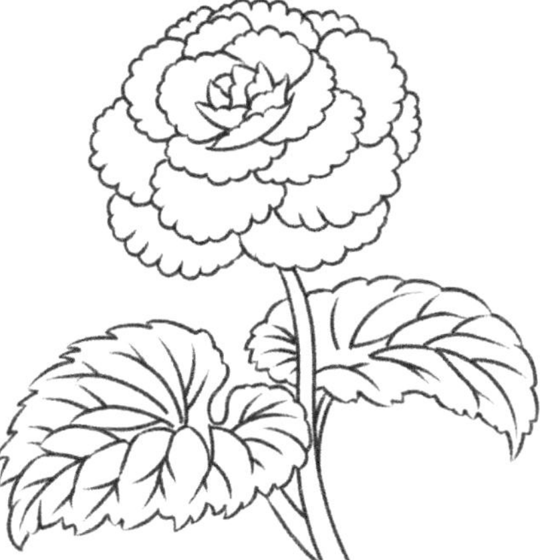

12

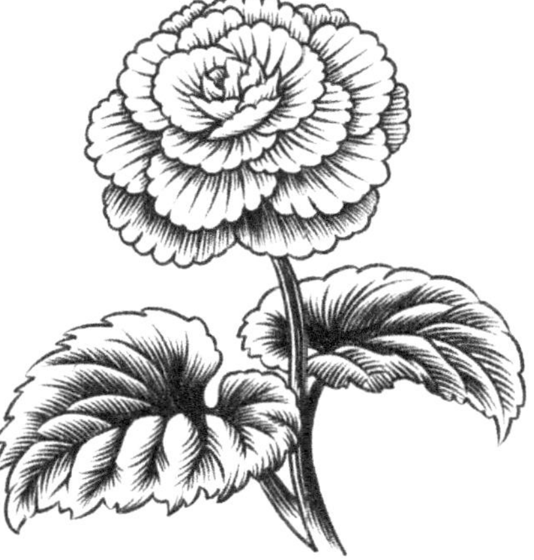

BIRD OF PARADISE

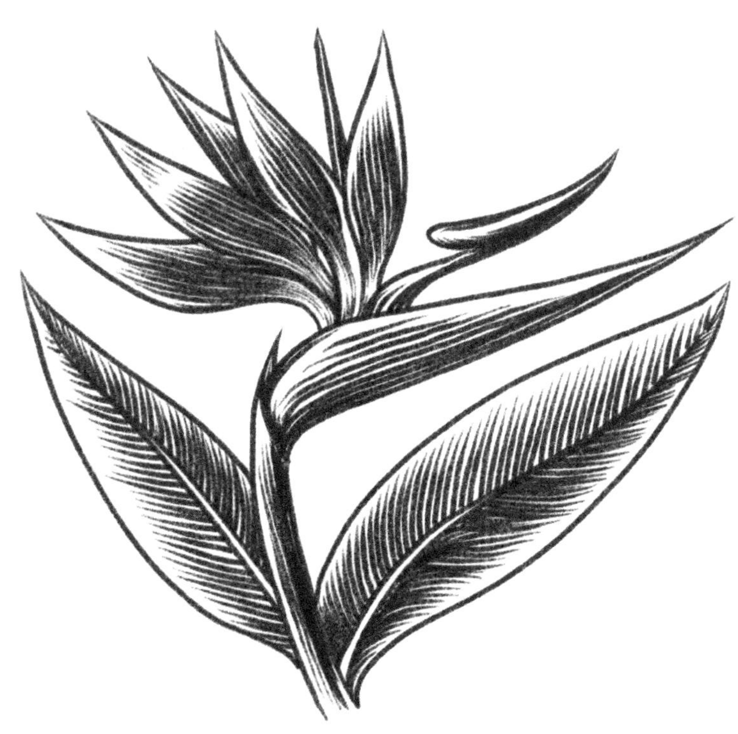

The Bird of Paradise represents joy, freedom, and paradise. It can symbolise exotic beauty and the anticipation of wonderful adventures or new beginnings.

01

02

03

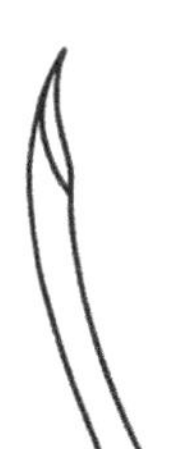

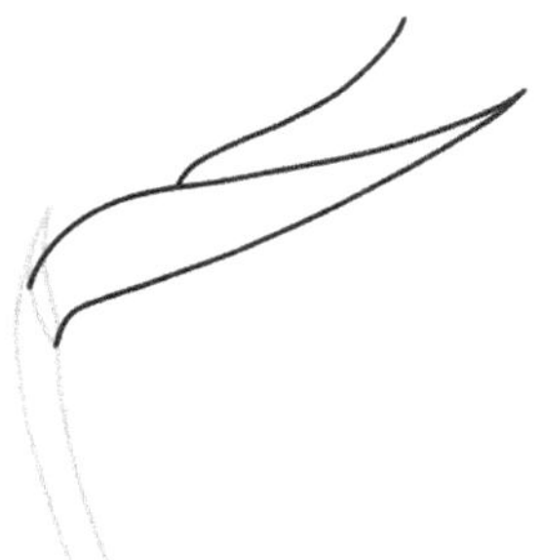

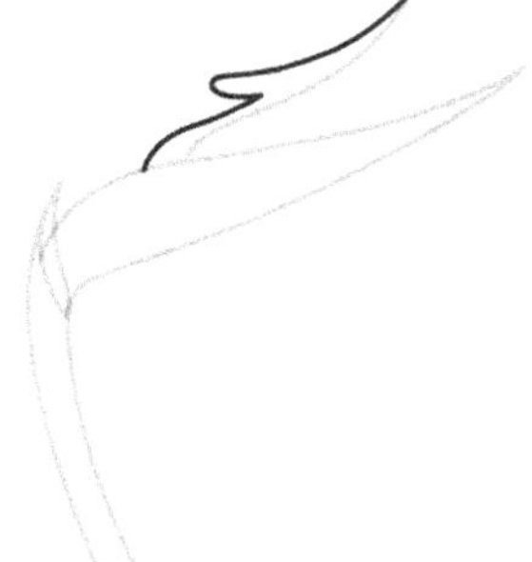

04

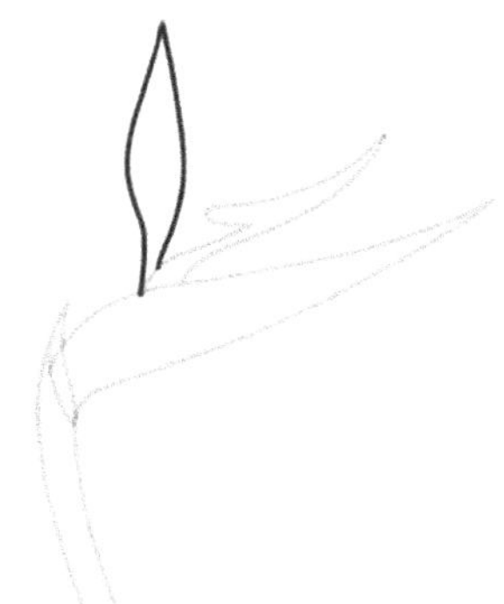

05

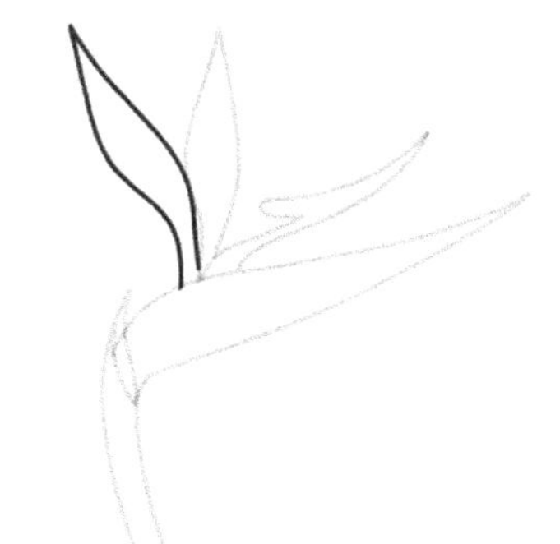

06

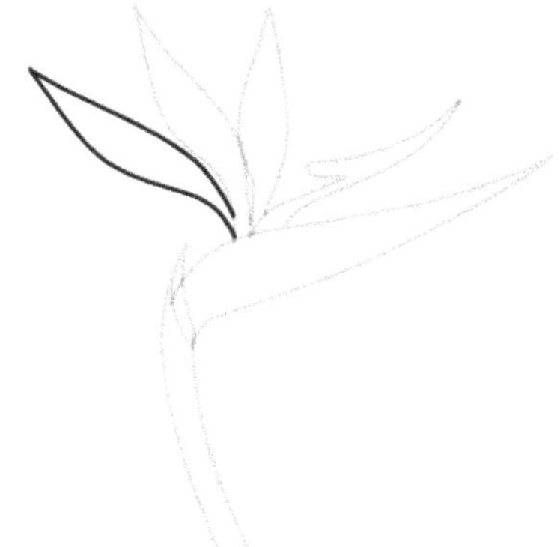

07

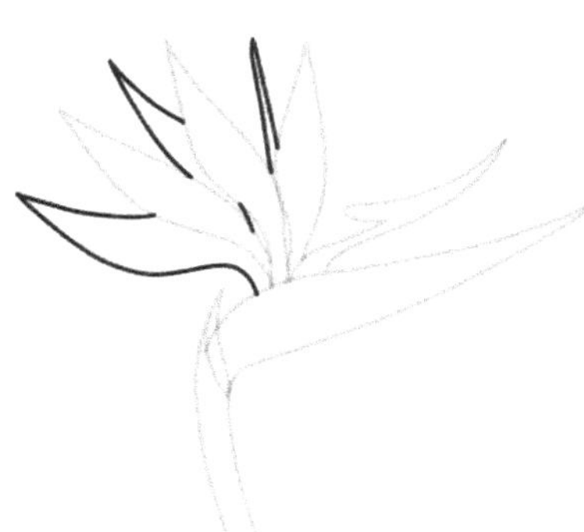

08

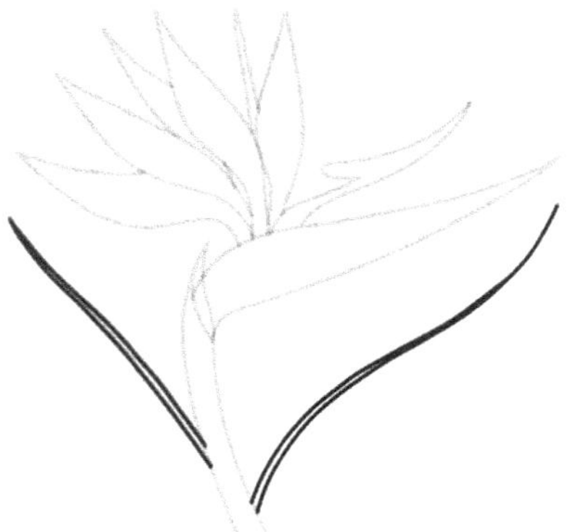

09

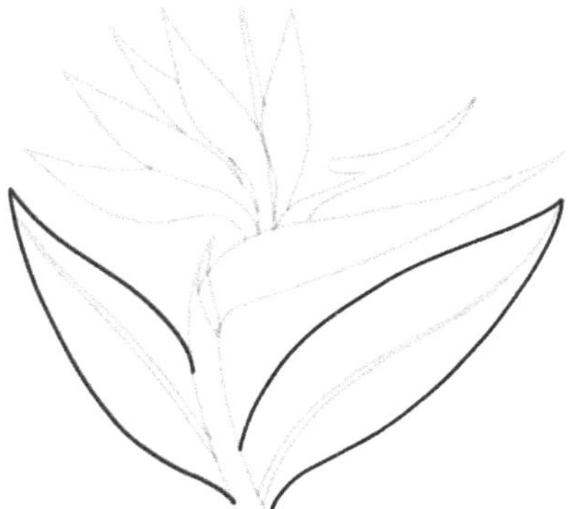

10

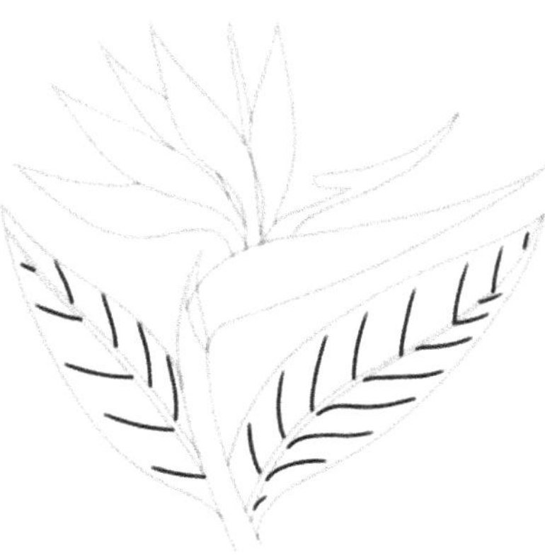

11

12

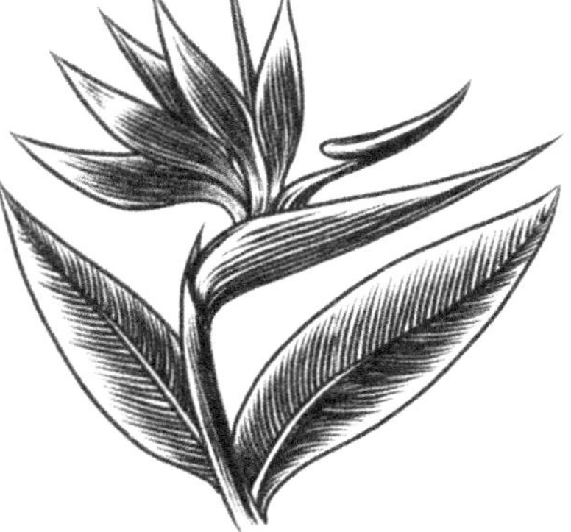

HOW TO DRAW FLOWERS

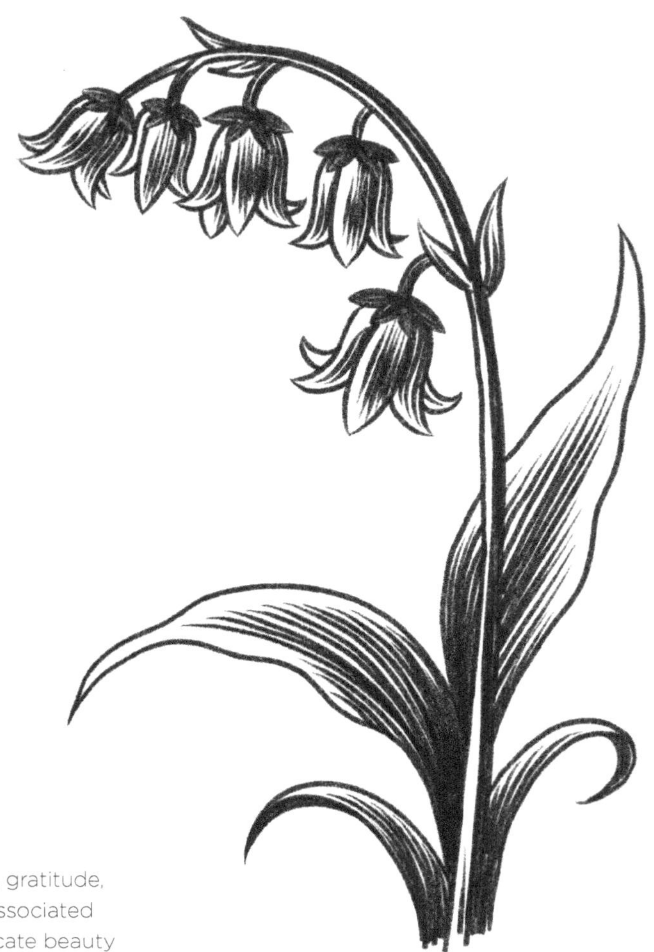

BLUEBELL

HOW TO DRAW FLOWERS

Bluebells symbolise humility, gratitude, and everlasting love, often associated with constancy and the delicate beauty found in nature's quiet moments.

01

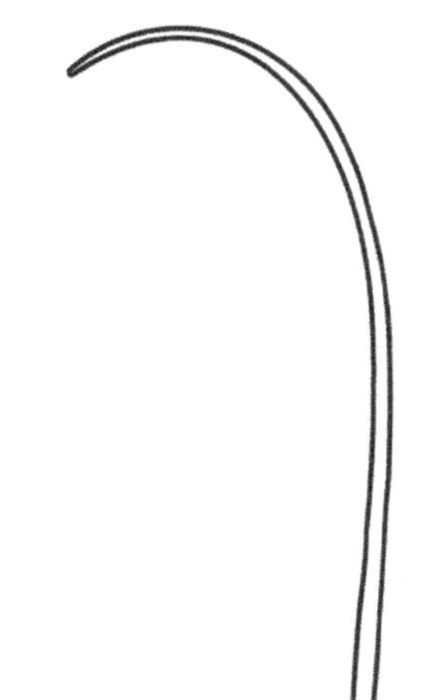

02

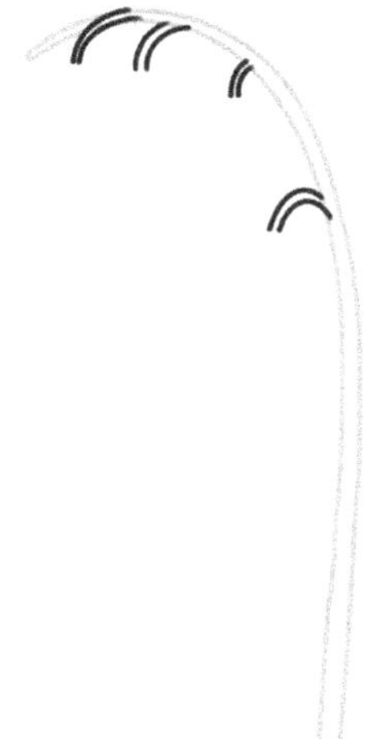

03

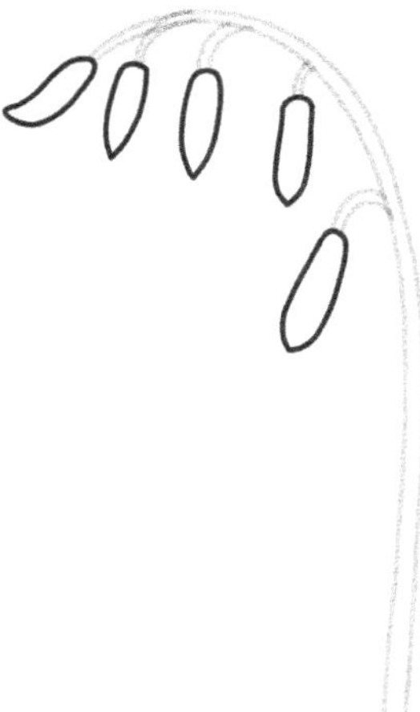

04

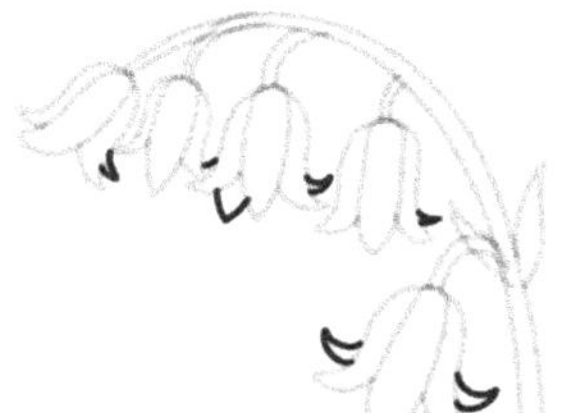

05

06

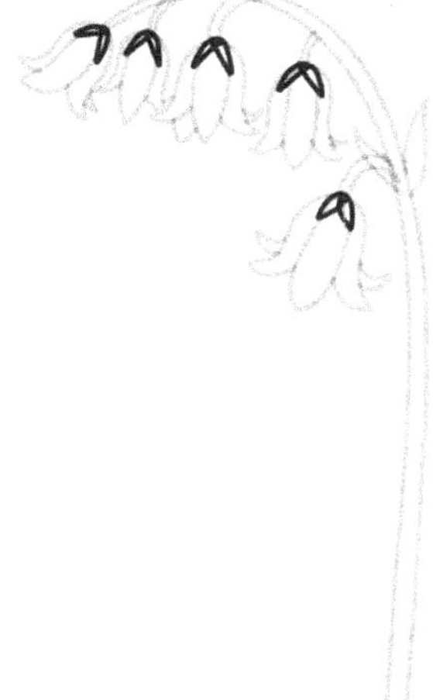

07

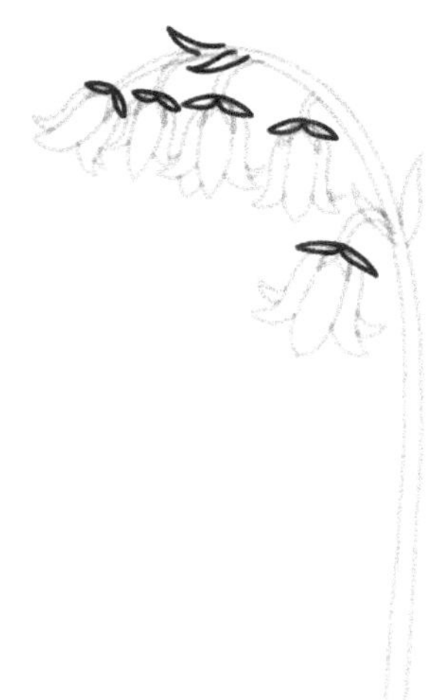

08

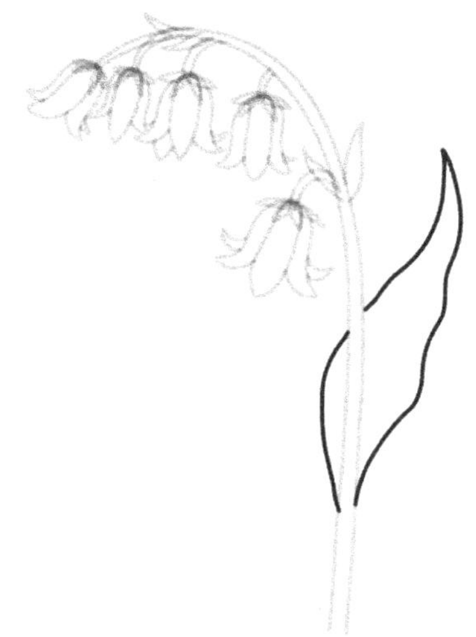

09

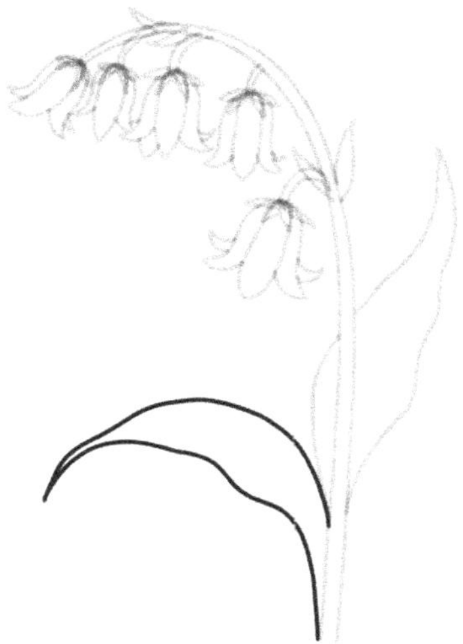

10

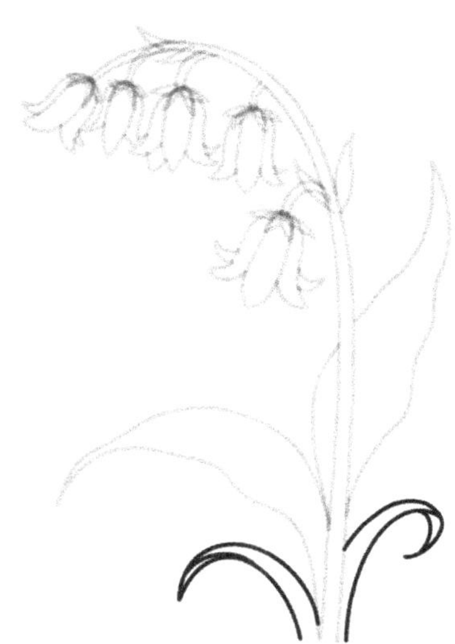

11

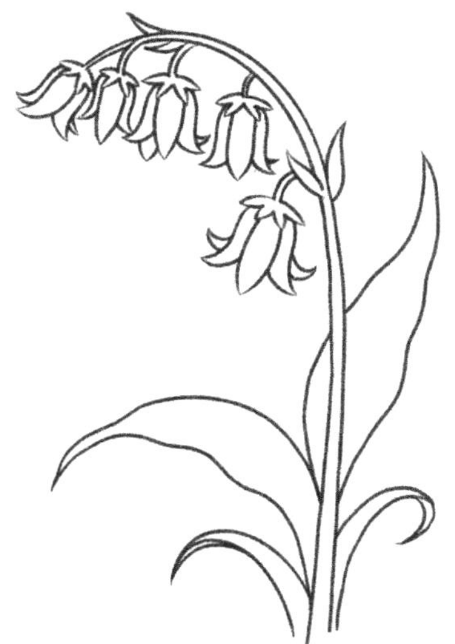

12

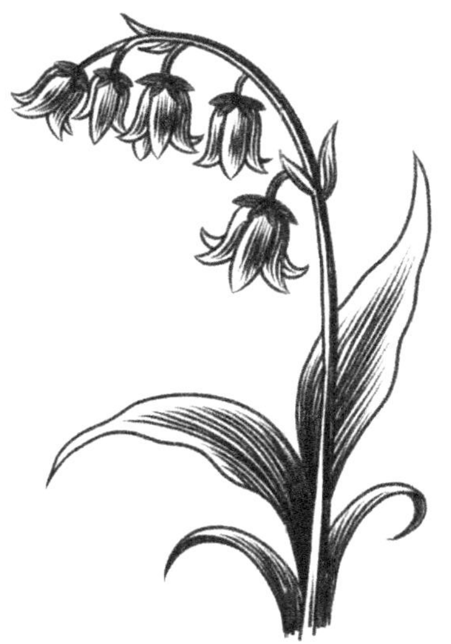

BUTTERCUP

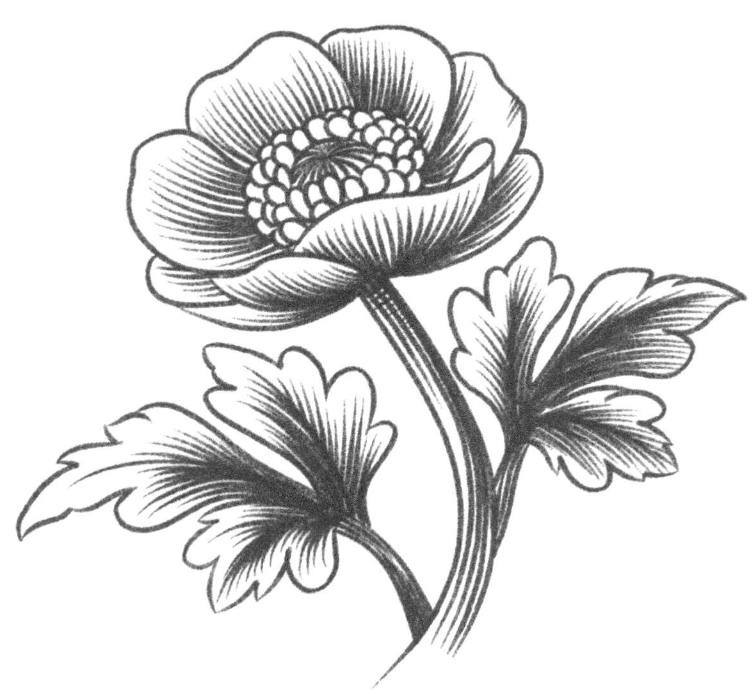

Buttercups represent cheerfulness and youthful joy, often symbolising innocence, playfulness, and the bright simplicity of childhood memories.

01

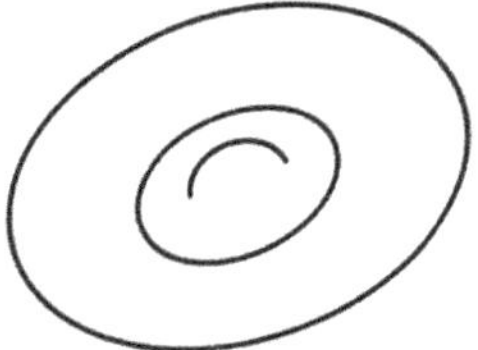

02

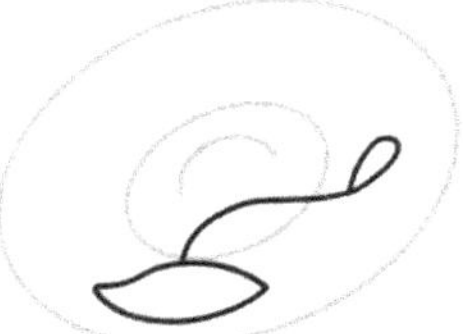

03

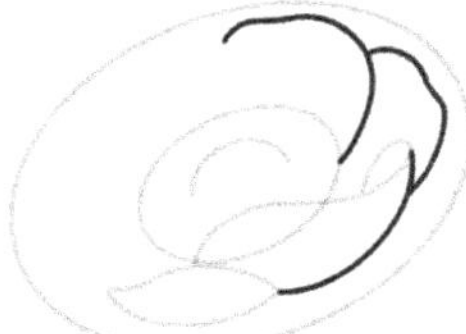

04

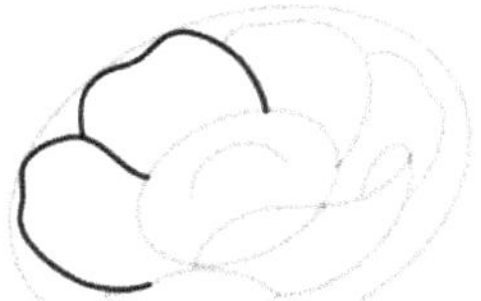

05

06

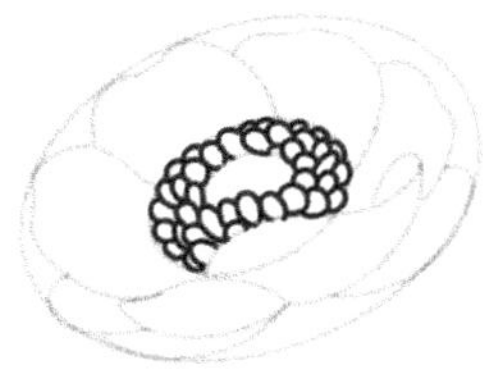

07

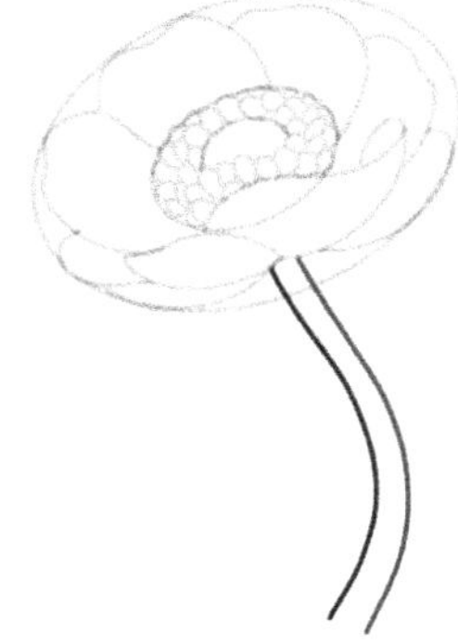

08

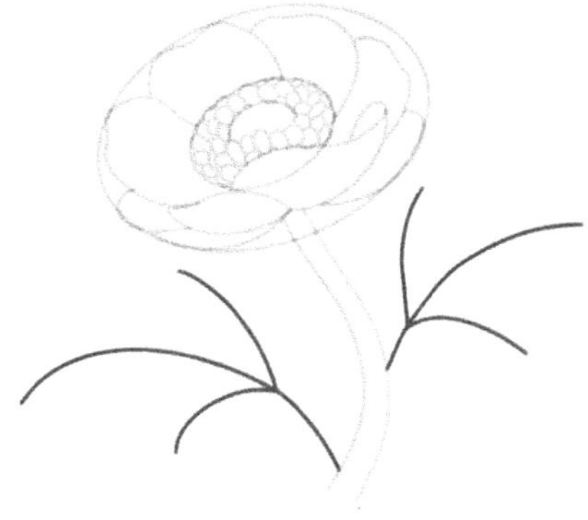

09

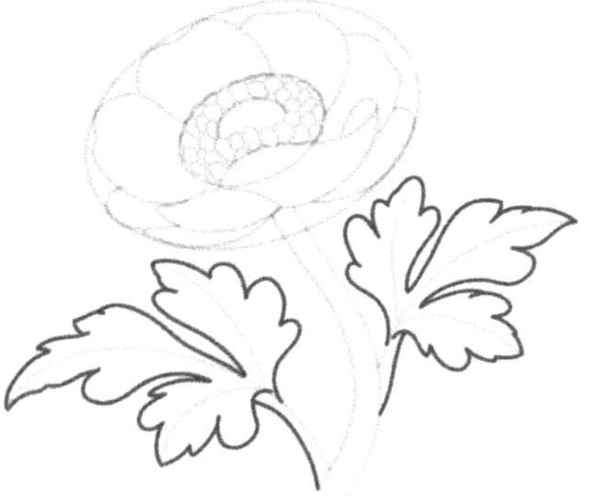

10

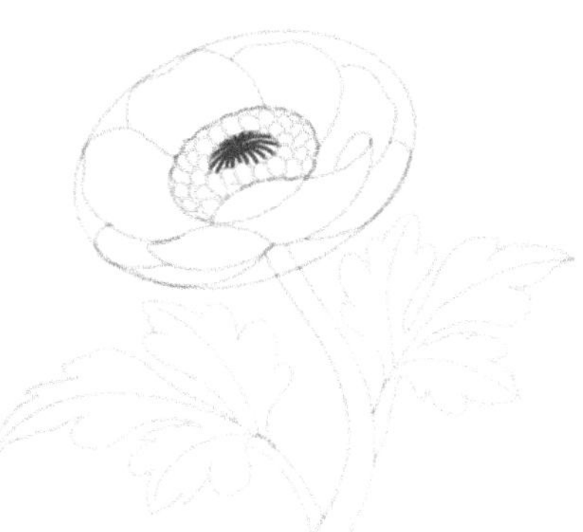

11

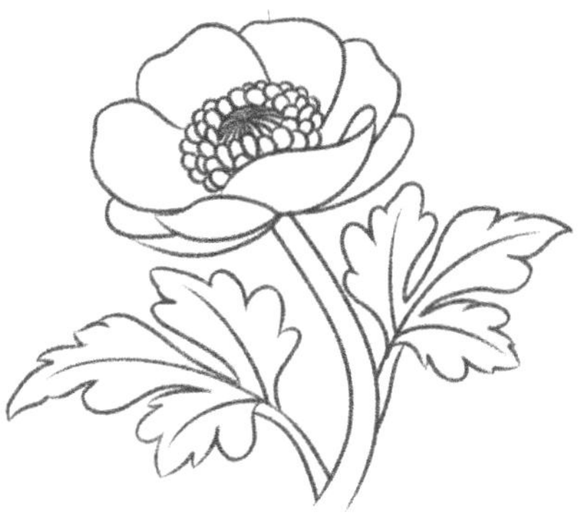

12

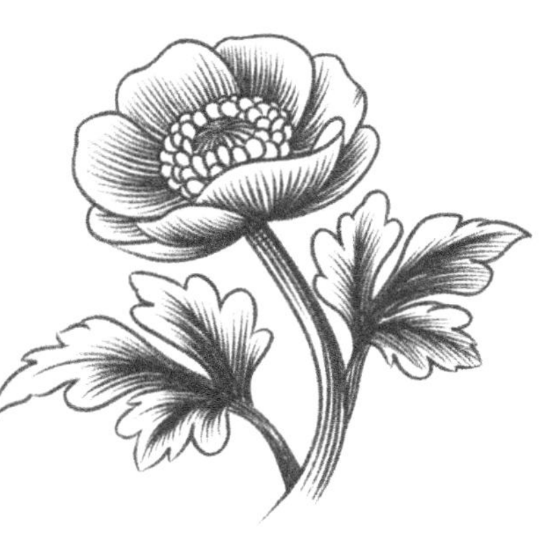

CAMELIA

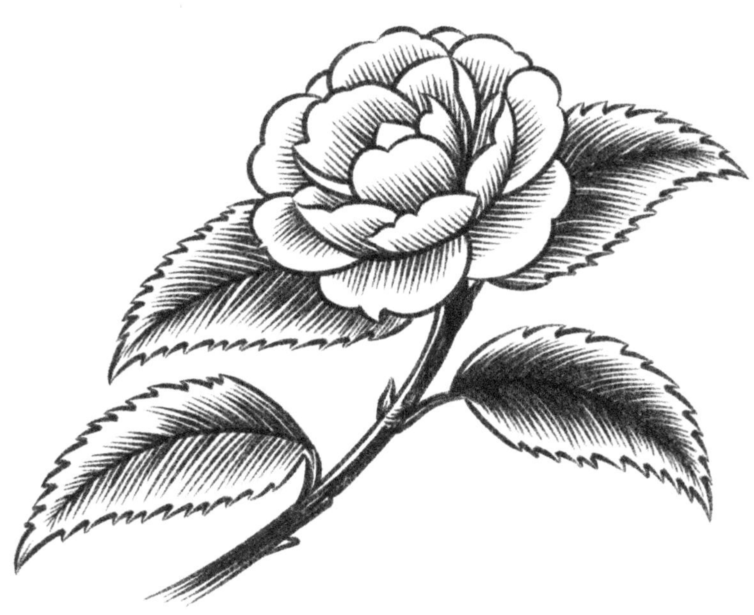

Camellias symbolise admiration, perfection, and refined beauty, often associated with deep longing and the steadfastness of love.

---

01   **02**   **03**

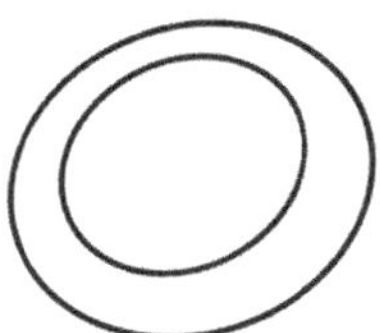
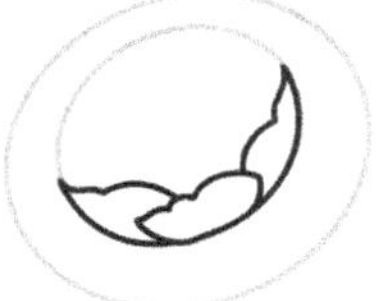
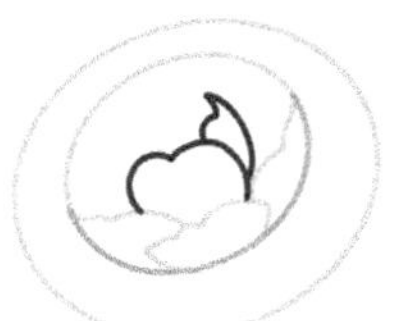

04

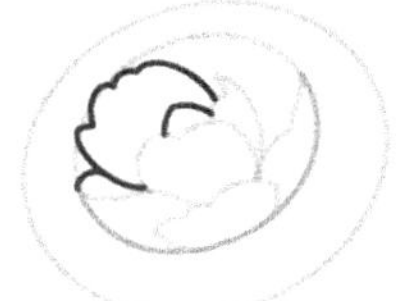

05

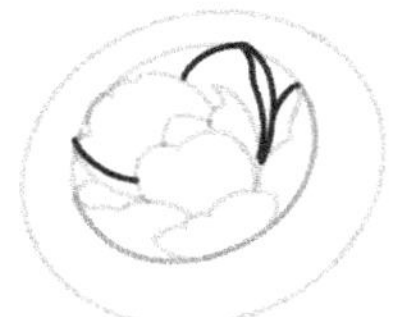

06

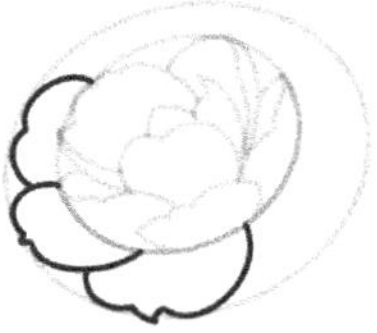

07

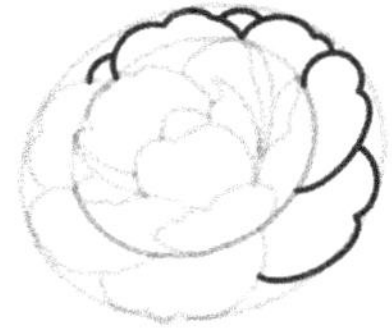

08

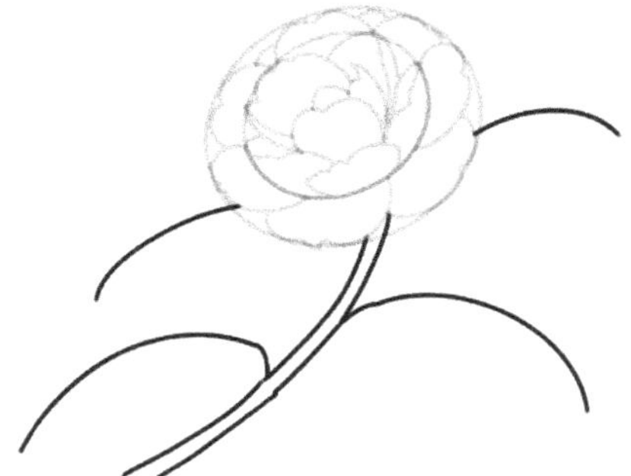

09

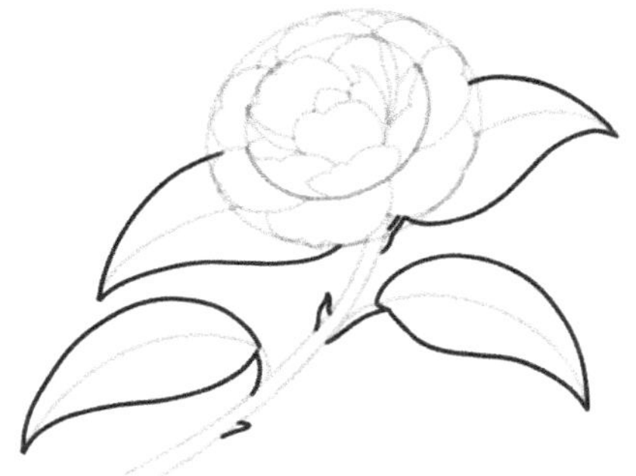

10

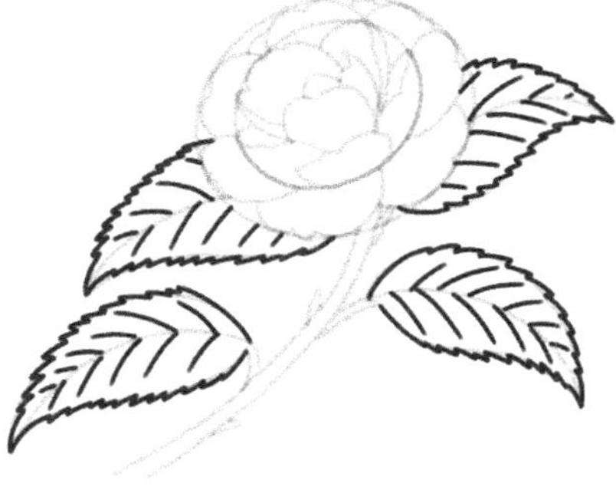

11

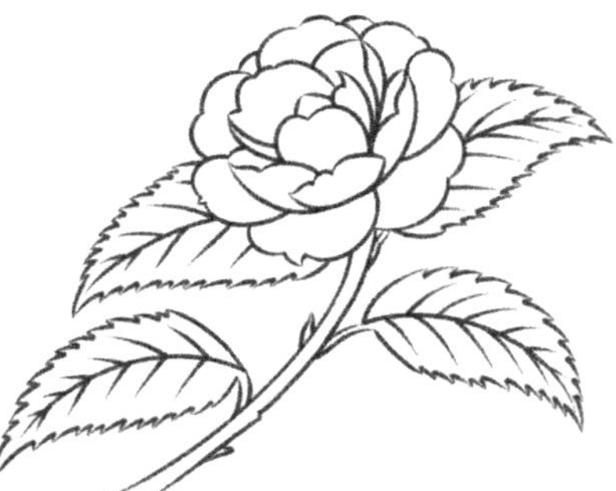

12

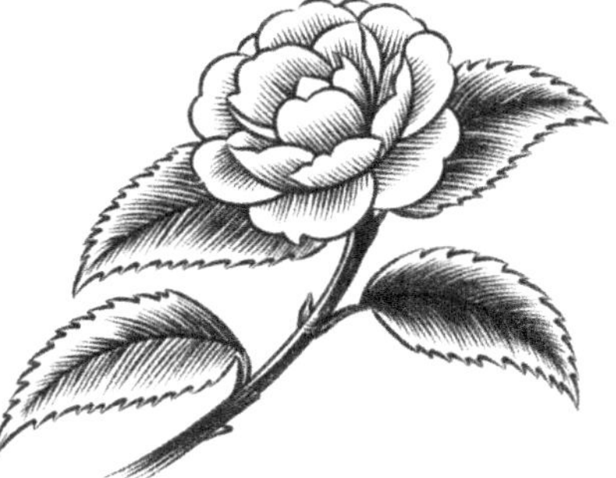

CARNATION

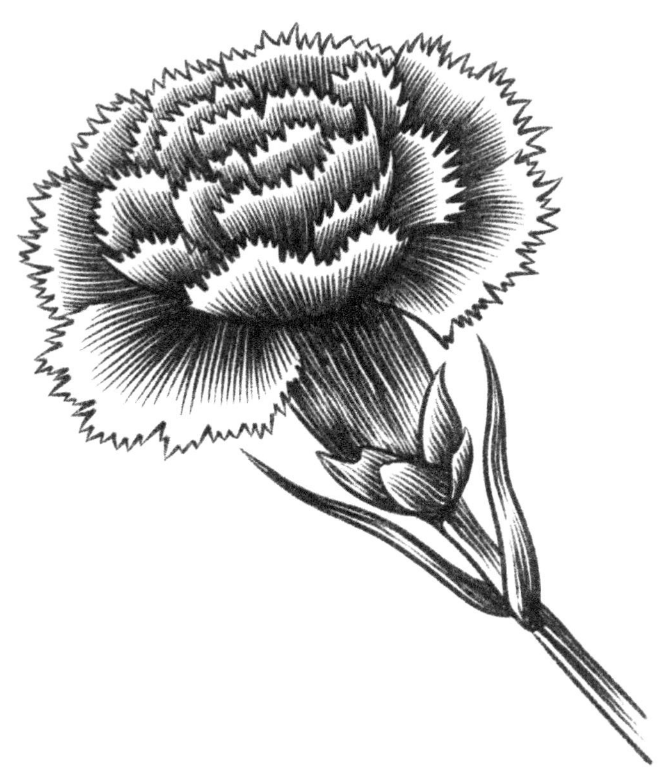

Carnations represent fascination and distinction, often symbolising love, admiration, and, in some cases, a mother's eternal affection.

01

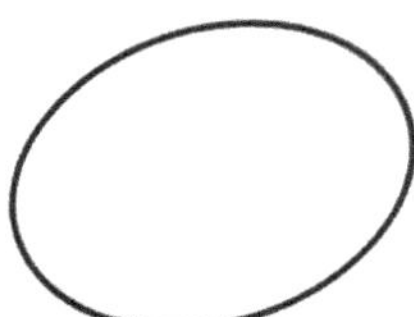

02

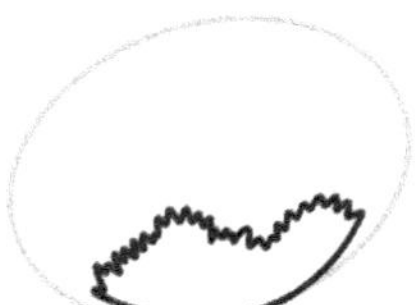

03

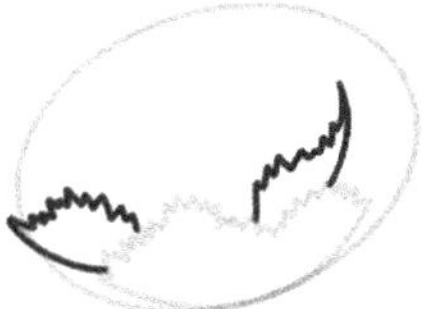

04

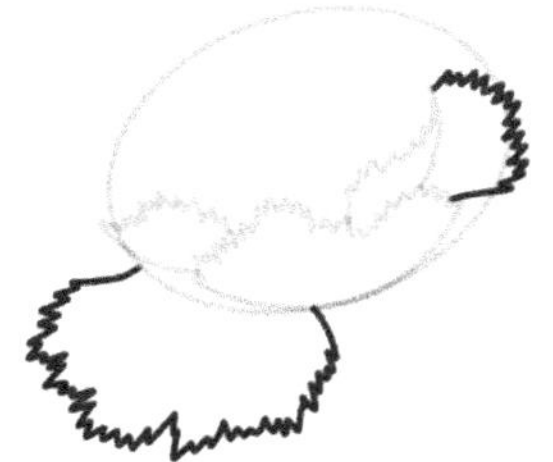

05

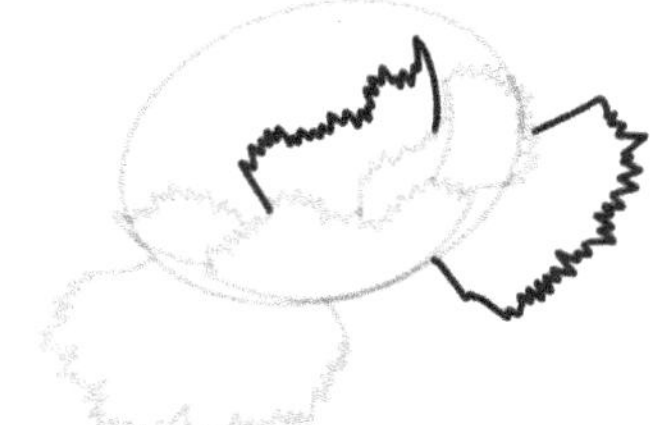

06

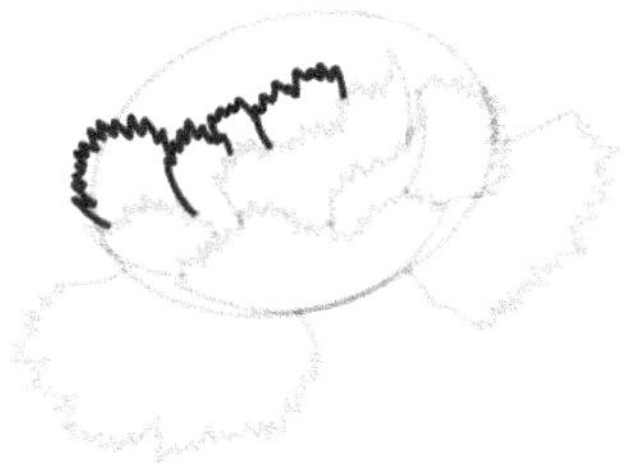

07

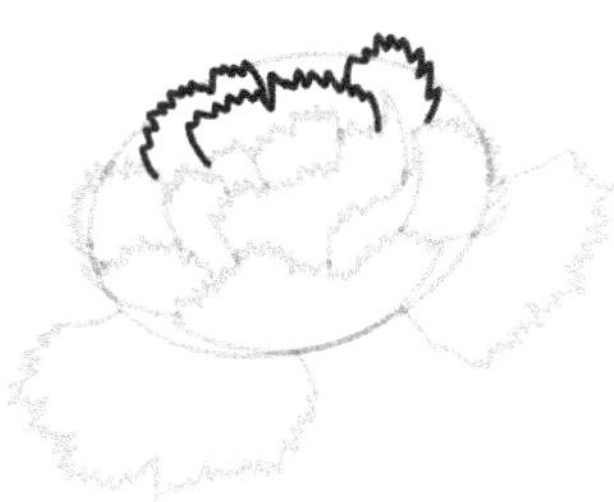

08

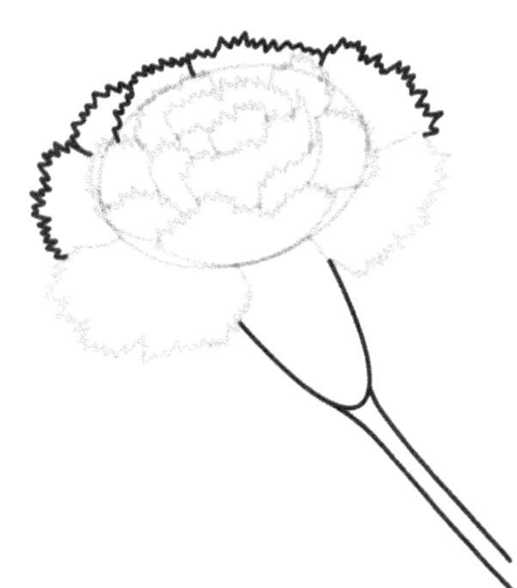

09

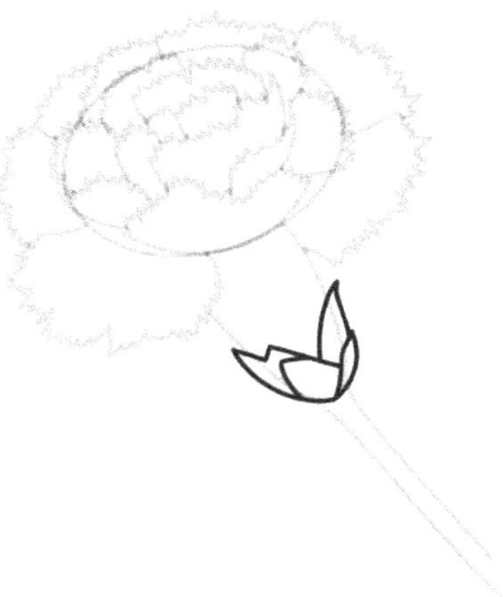

10

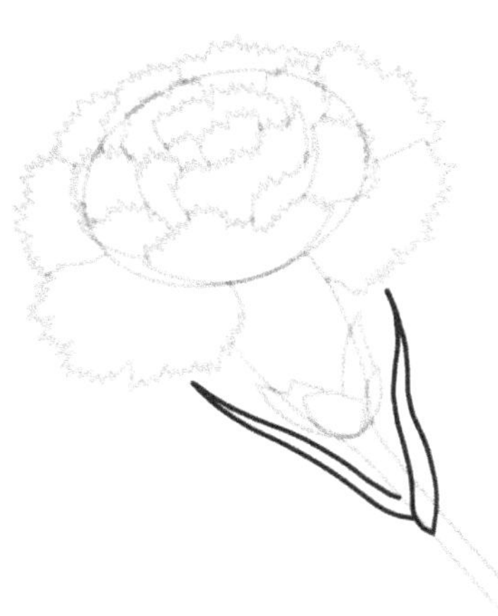

11

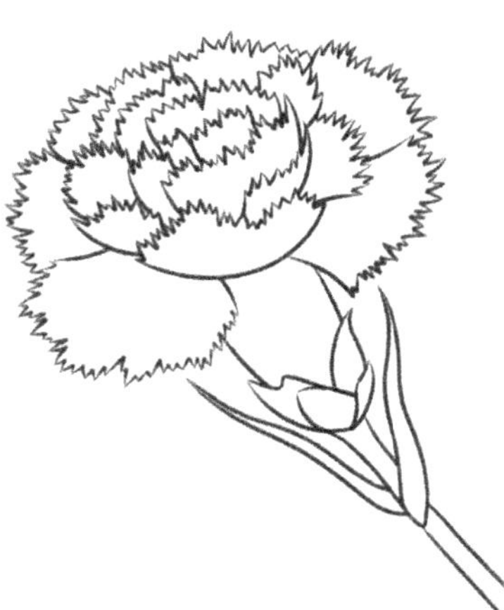

12

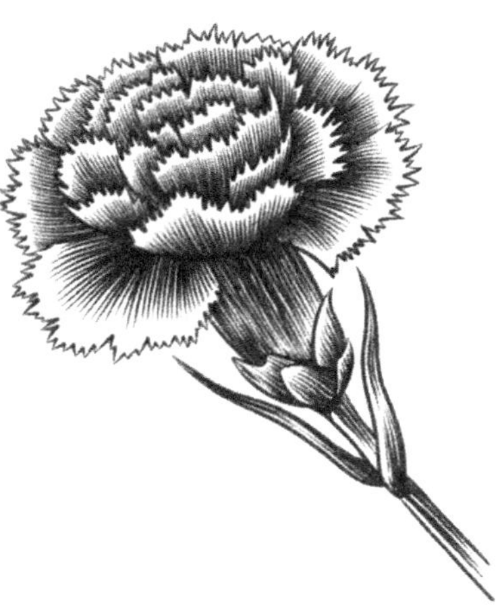

HOW TO DRAW FLOWERS

CHRYSANTHEMUM

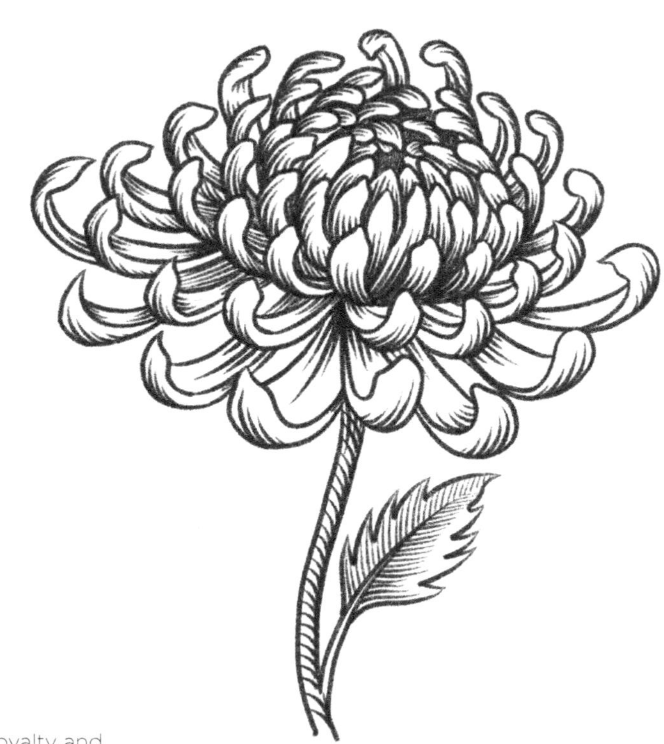

Chrysanthemums symbolise loyalty and devotion, often representing longevity, joy, and in some cultures, a celebration of life and honour in death.

01

02

03

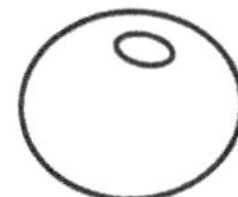

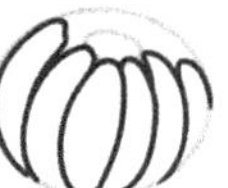

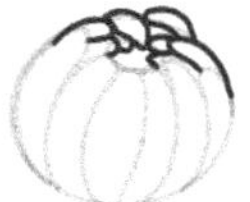

04

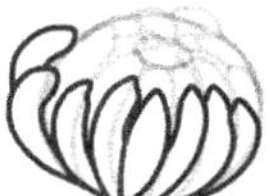

05

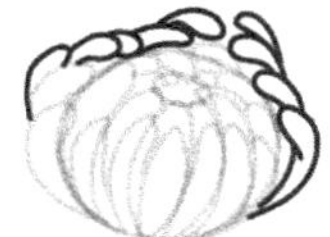

06

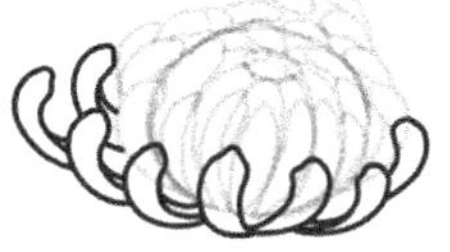

07

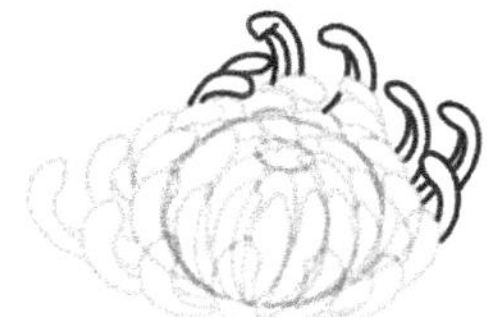

08

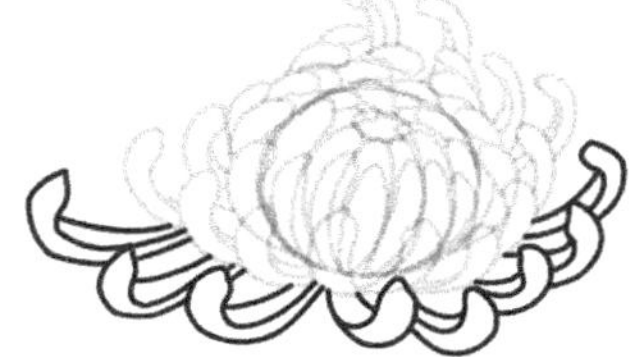

09

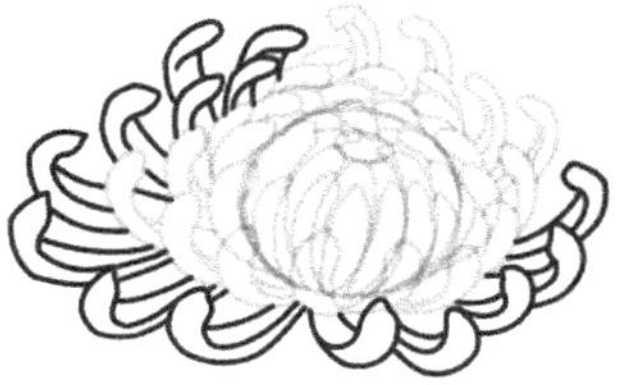

10

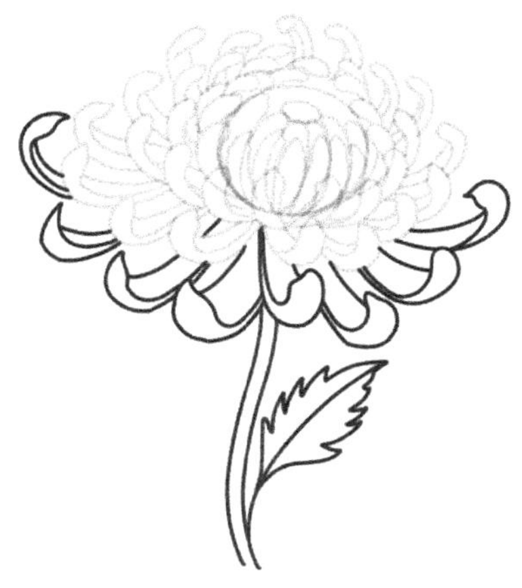

11

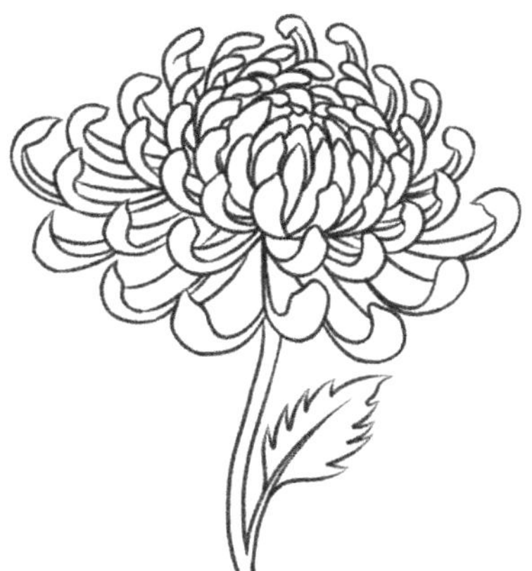

12

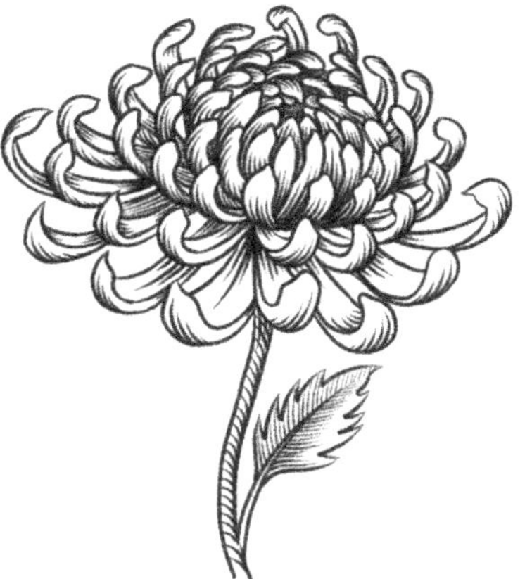

COMMON MALLOW

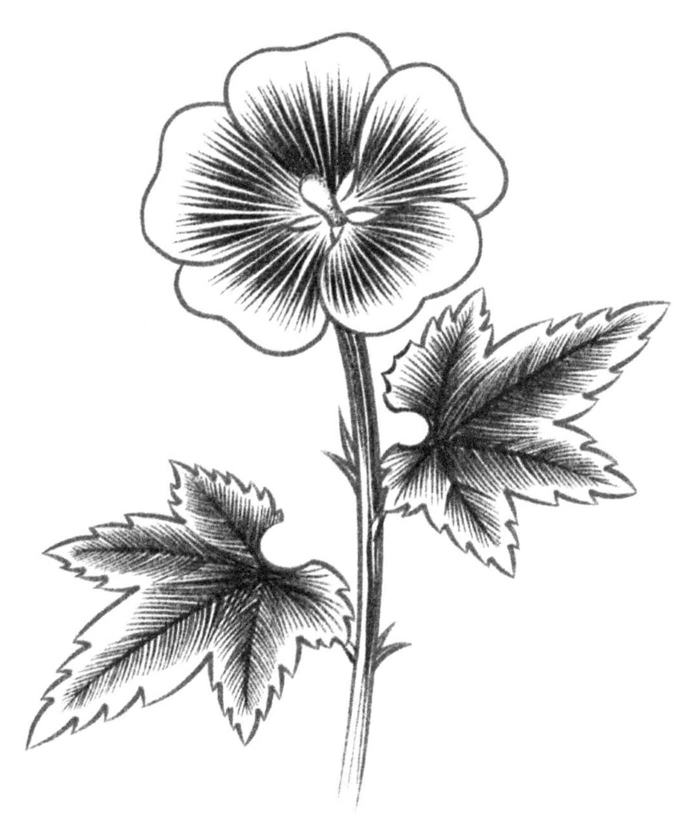

Common Mallow symbolises healing and protection, often associated with peace, soothing comfort, and resilience in the face of hardship.

01

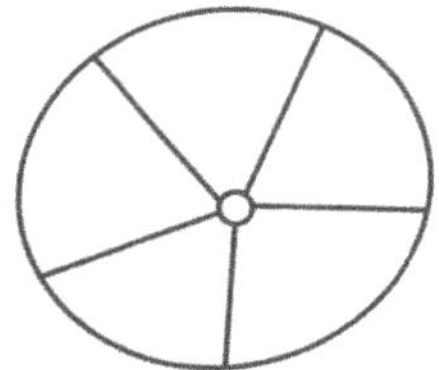

02

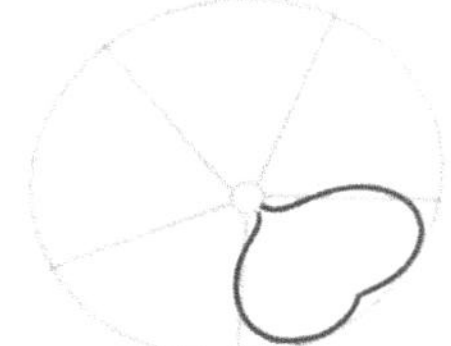

03

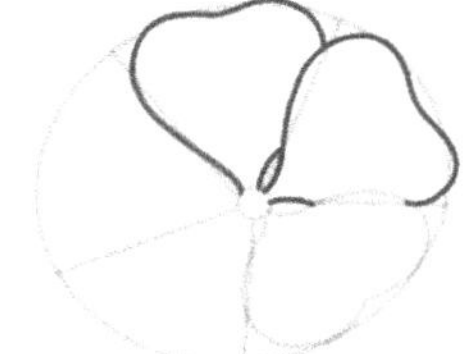

04

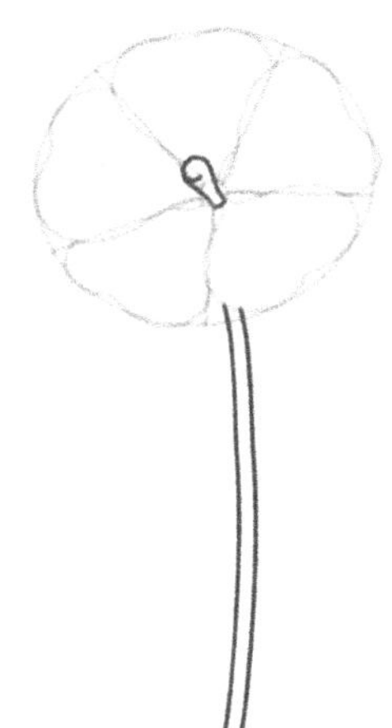

05

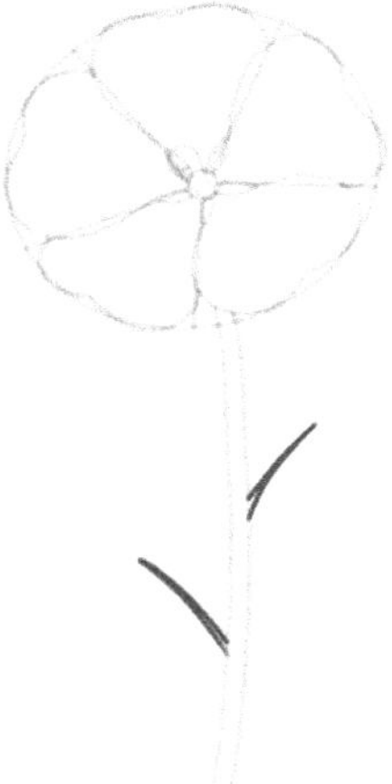

06

07

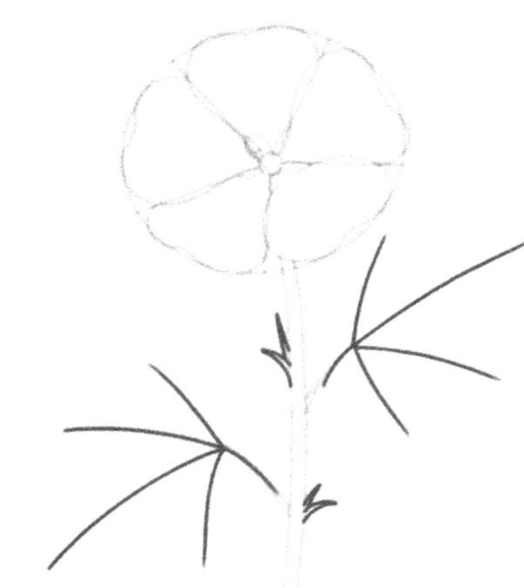

08

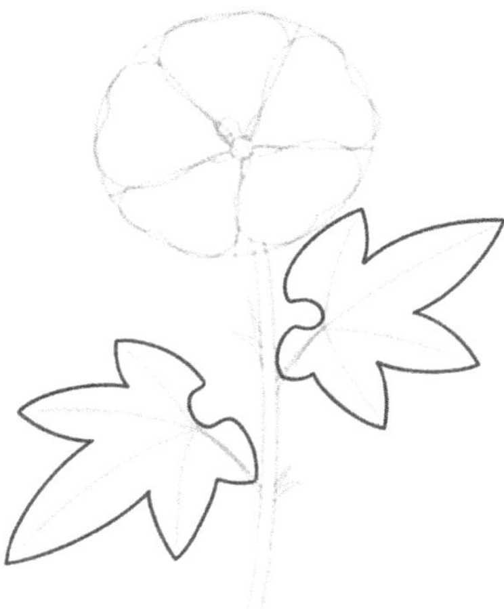

09

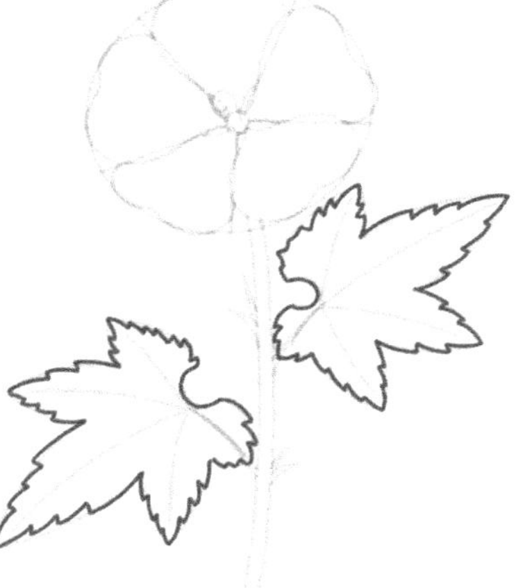

10

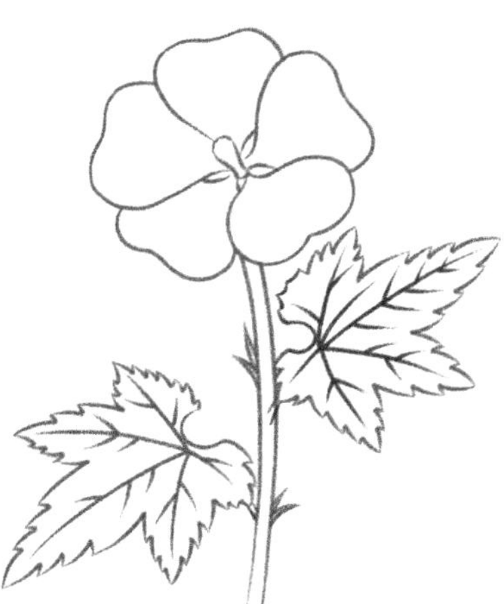

11

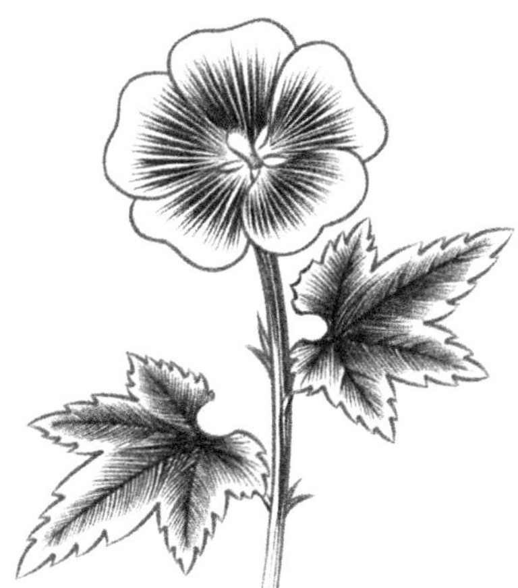

12

COSMOS

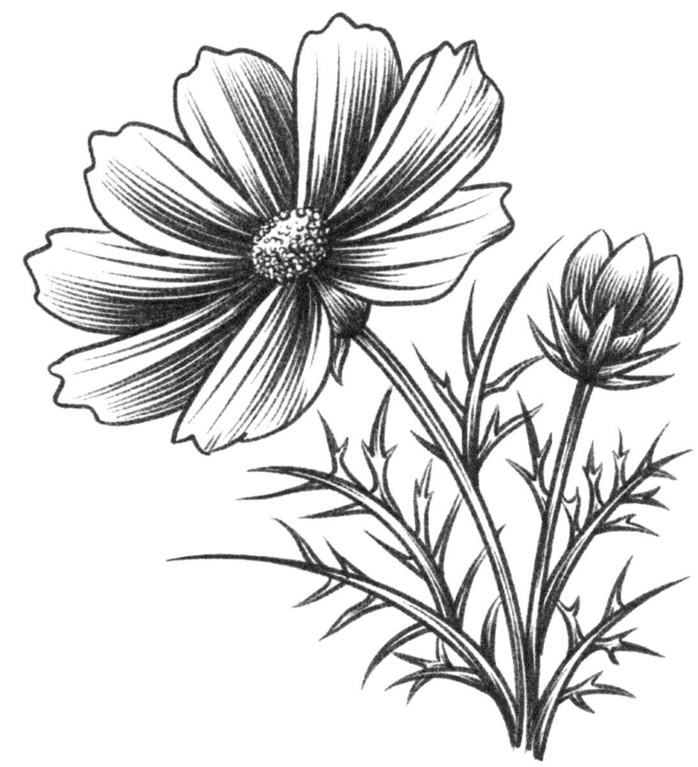

Cosmos symbolise harmony and balance, often representing peace, tranquillity, and the orderly beauty of the universe.

01

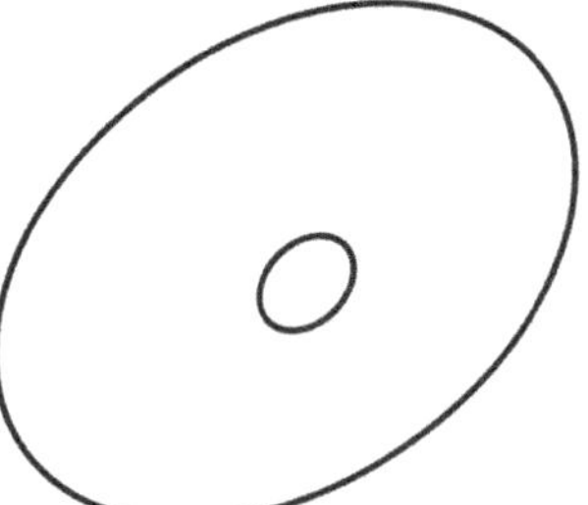

02

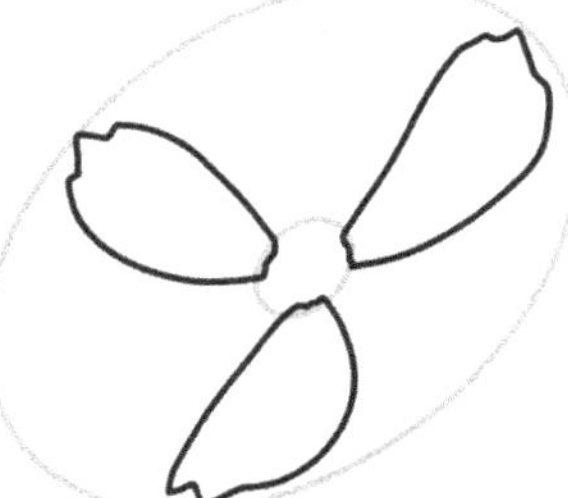

03

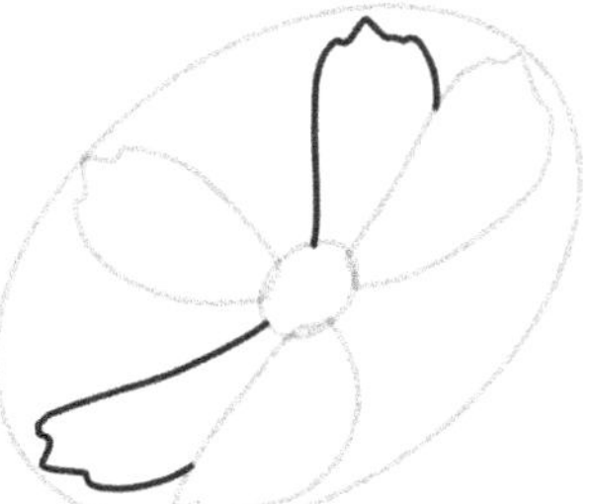

04

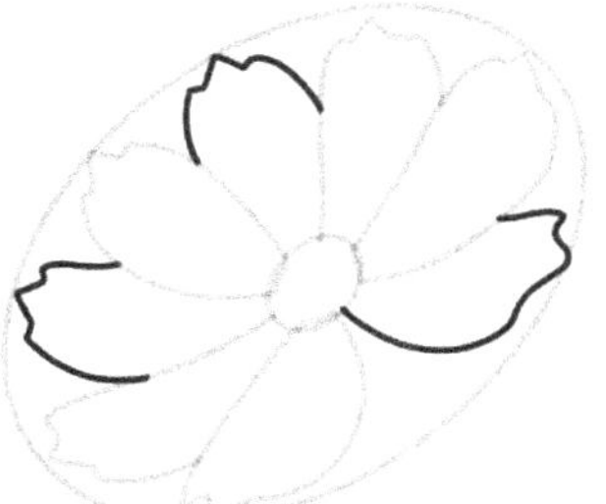

05

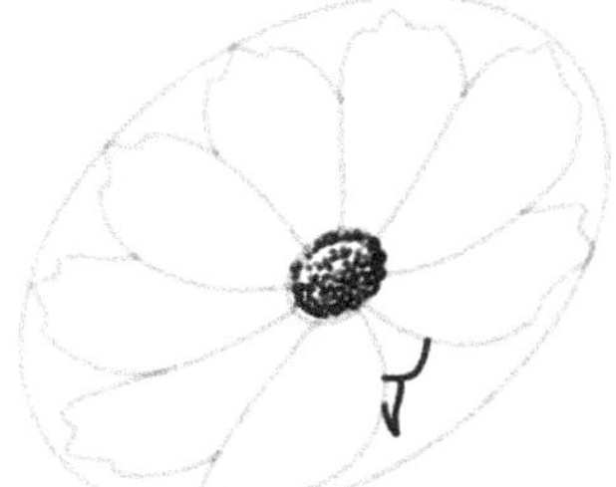

06

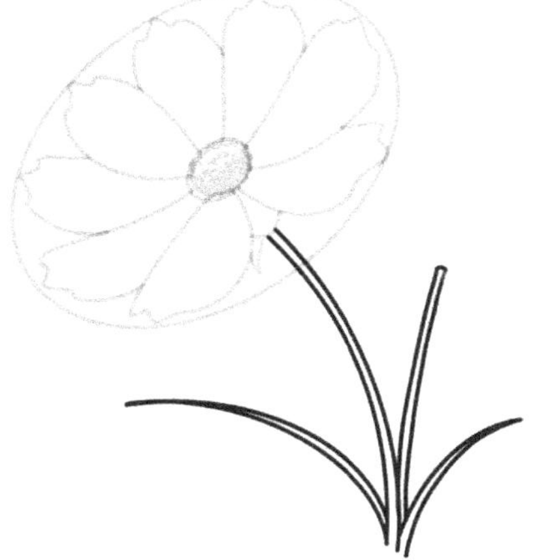

07

08

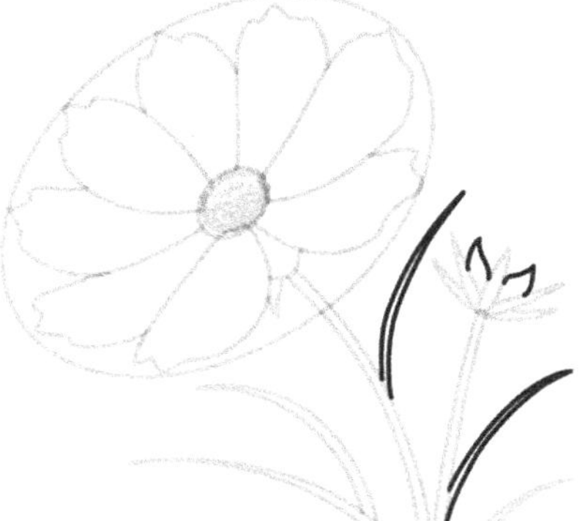

09

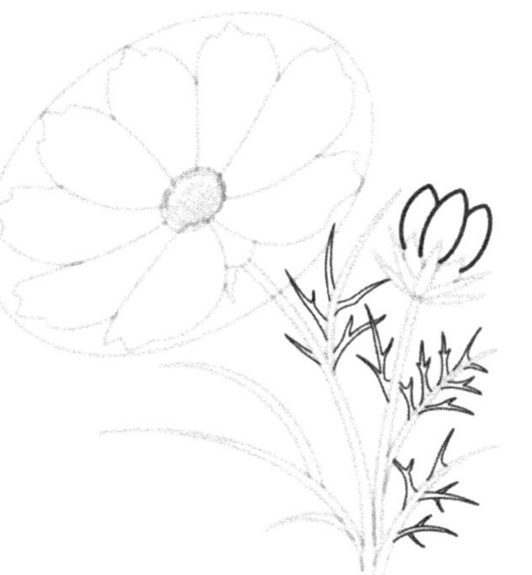

10

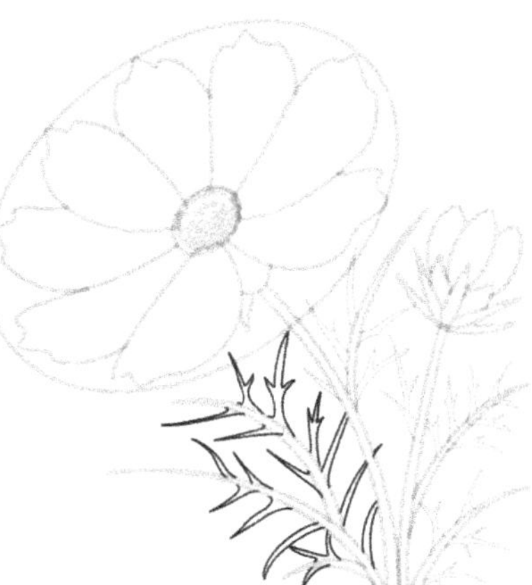

11

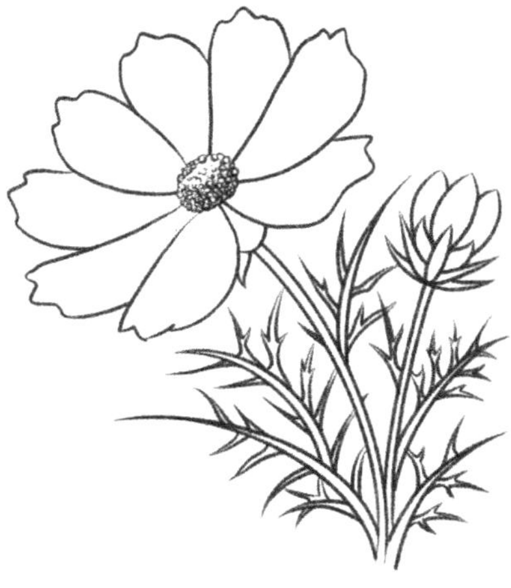

12

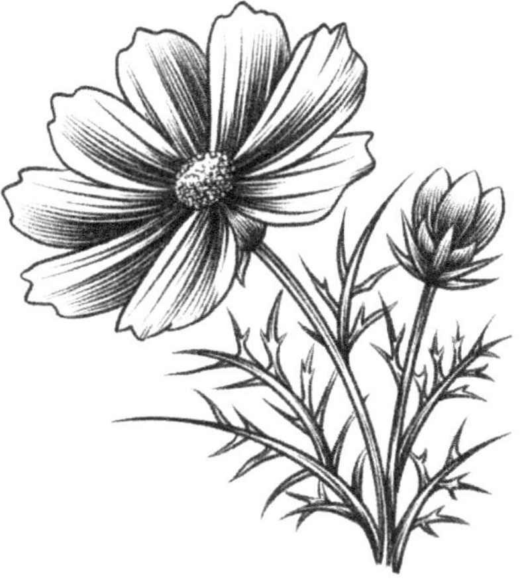

DAFFODIL

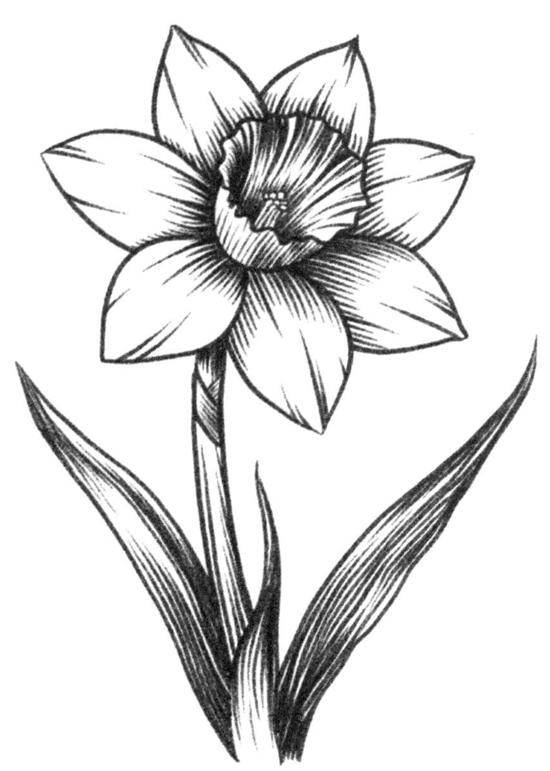

Daffodils represent renewal and hope,
symbolising new beginnings, rebirth,
and the arrival of spring's joyful energy.

01

02

03

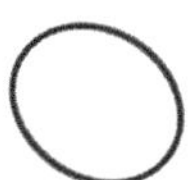

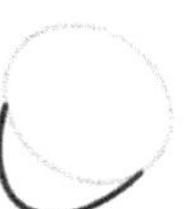

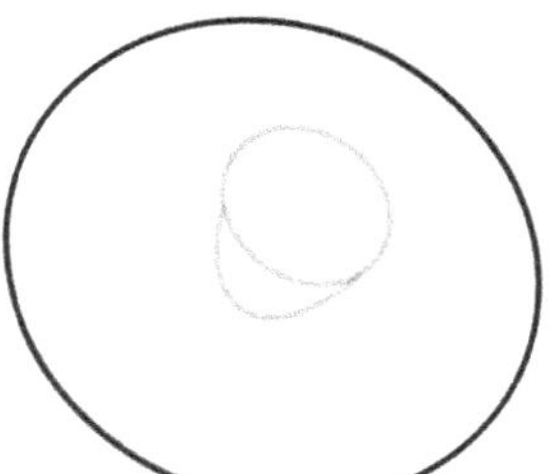

04

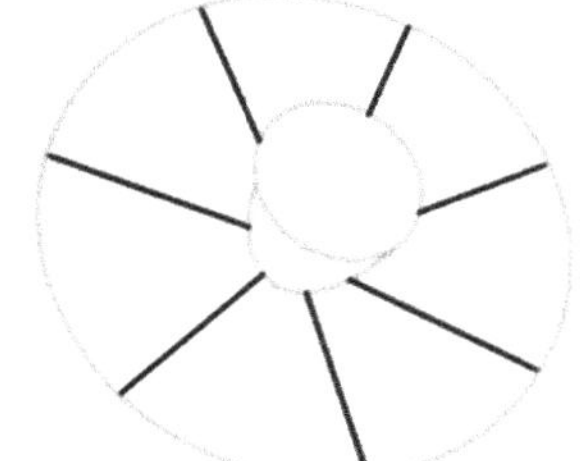

05

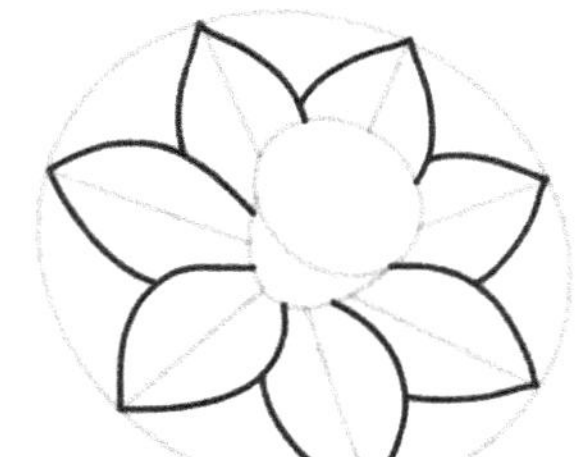

06

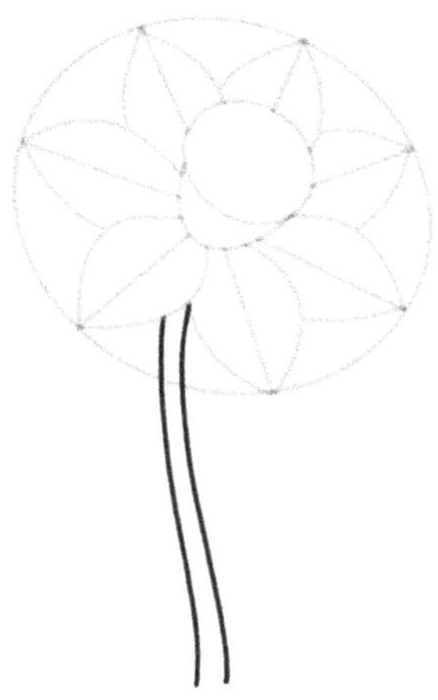

07

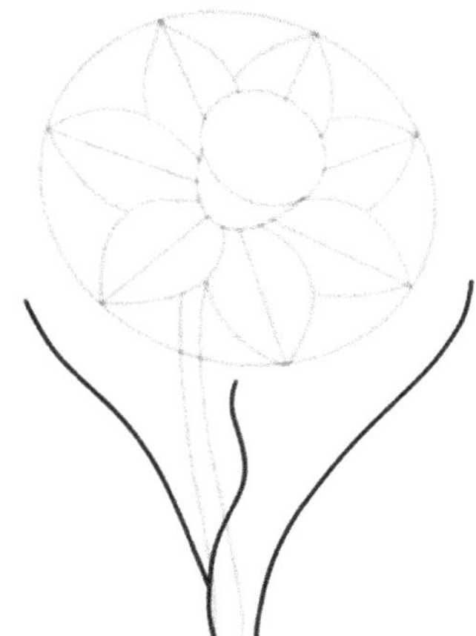

08

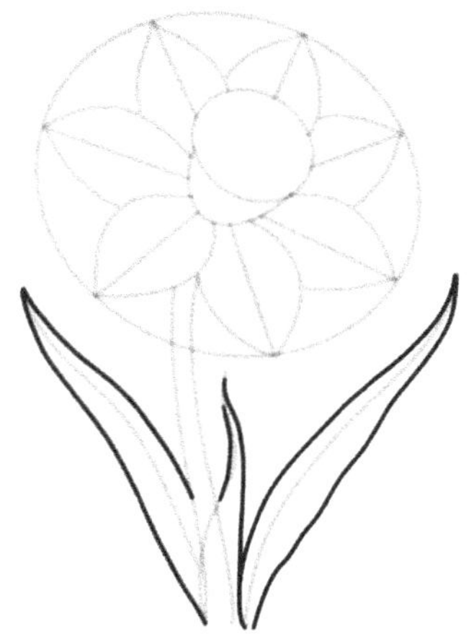

09

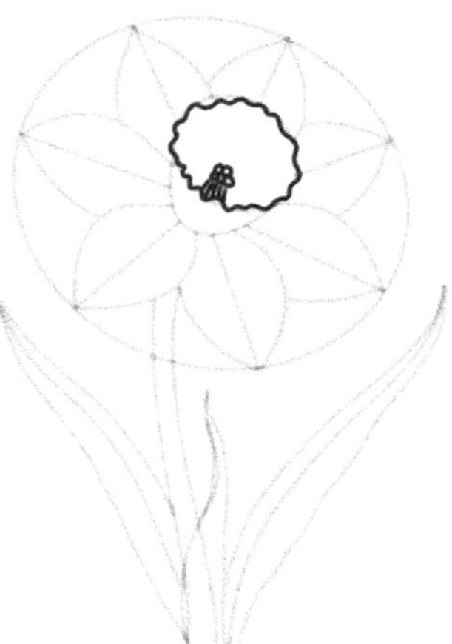

10

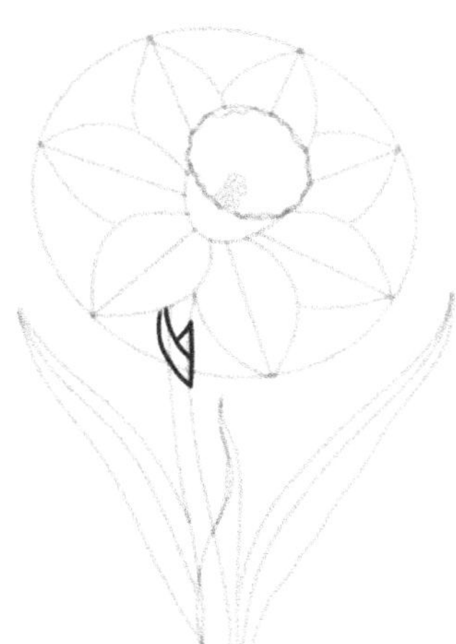

11

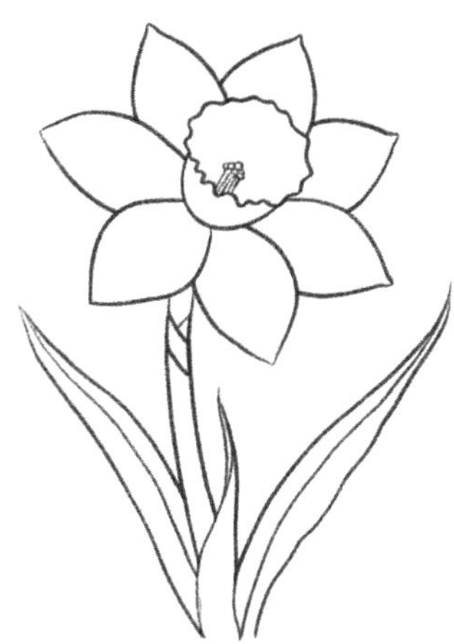

12

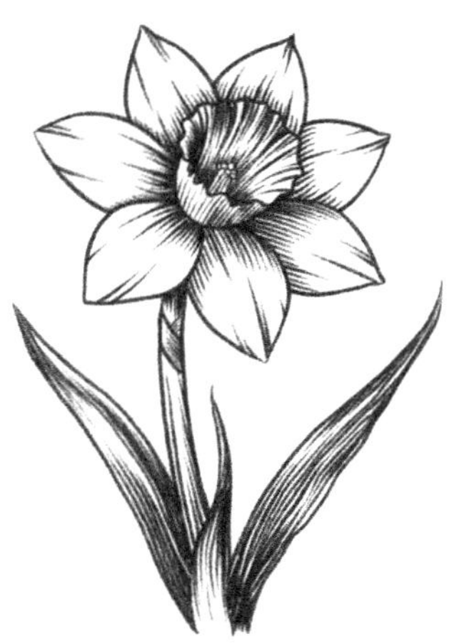

DAISY

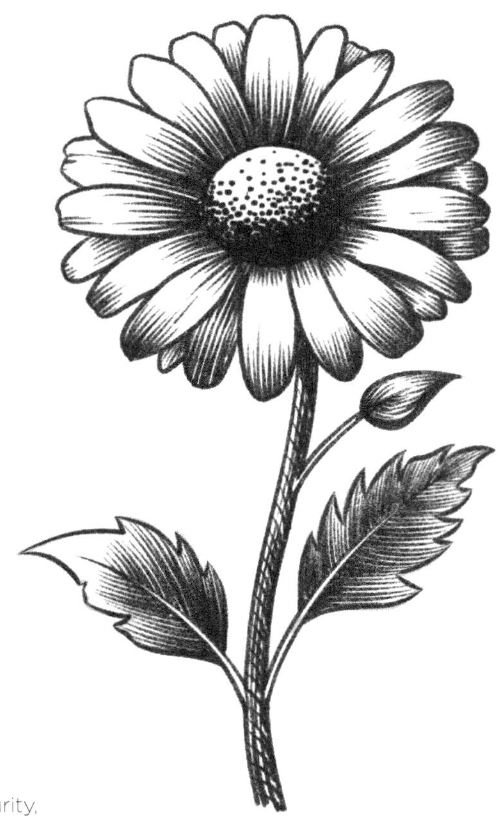

Daisies symbolise innocence and purity, often associated with loyal love, new beginnings, and the simplicity of joy.

01

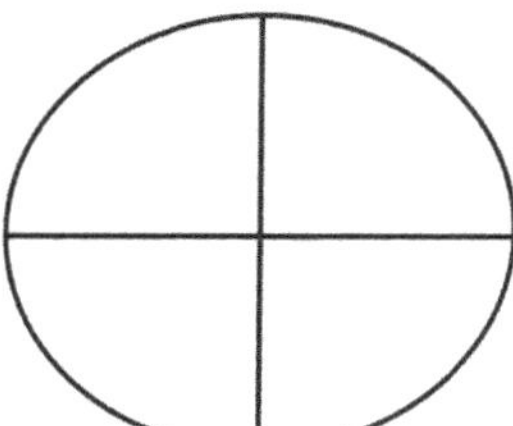

02

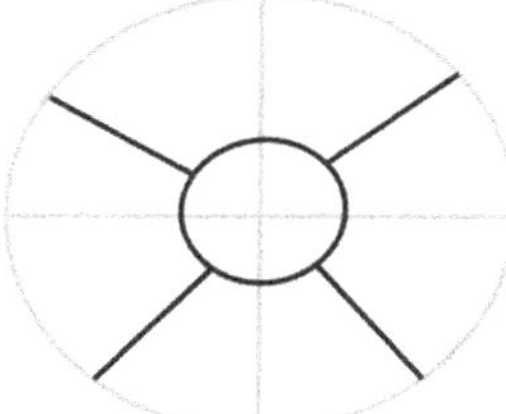

03

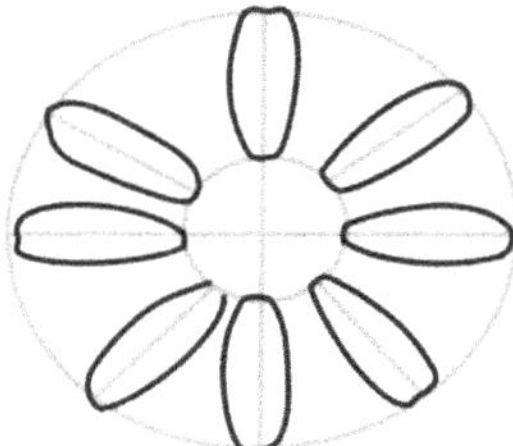

04

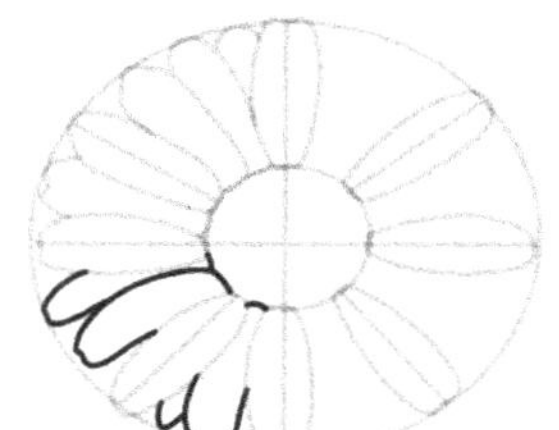

05

06

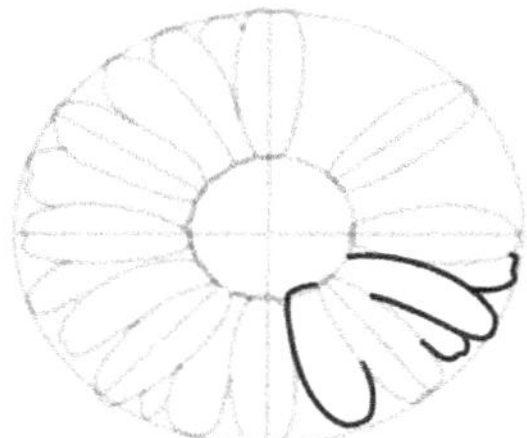

07

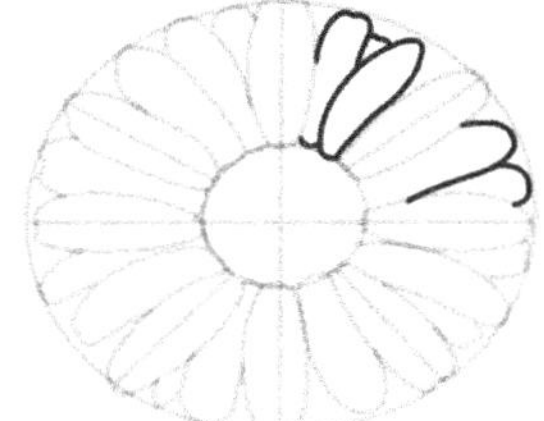

08

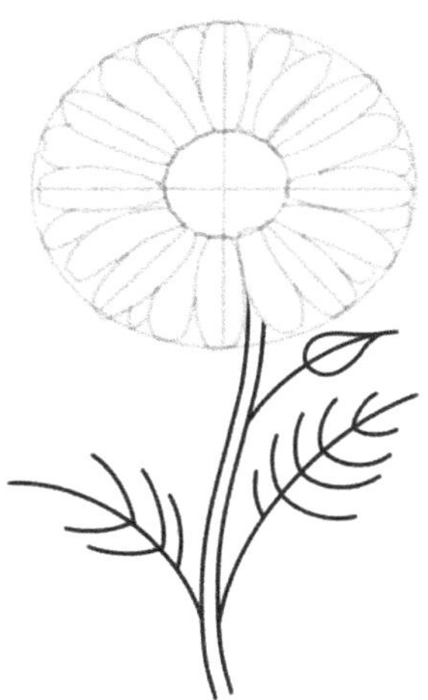

09

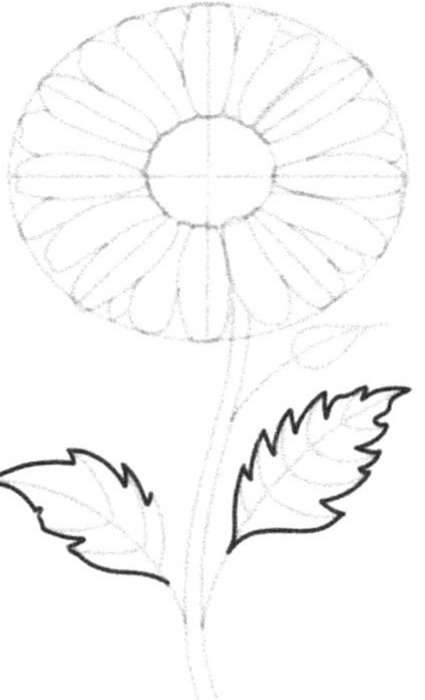

10

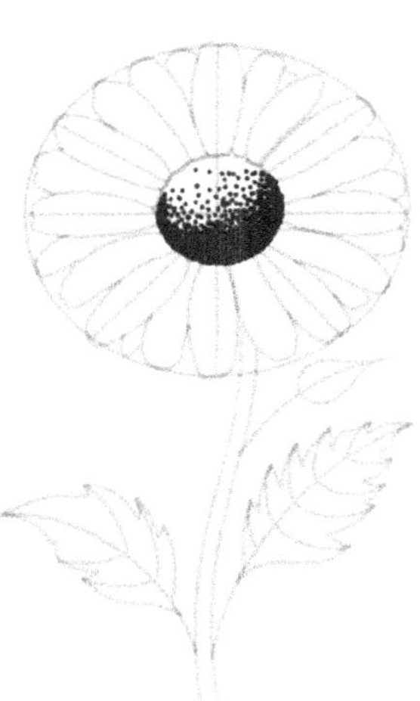

11

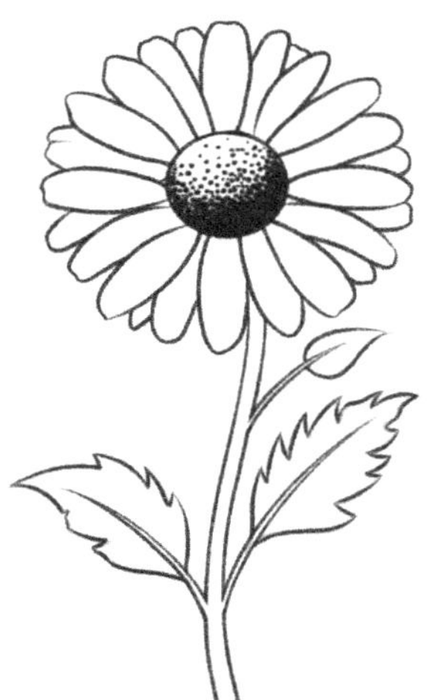

12

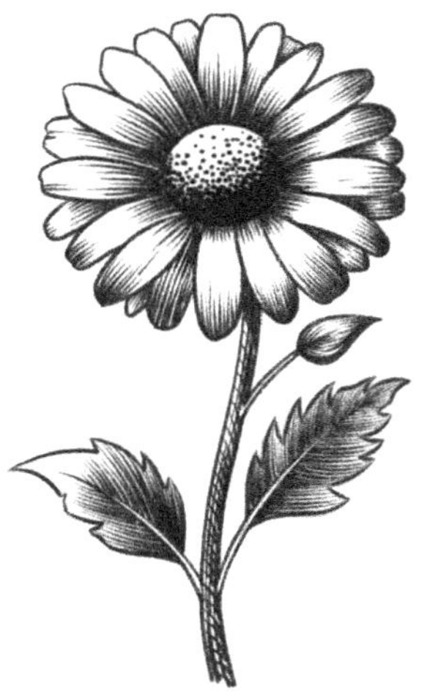

HOW TO DRAW FLOWERS

FORGET ME NOT

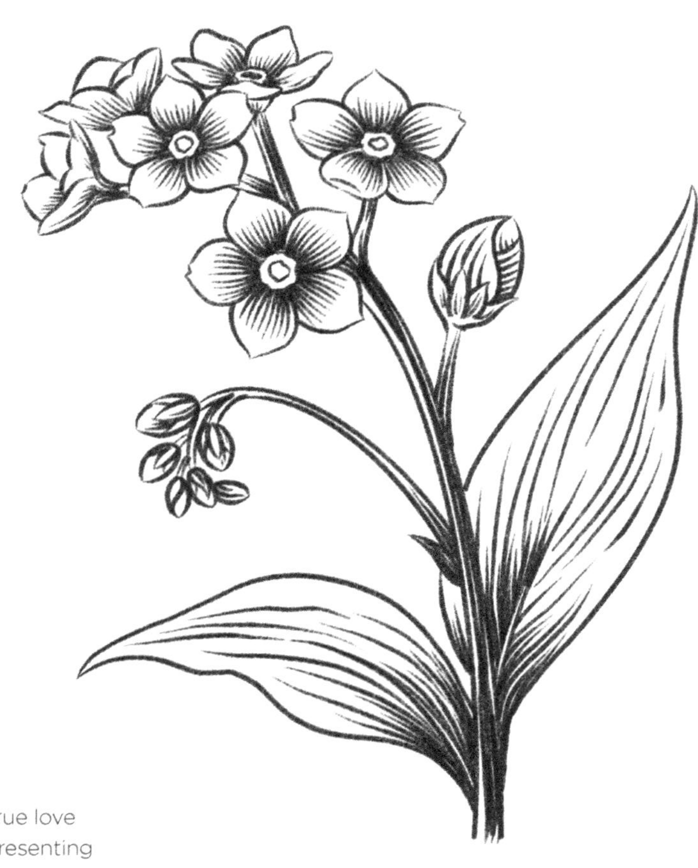

Forget-Me-Nots symbolise true love and remembrance, often representing enduring connections and cherished memories that withstand the passage of time.

01

02

03

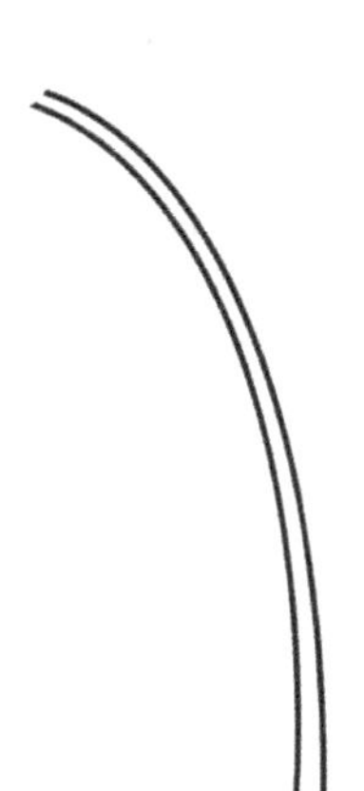

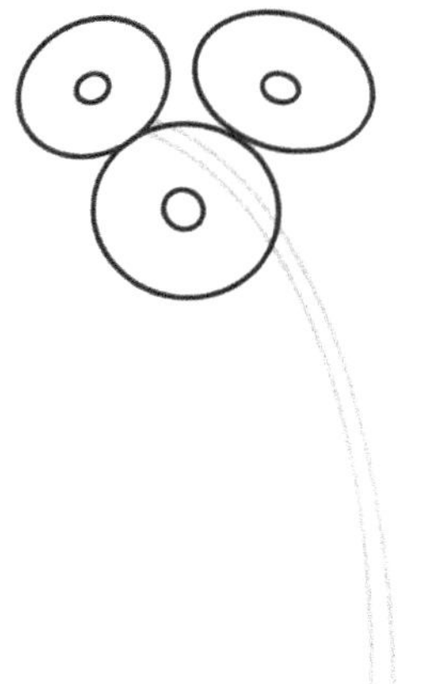

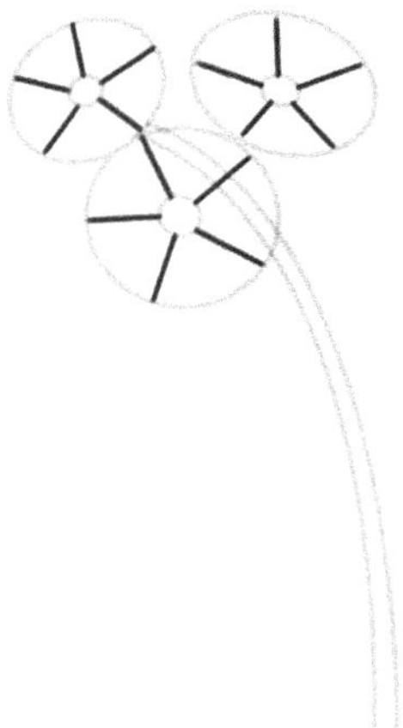

04
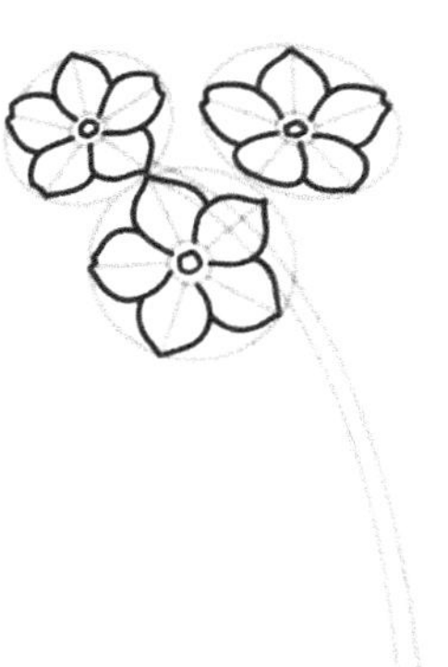

05
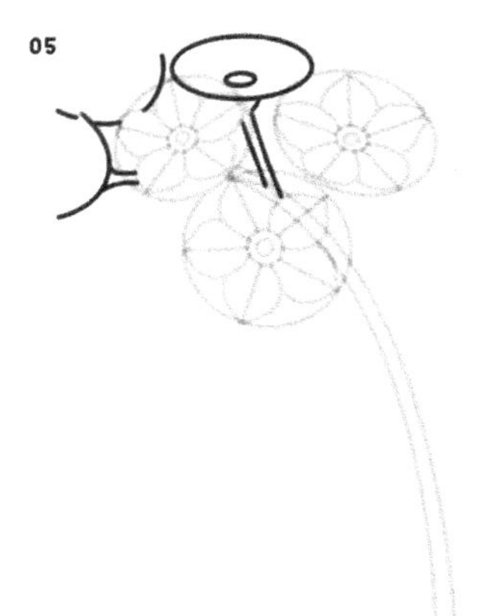

06
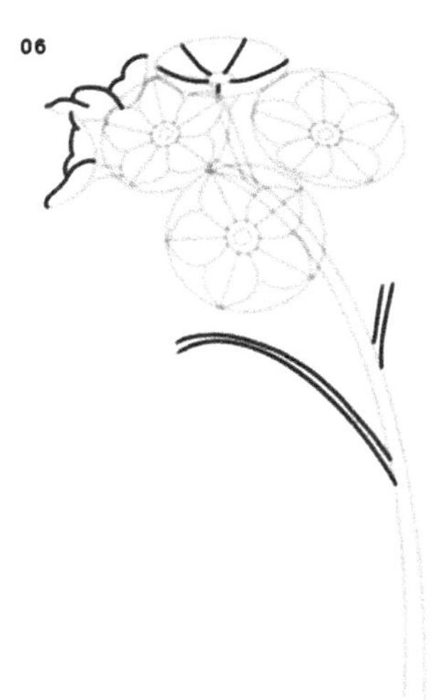

07
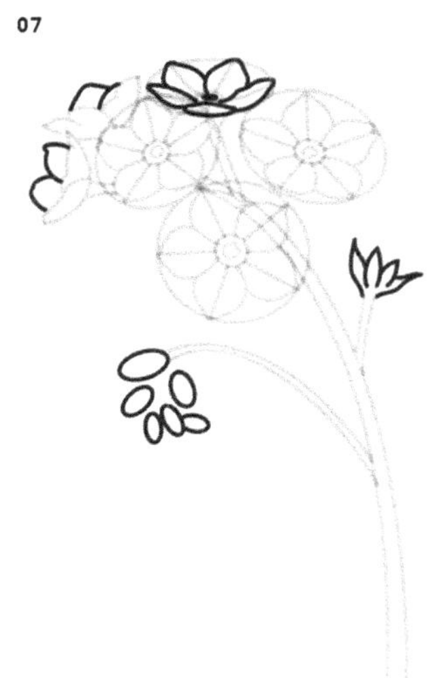

08
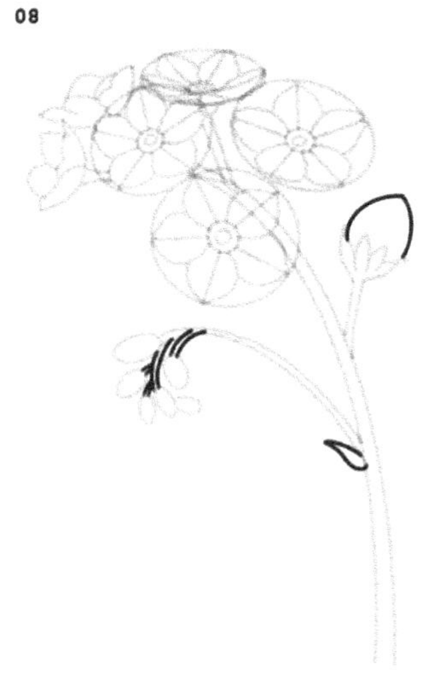

09
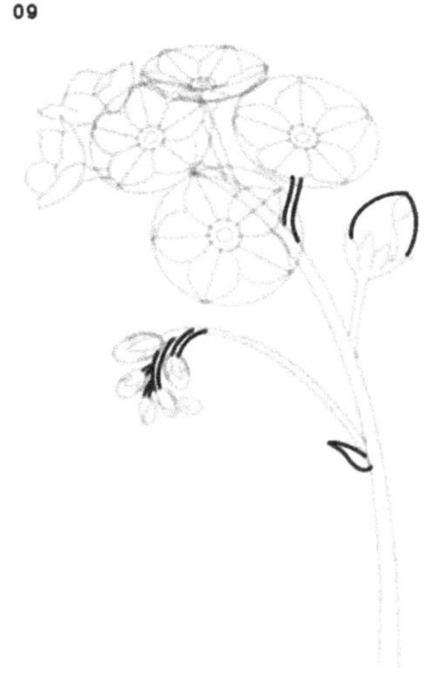

10
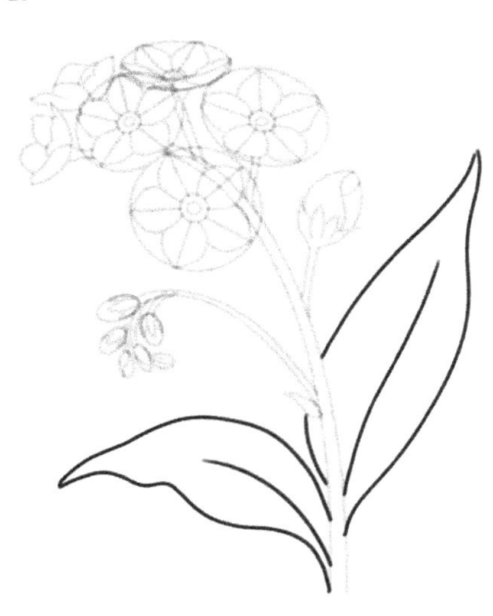

11
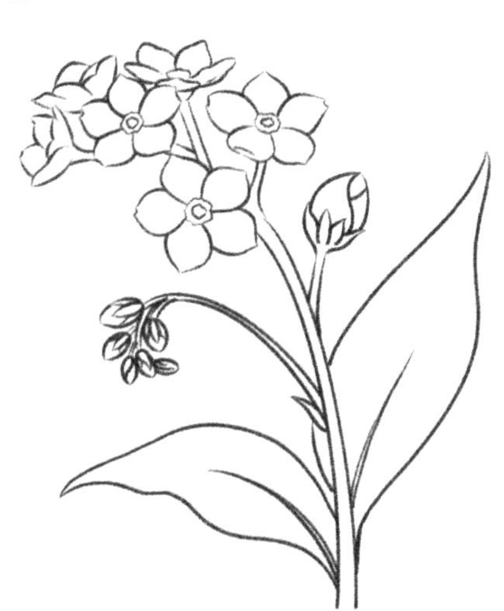

12
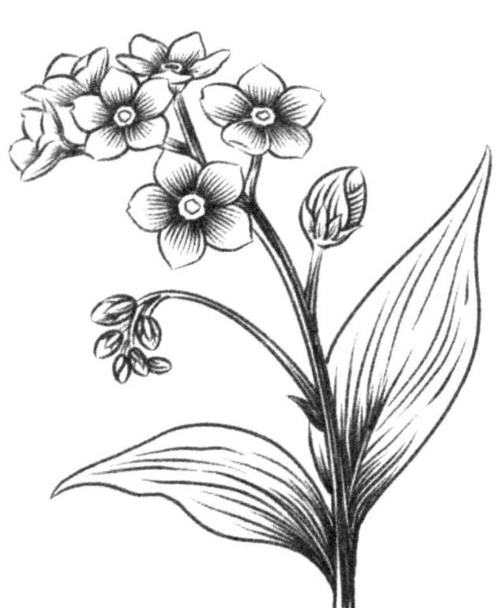

FRANGIPANI

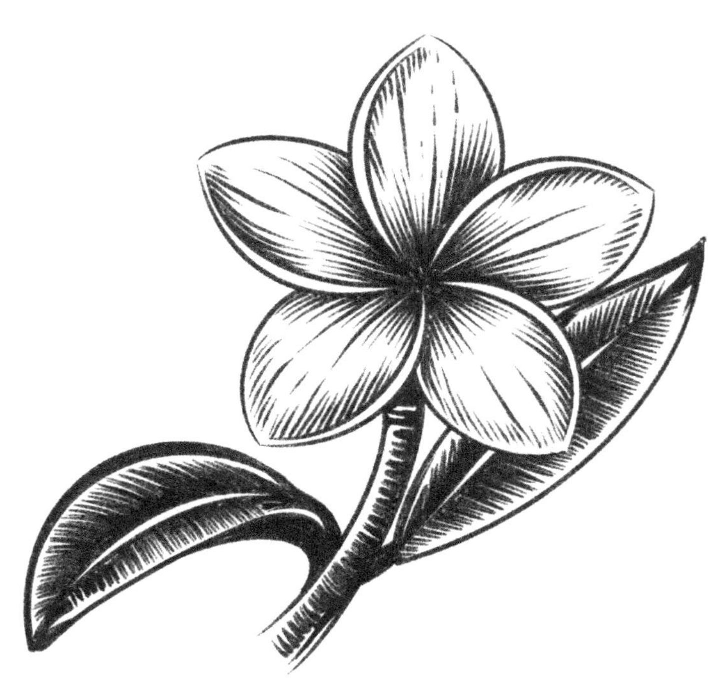

Frangipani symbolises spiritual
devotion, often associated with grace,
beauty, and the resilience of the soul.

01

02

03

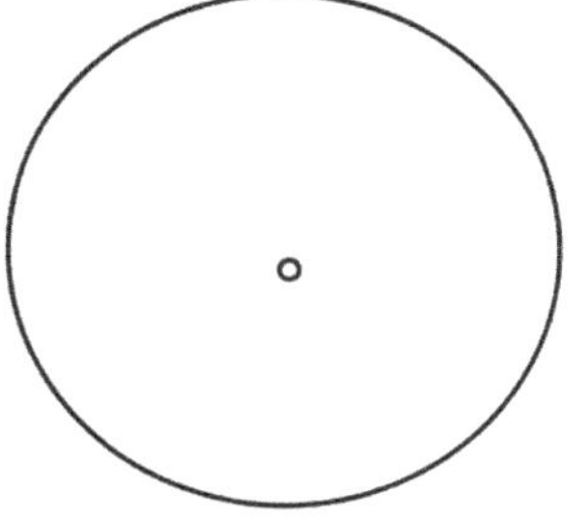

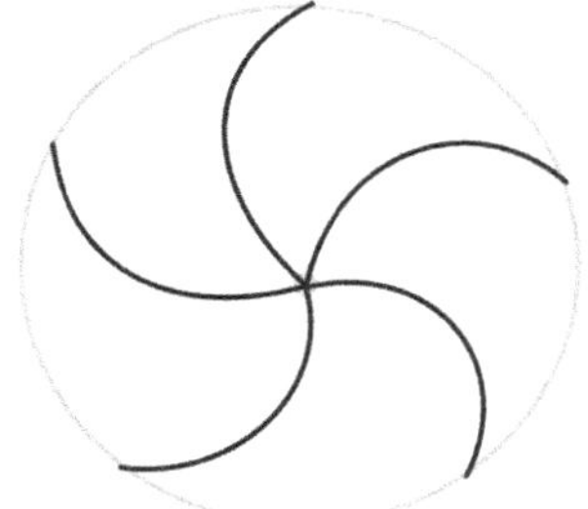

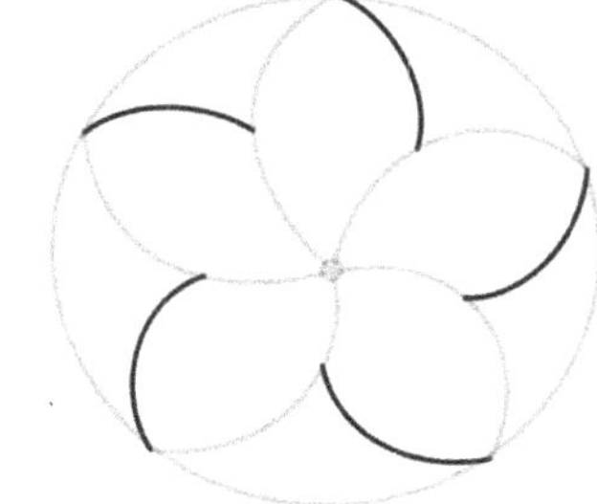

04

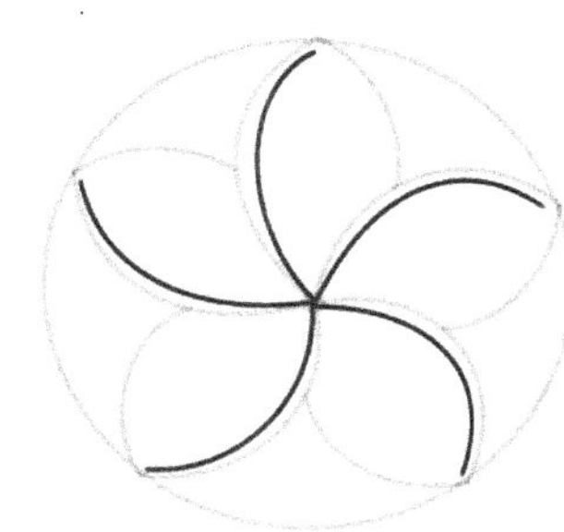

05

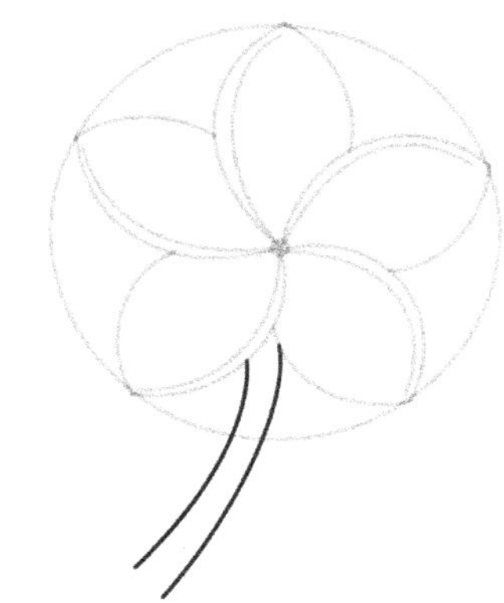

06

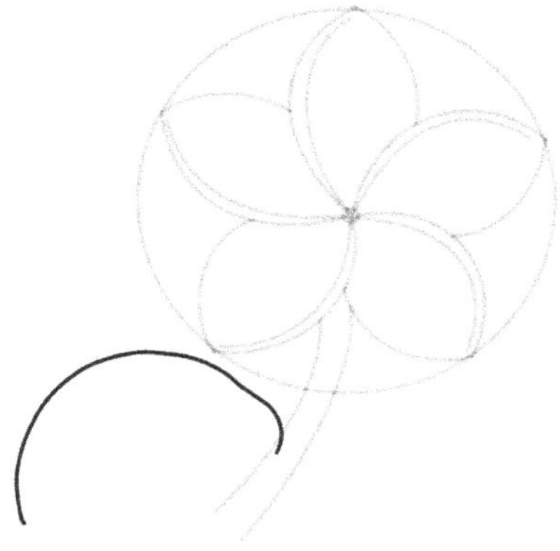

07

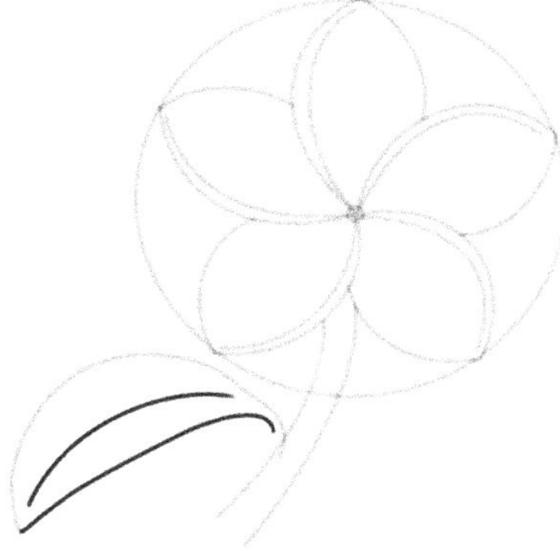

08

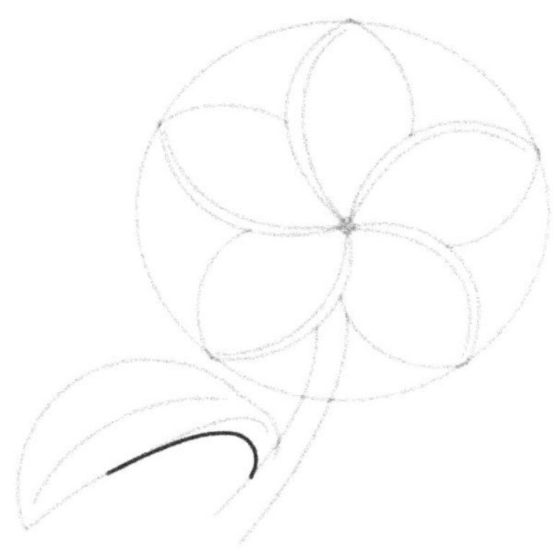

09

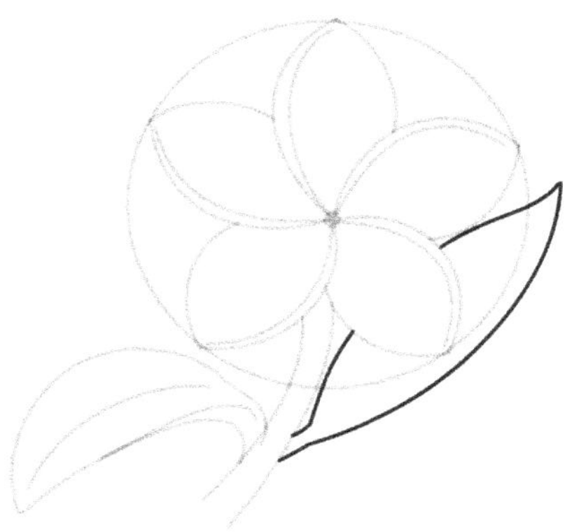

10

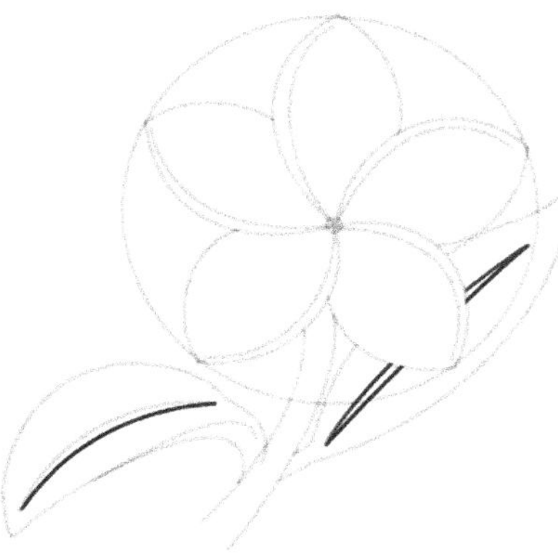

11

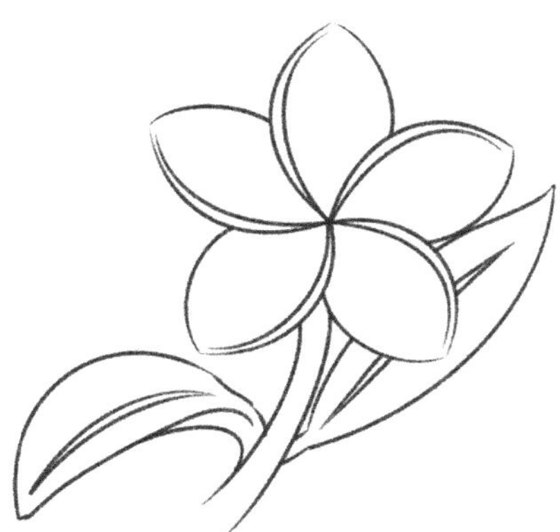

12

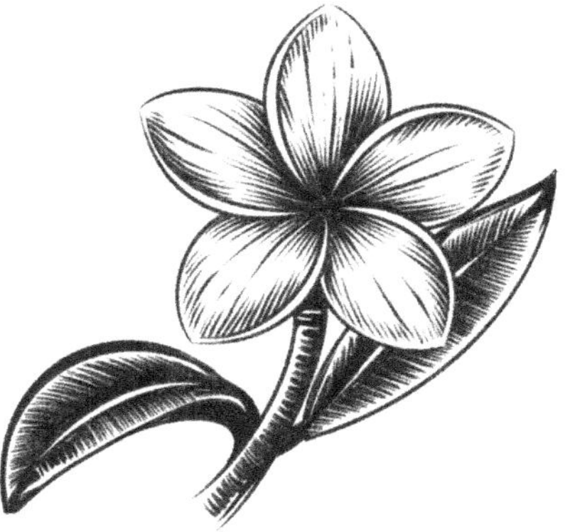

FREESIA

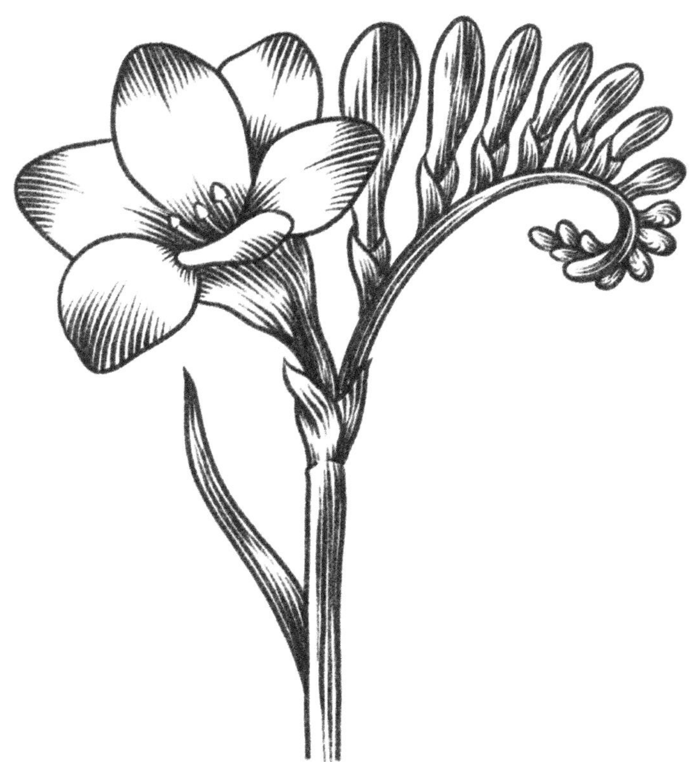

Freesias symbolise friendship, trust, and innocence, often representing thoughtfulness, purity, and the joyful promise of new beginnings and heartfelt connections.

01

02

03

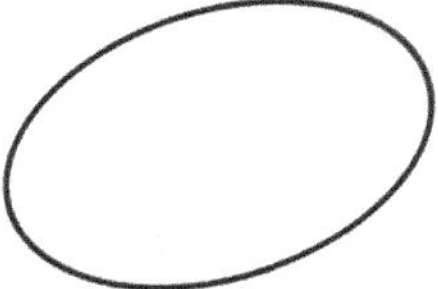

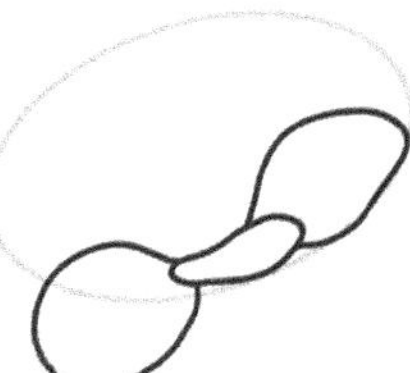

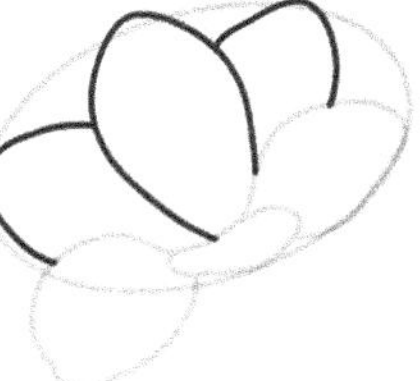

04

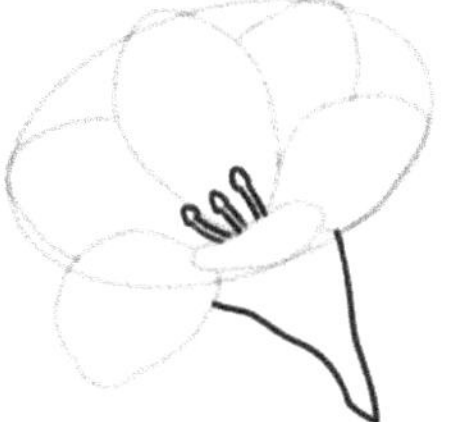

05

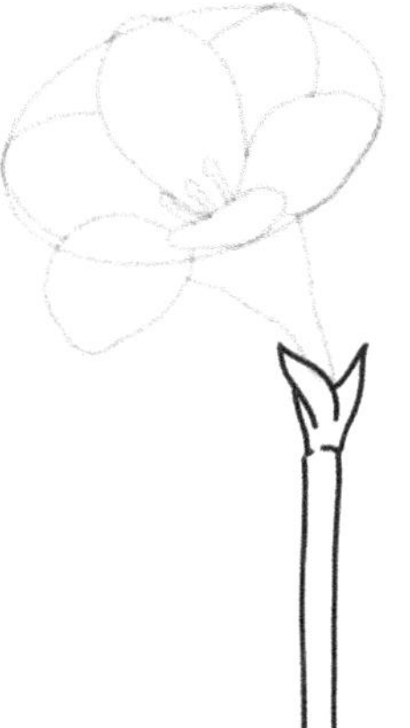

06

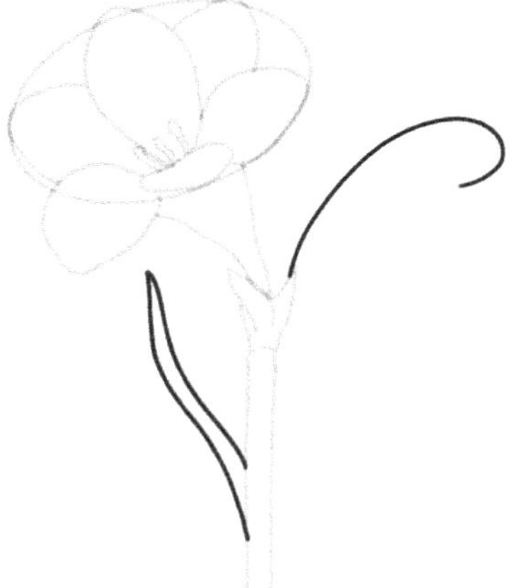

07

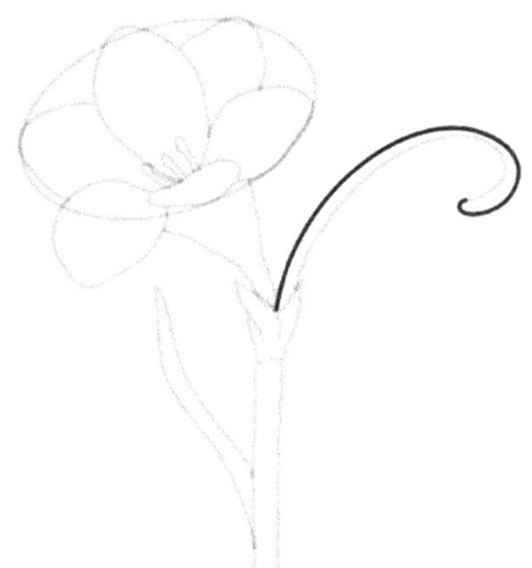

08

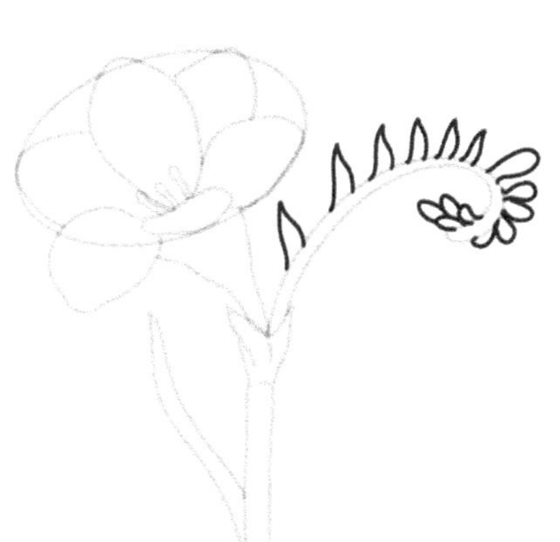

09

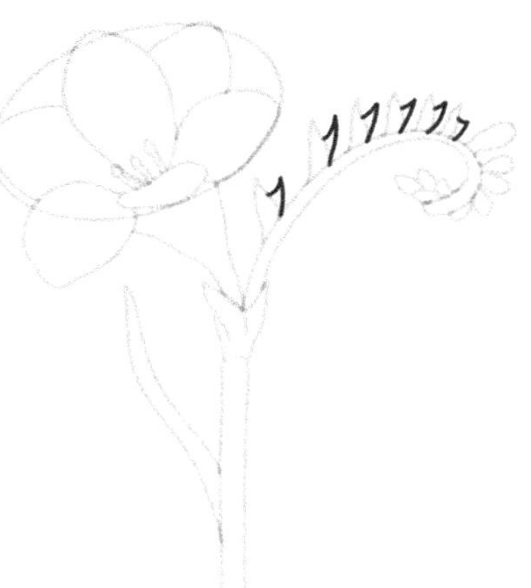

10

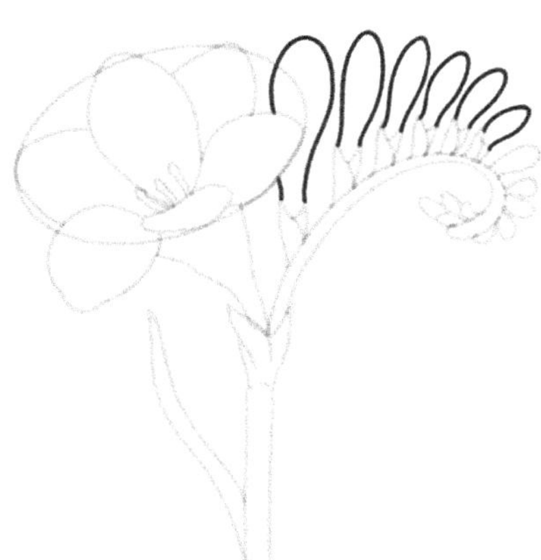

11

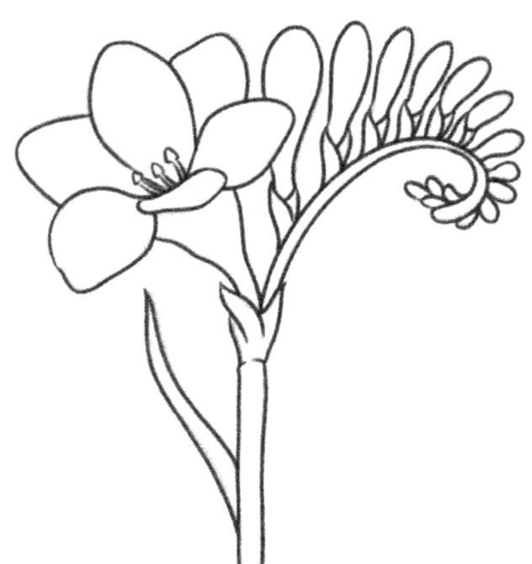

12

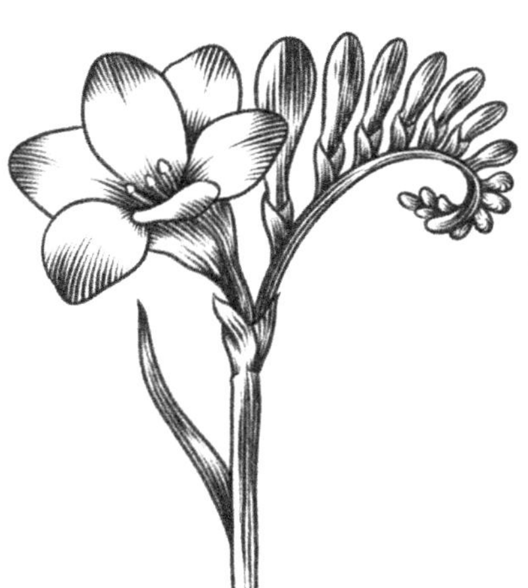

FUCHSIA

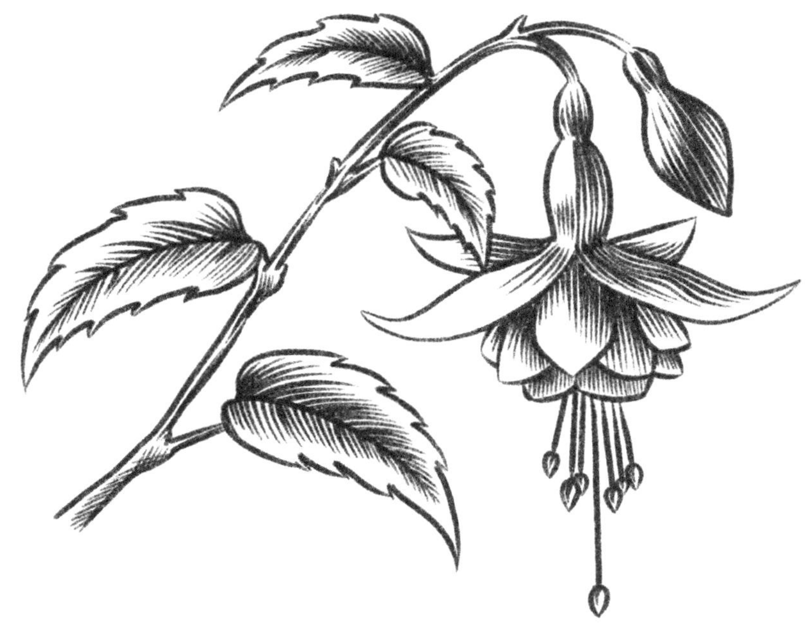

Fuchsias symbolise elegance, refined taste, and vibrant energy, often associated with confiding love, resilience, and the playful yet sophisticated beauty of the unconventional and bold spirit.

01   02   03

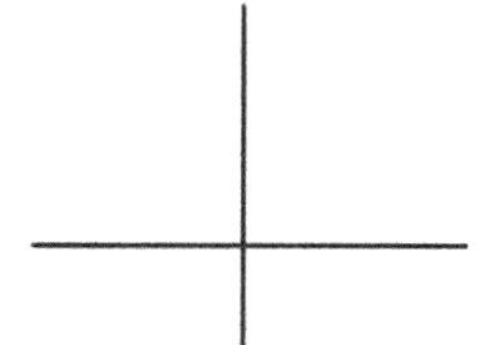

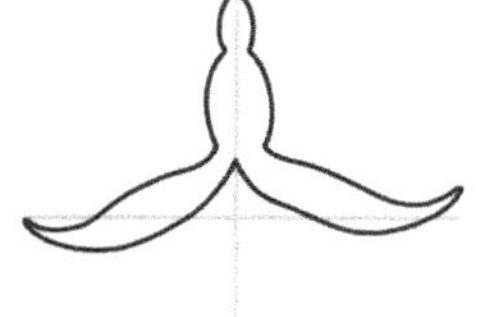

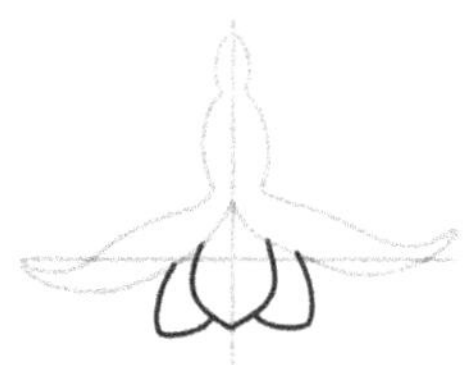

04

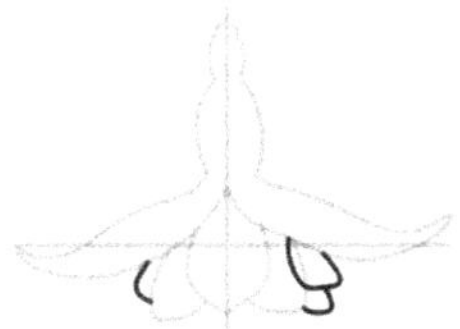

05

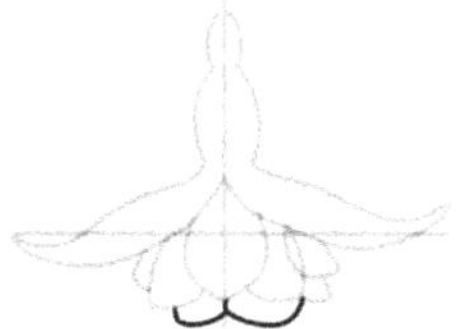

06

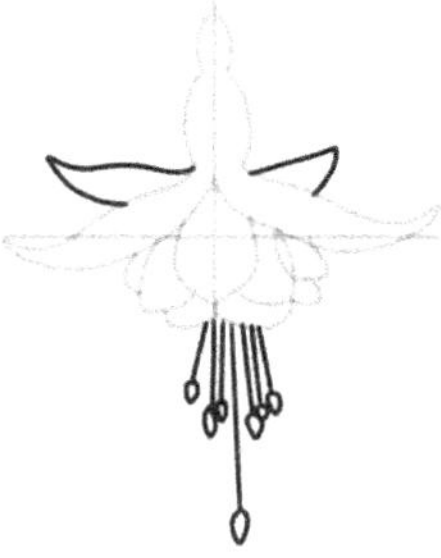

07

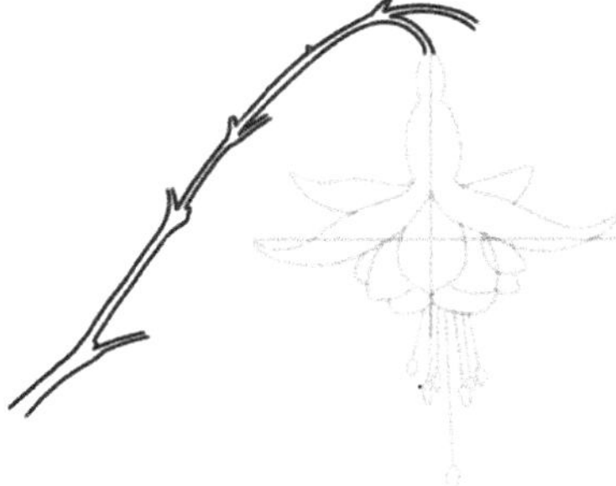

08

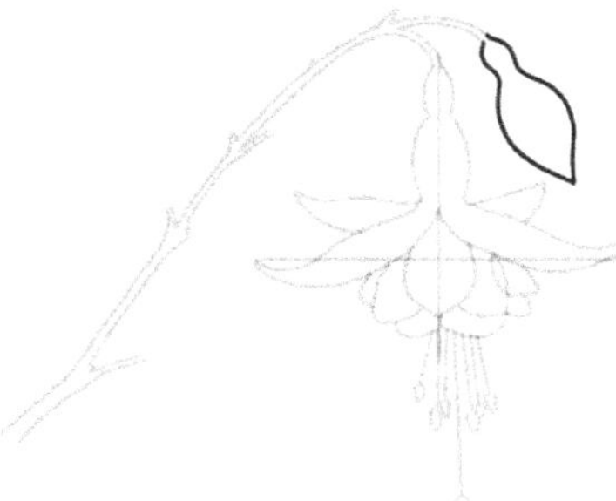

09

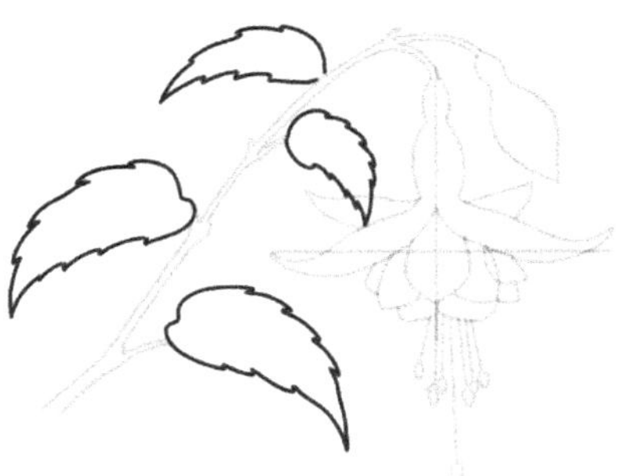

10

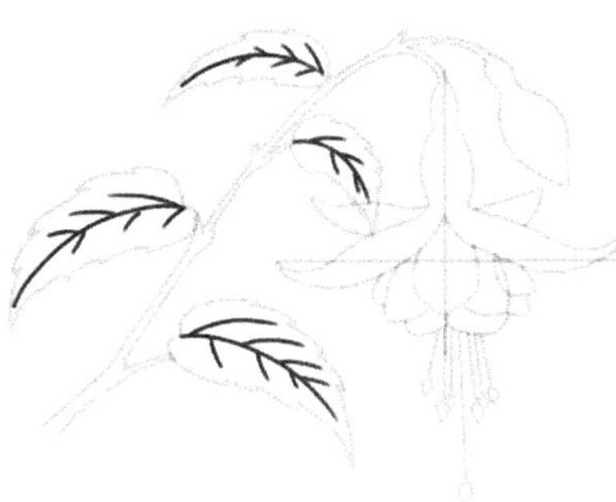

11

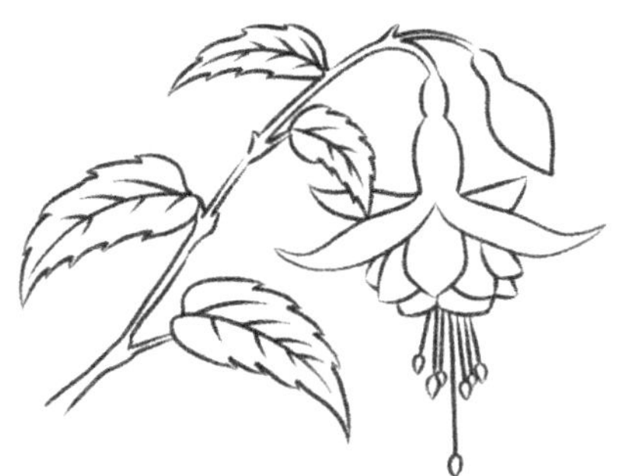

12

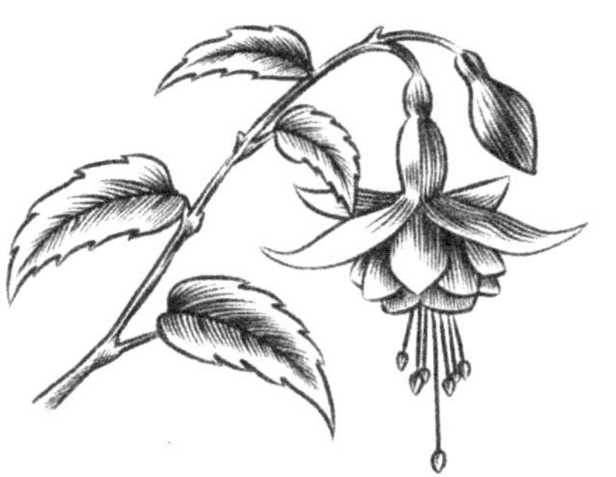

HOW TO DRAW FLOWERS

GARDENIA

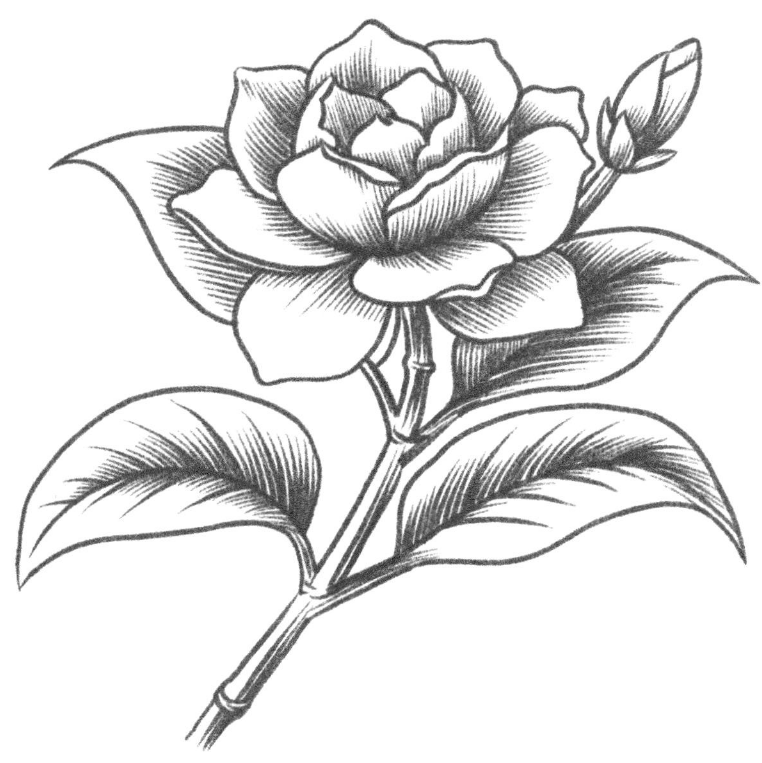

Gardenias symbolise purity, sweetness, and secret love, often associated with beauty, gentle joy, and the profound connections that flourish quietly beneath the surface.

01

02

03

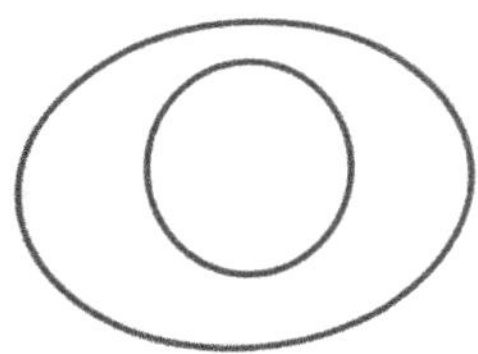

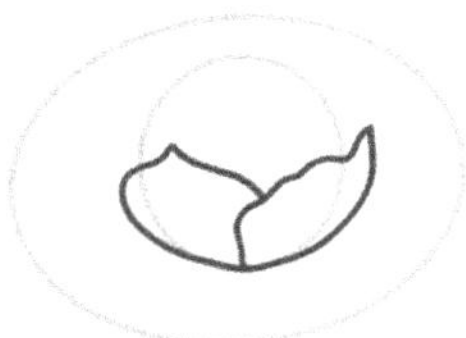

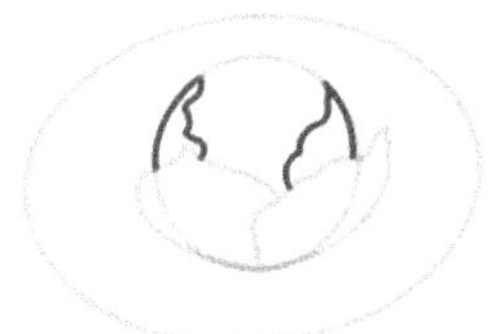

04

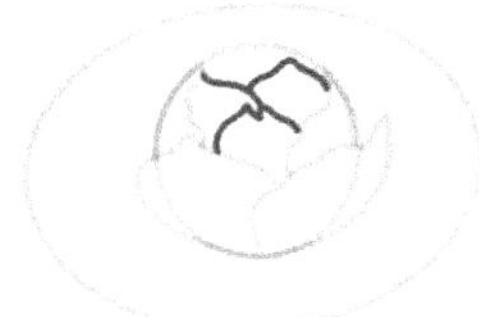

05

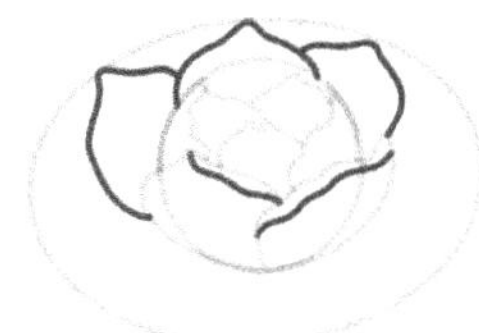

06

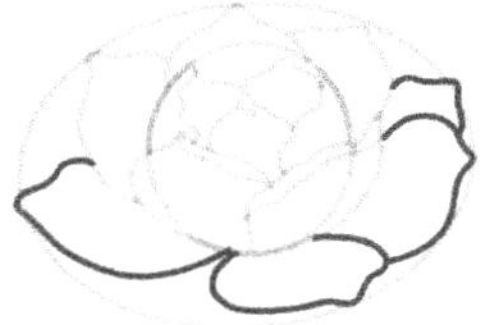

07

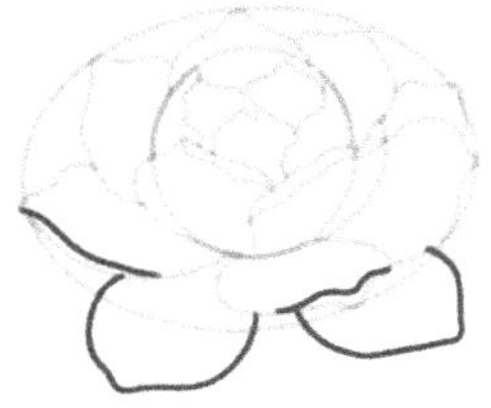

08

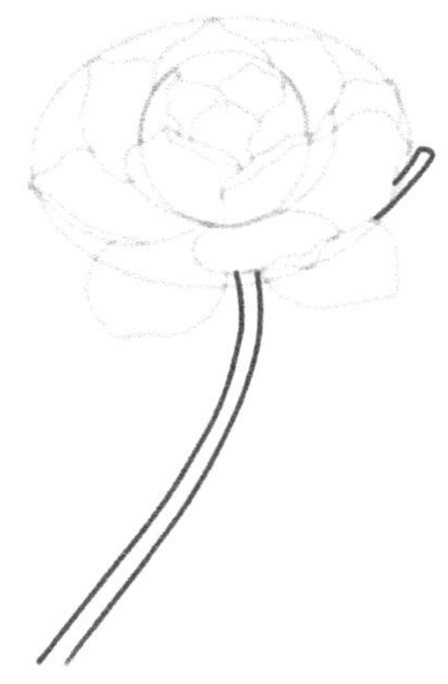

09

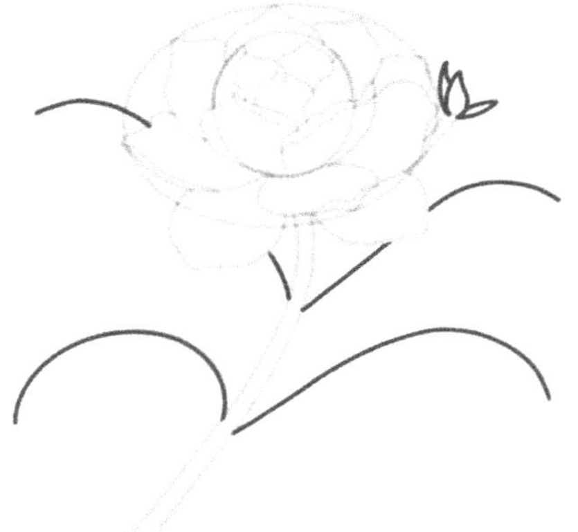

10

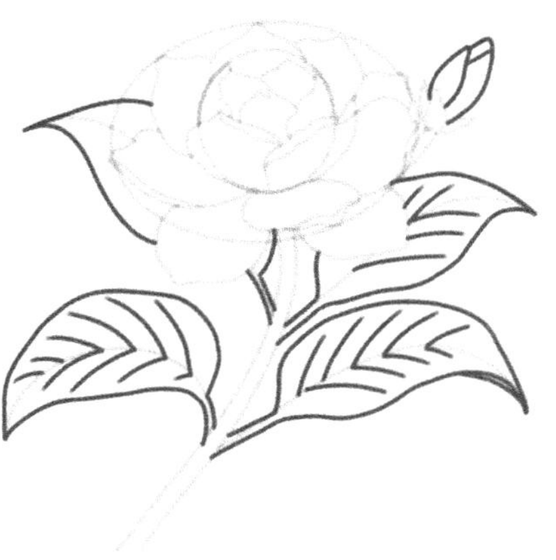

11

12

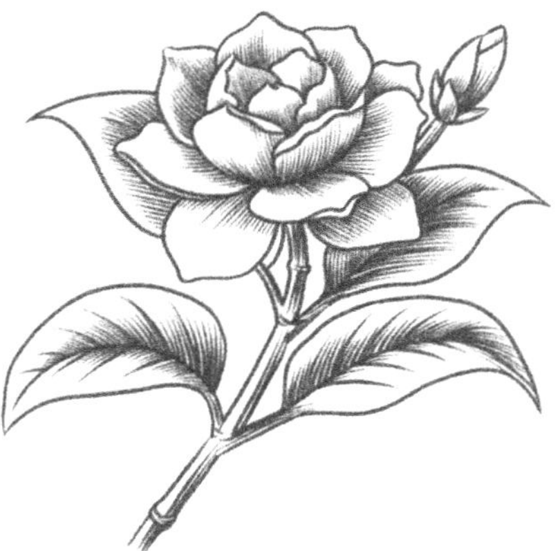

GERANIUM

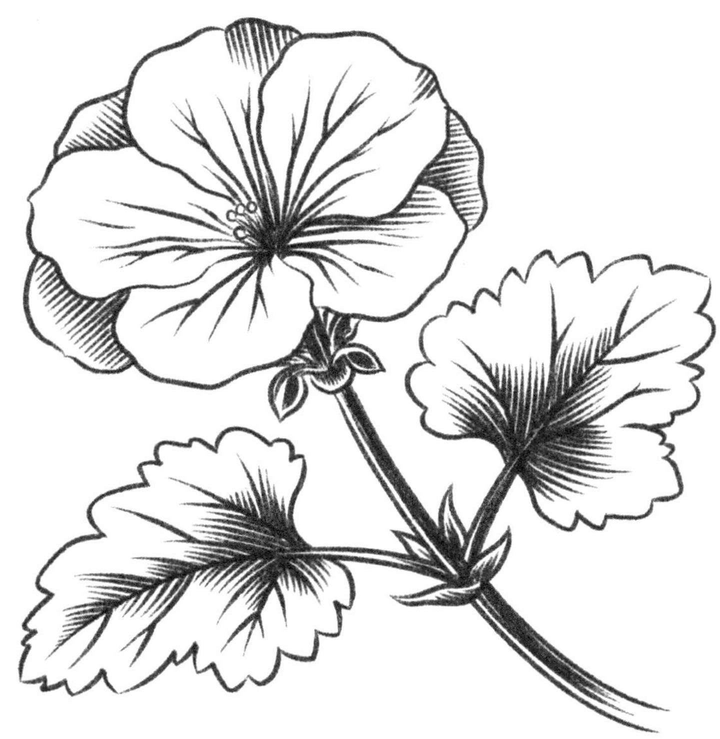

Geraniums symbolise friendship, positivity, and protection, often associated with comfort, good health, and the steady warmth found in loyal companionship and enduring support through life's challenges.

01

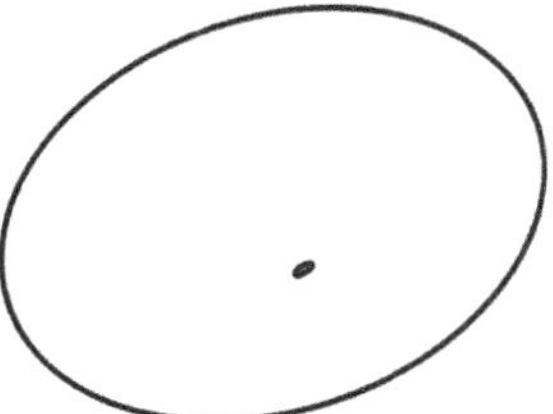

02

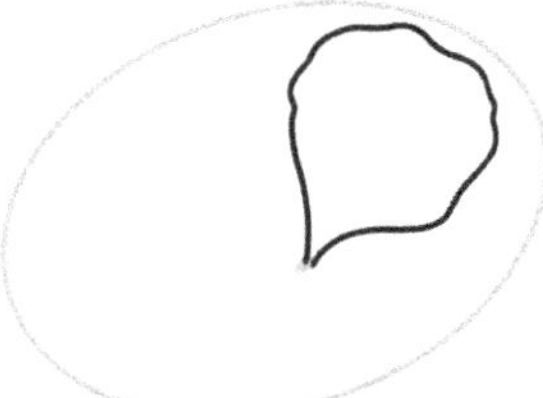

03

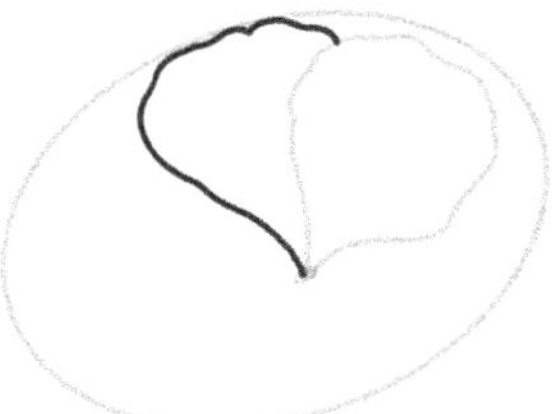

04

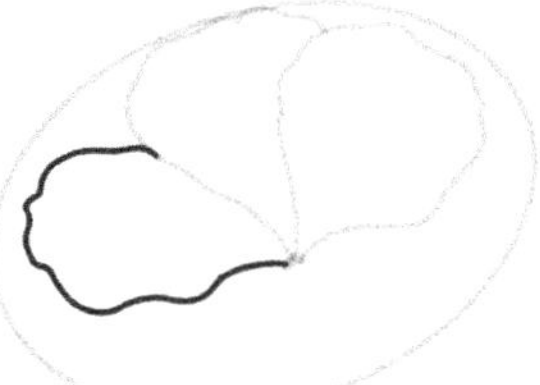

05

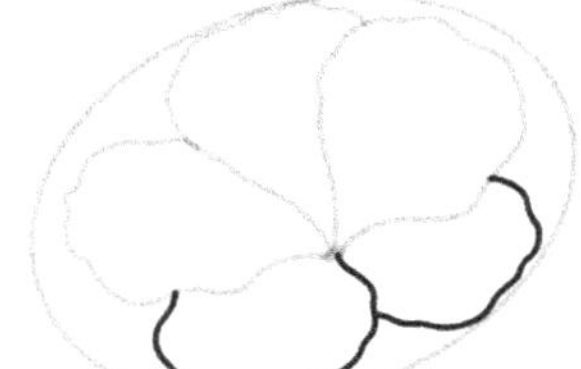

06

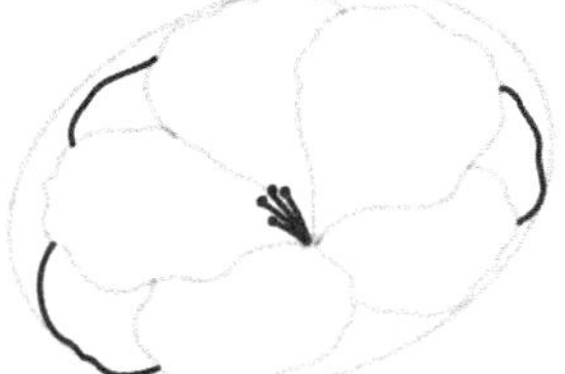

07

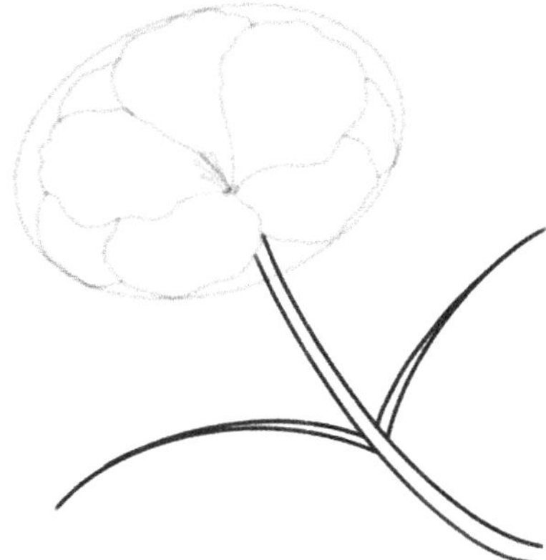

08

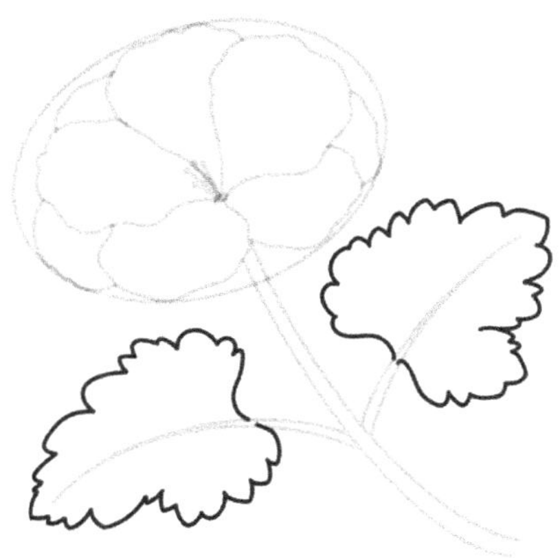

09

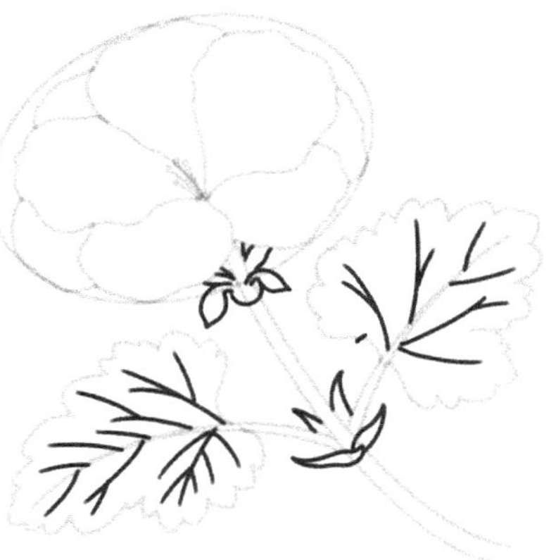

10

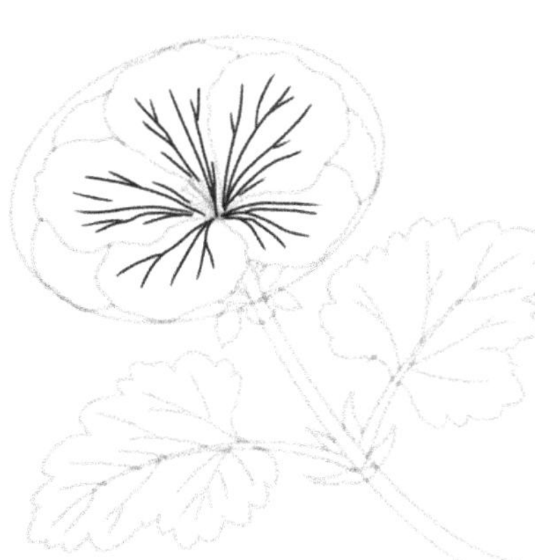

11

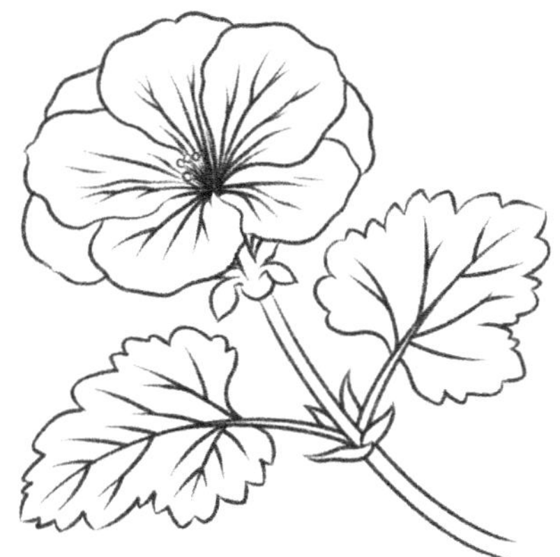

12

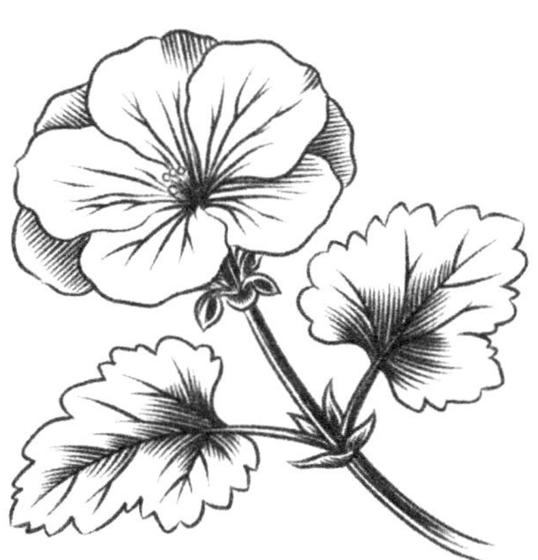

GERBERA

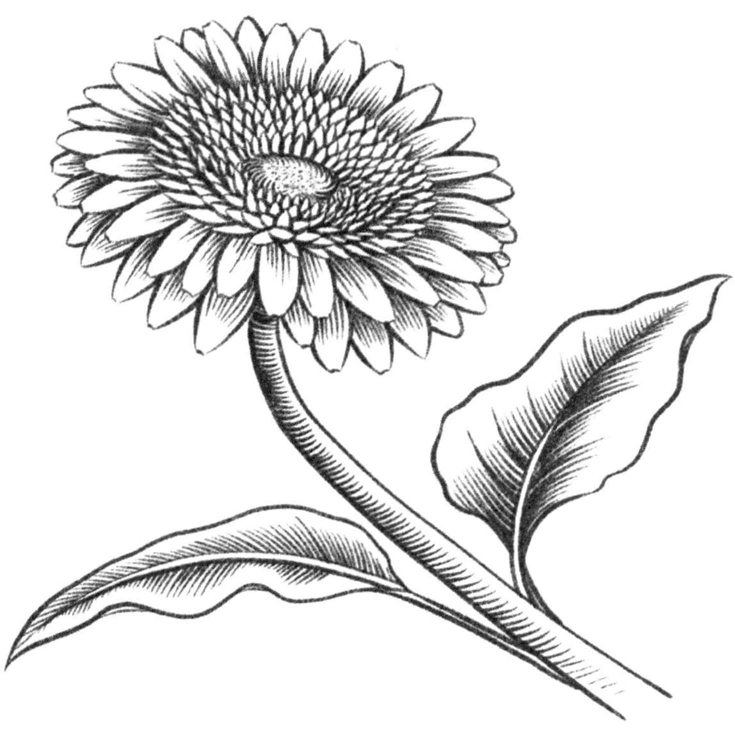

Gerberas symbolise cheerfulness, purity, and innocence, often associated with optimism, vibrant energy, and the uplifting joy that brightens even the simplest moments in life.

01

02

03

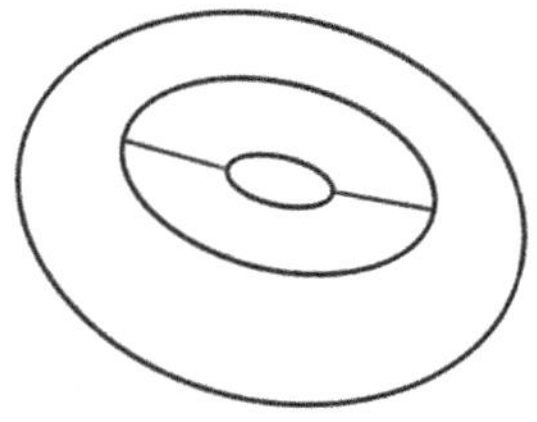

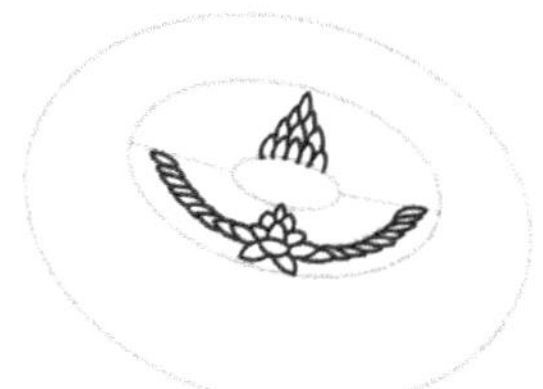

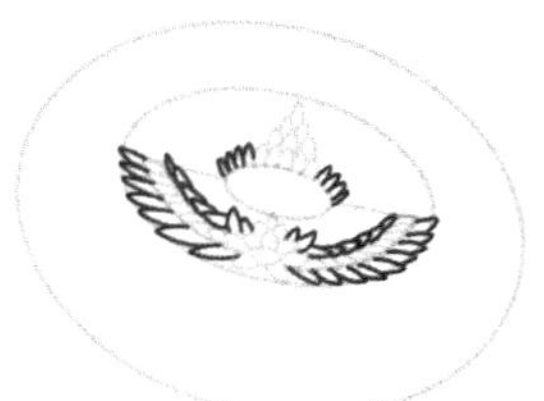

04

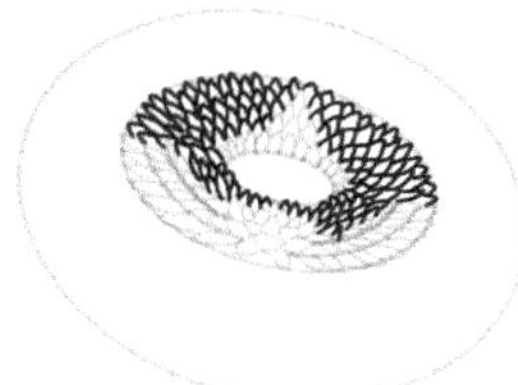

05

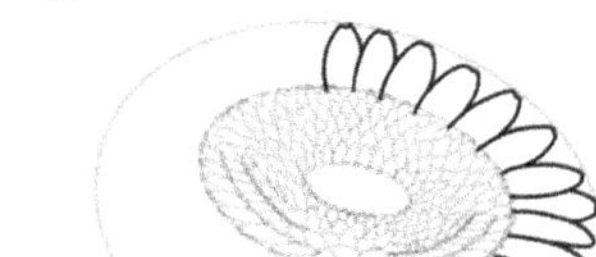

06

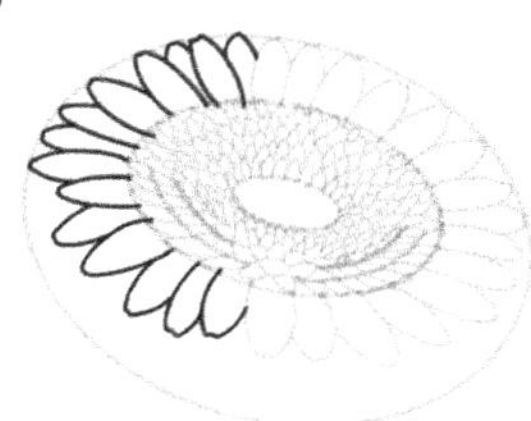

07

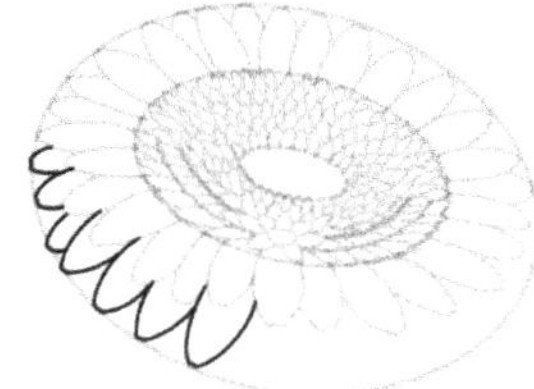

08

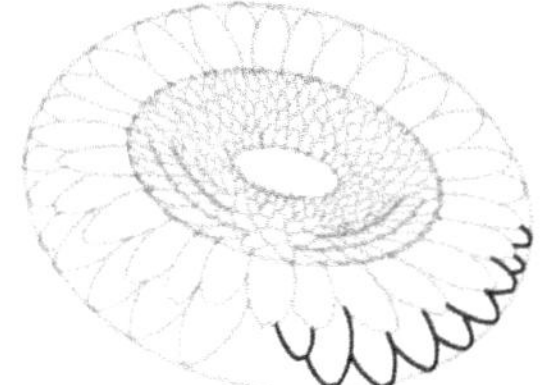

09

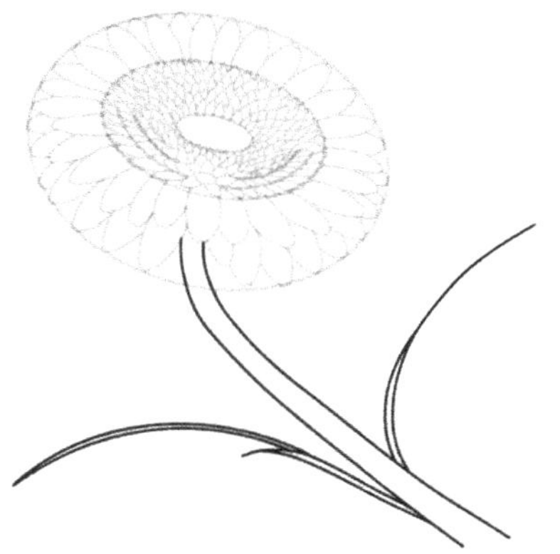

10

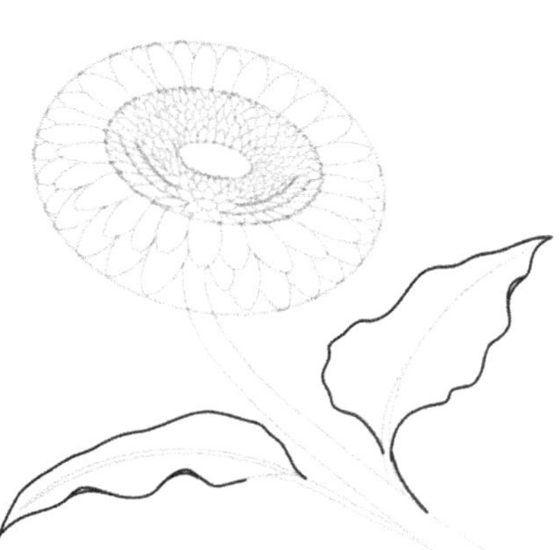

11

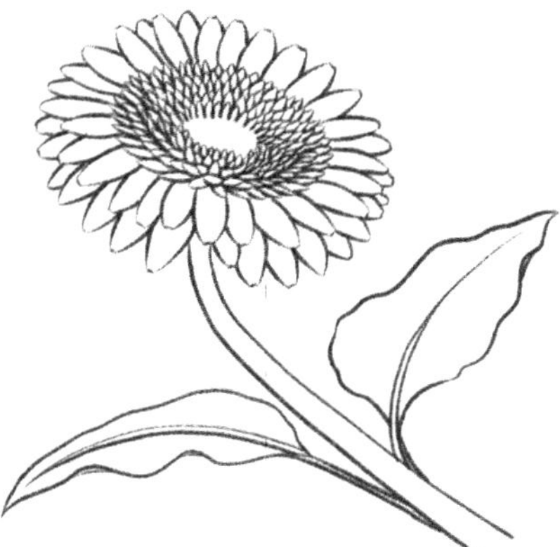

12

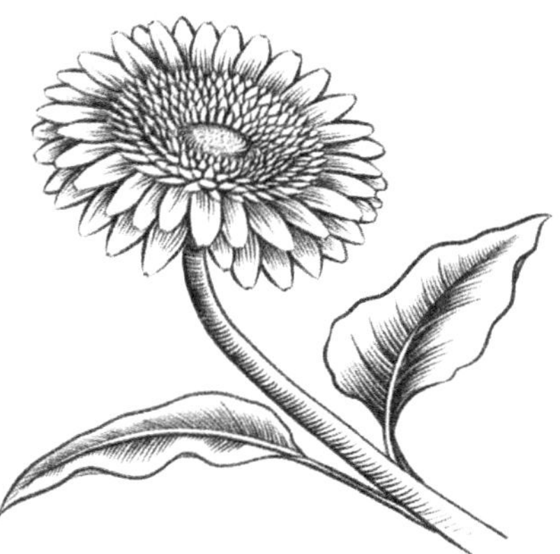

HIBISCUS

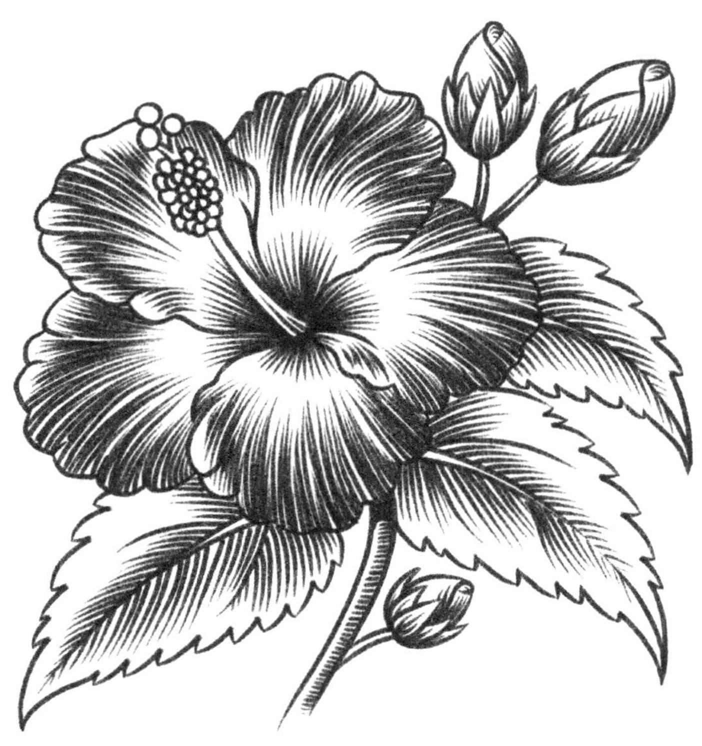

Hibiscus symbolises delicate beauty, femininity, and passion, often associated with fleeting moments, grace, and the vibrant allure of tropical warmth and charm.

01

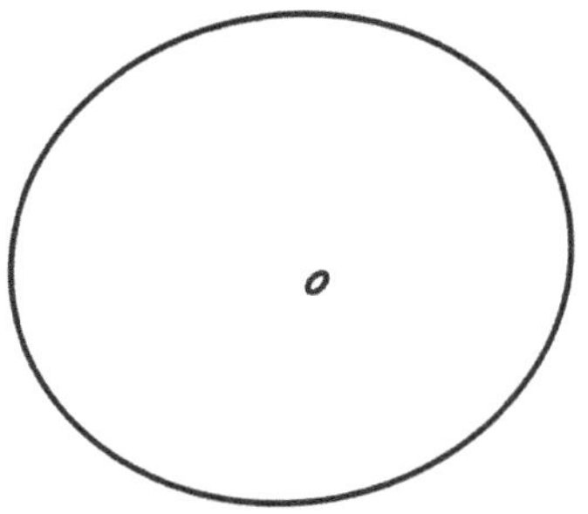

02

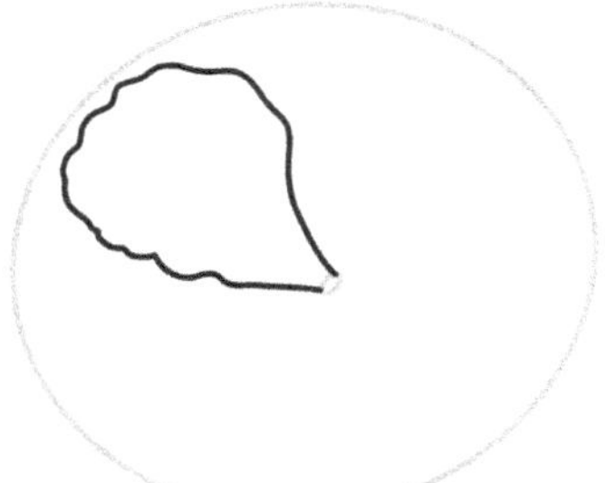

03

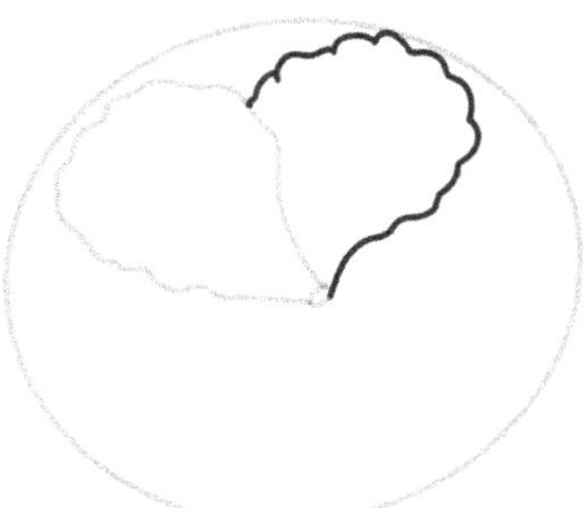

04

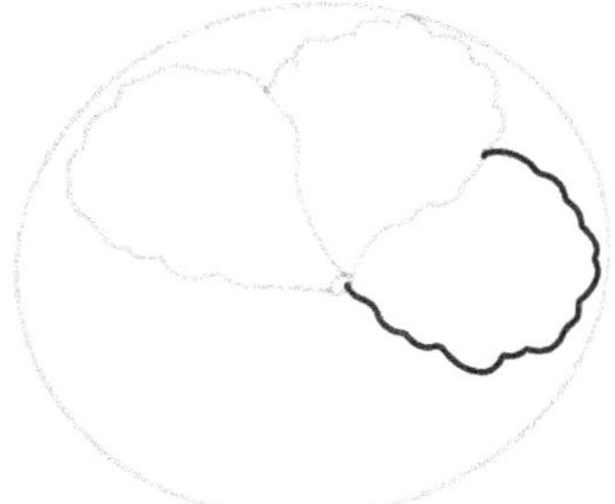

05

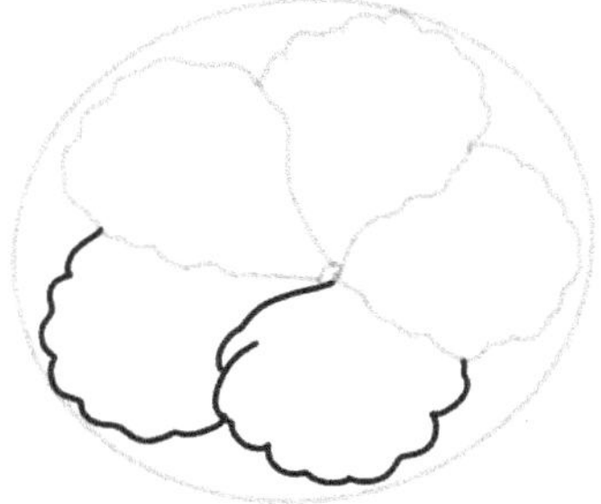

06

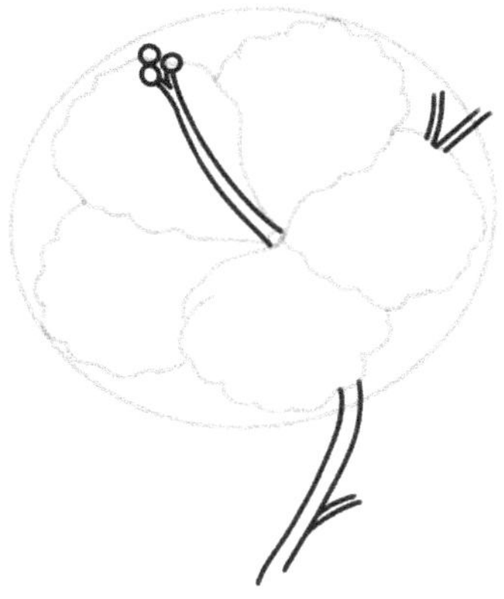

07

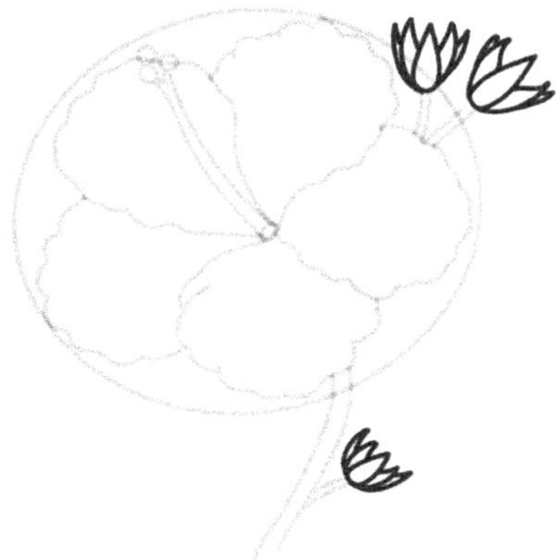

08

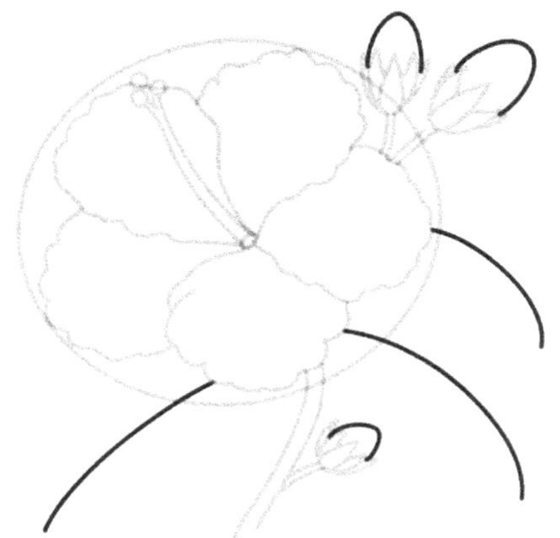

09

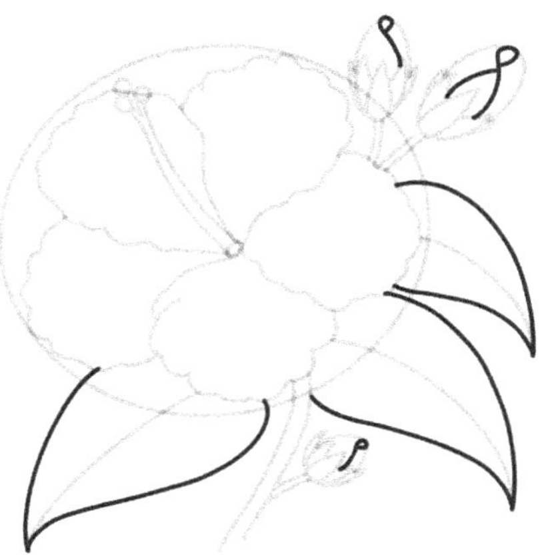

10

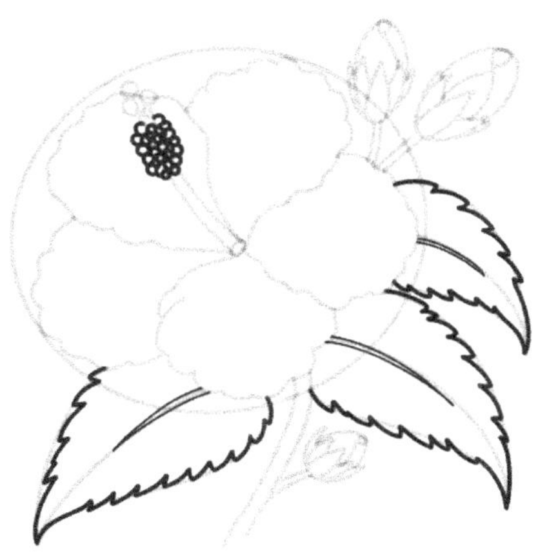

11

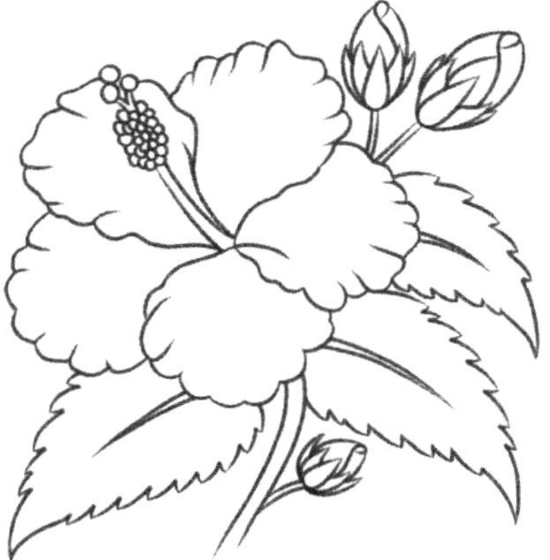

12

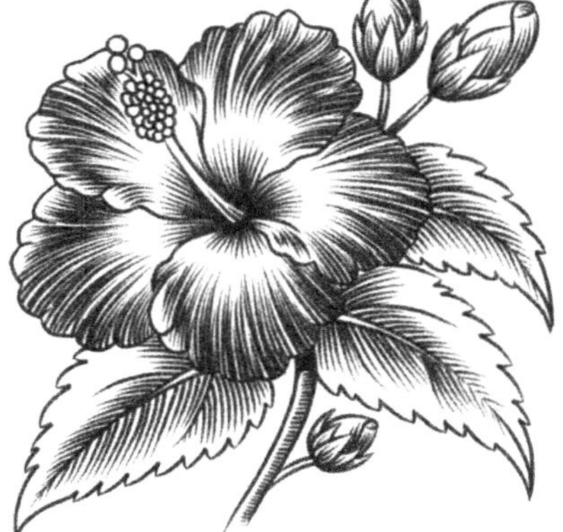

HOW TO DRAW FLOWERS

IRIS

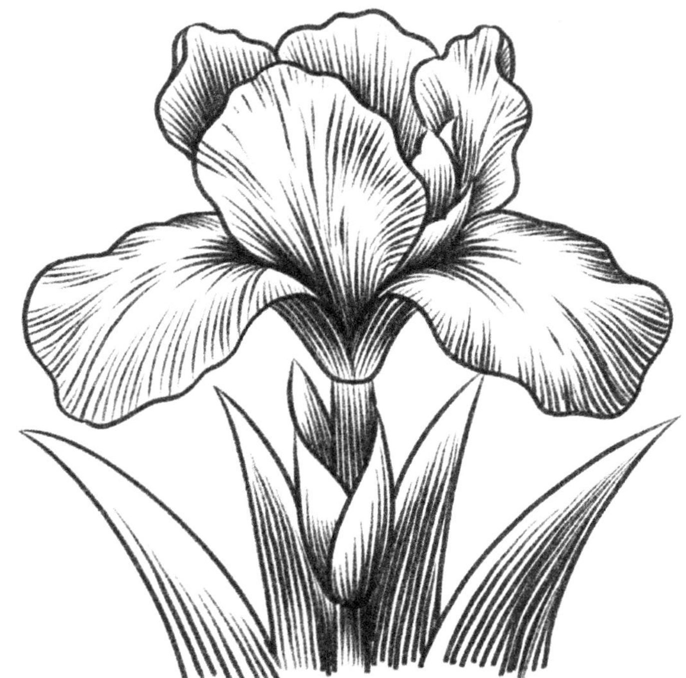

Irises symbolise wisdom, courage, and faith, often associated with hope, communication, and the mystical bridge between earthly and spiritual realms, embodying clarity, intuition, and deep inspiration.

01

02

03

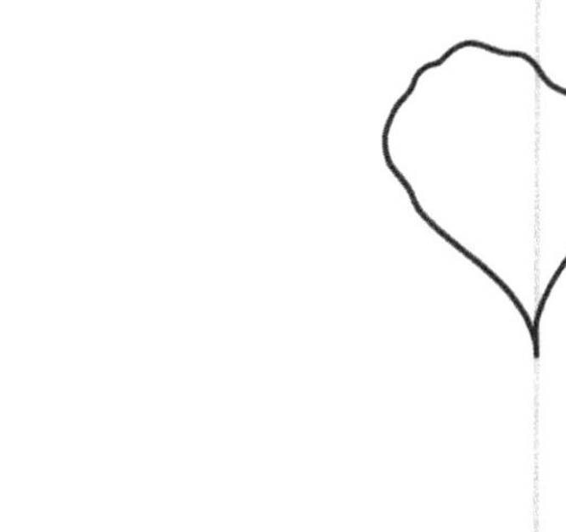

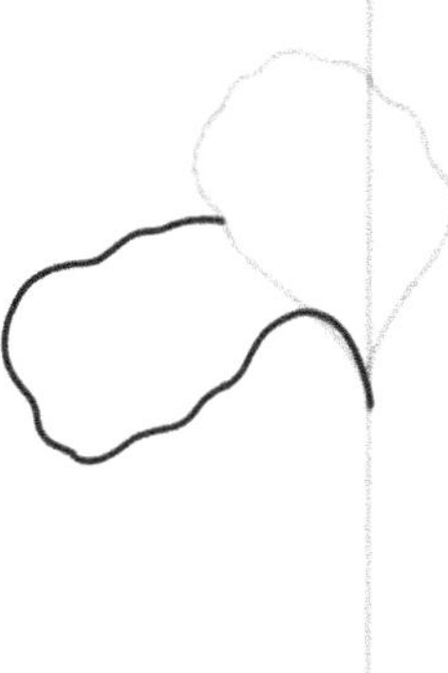

04

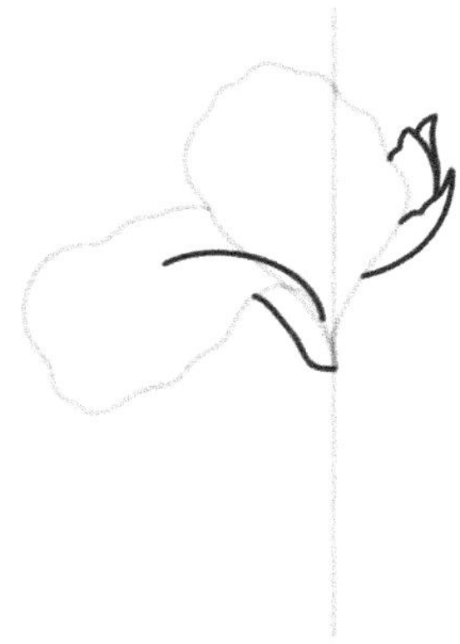

05

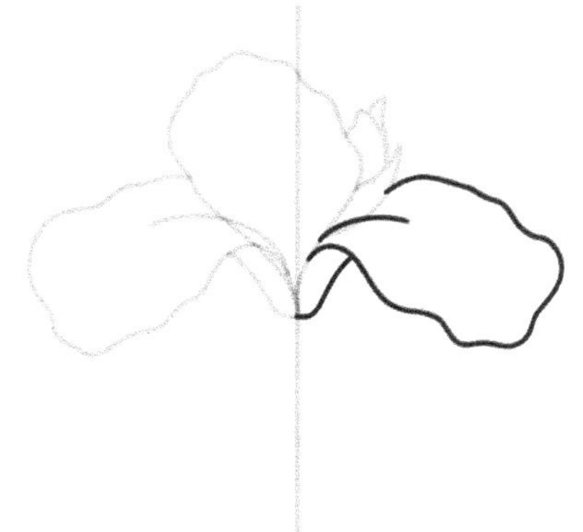

06

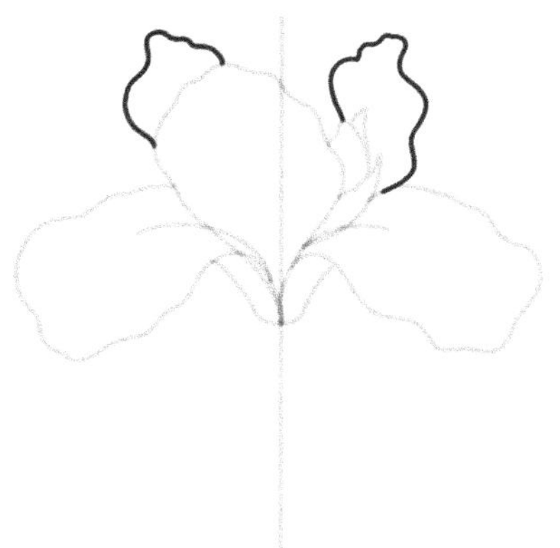

07

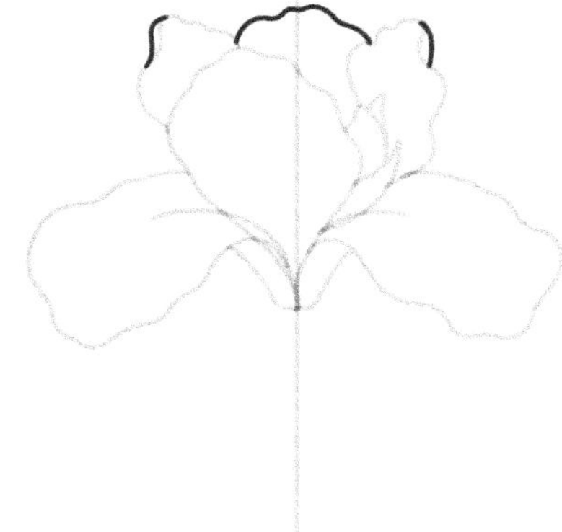

08

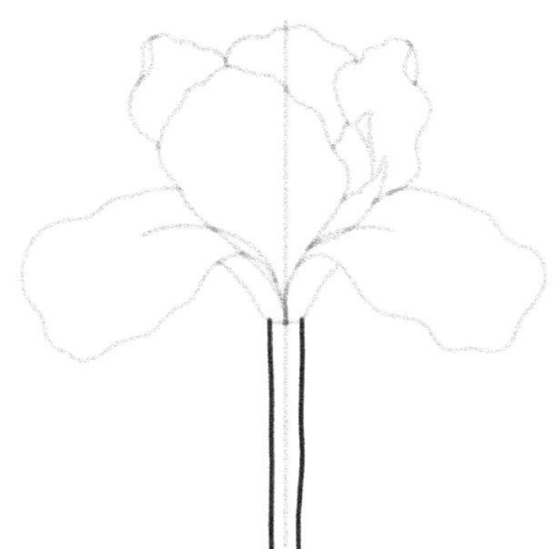

09

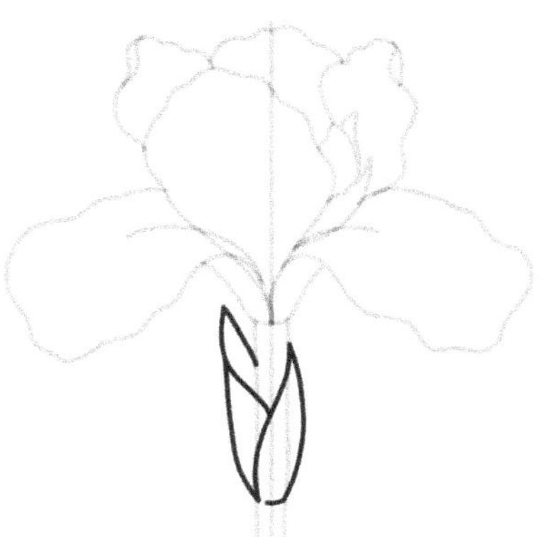

10

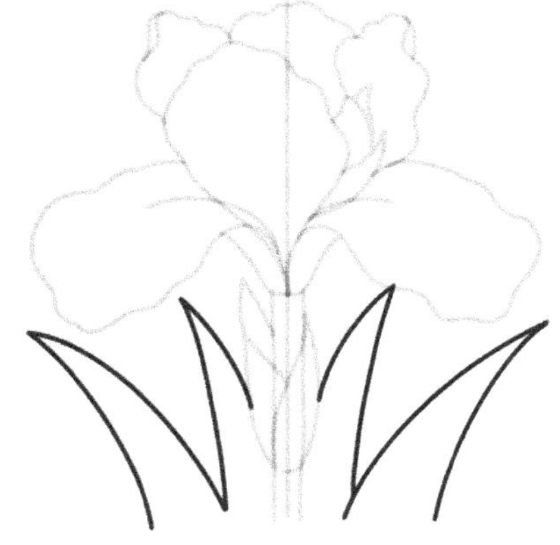

11

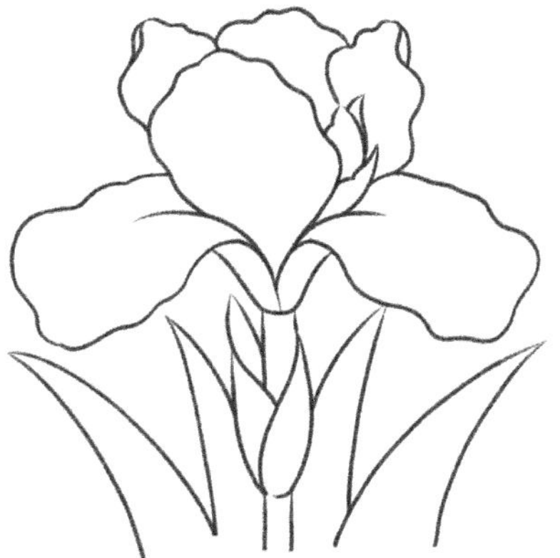

12

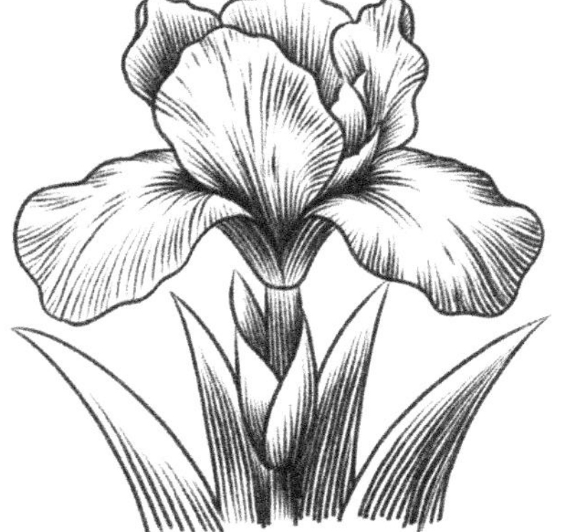

HOW TO DRAW FLOWERS

HOW TO DRAW FLOWERS

JASMINE

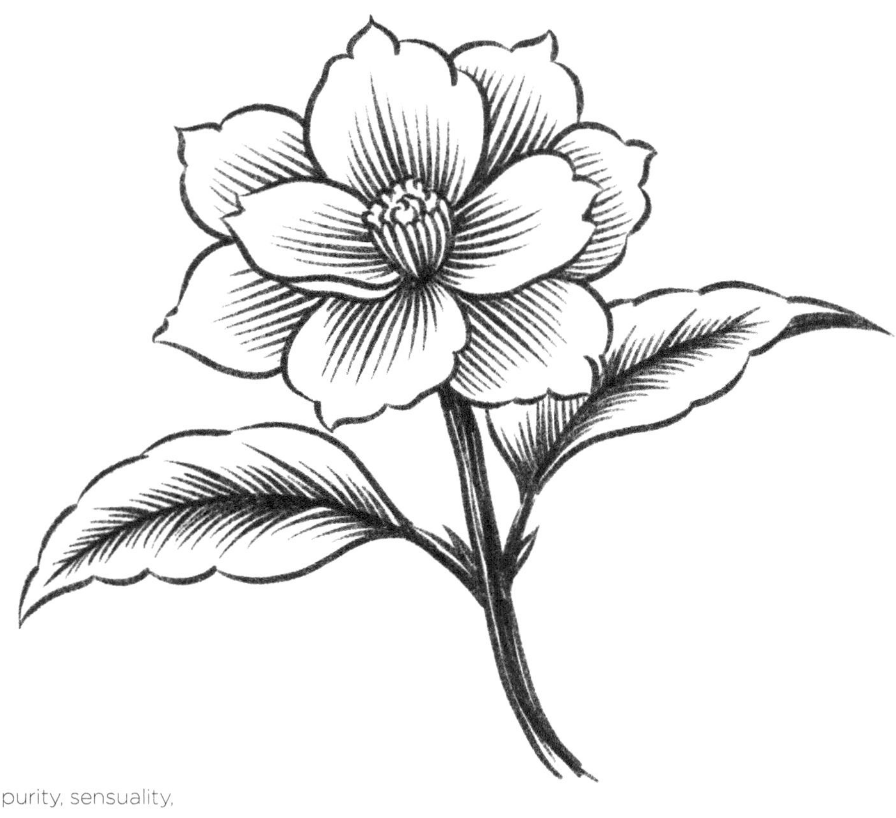

Jasmine symbolises purity, sensuality, and grace, often associated with love, beauty, and the enchanting allure of a tranquil evening, evoking feelings of peace and spiritual harmony.

01

02

03

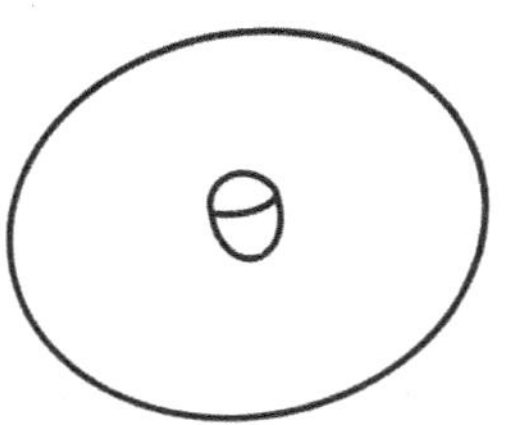

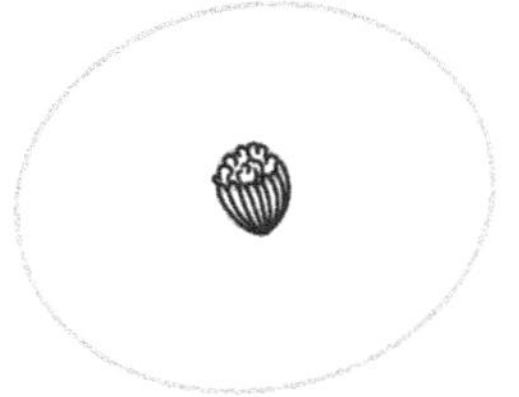

04

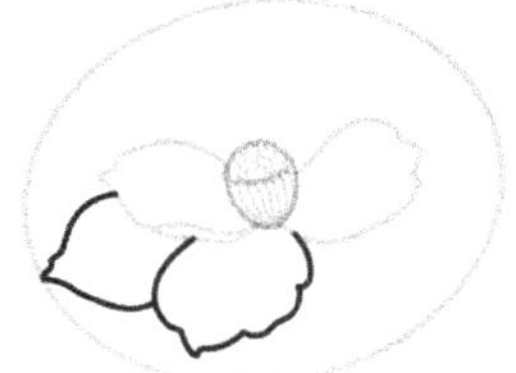

05

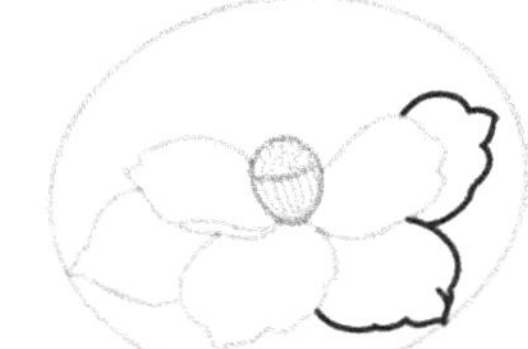

06

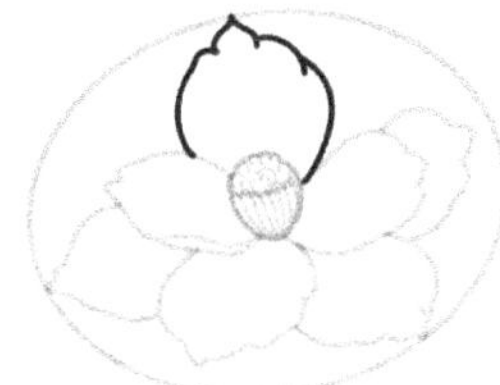

07

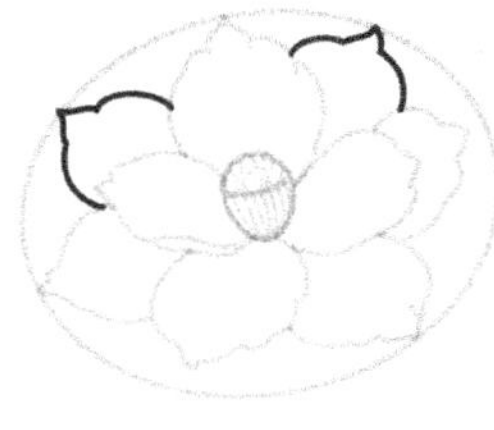

08

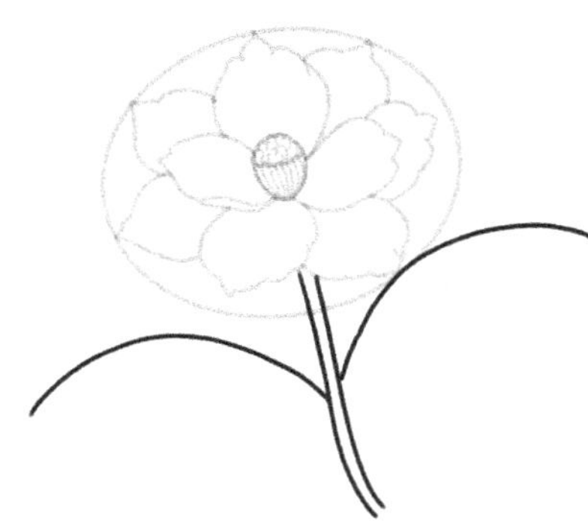

09

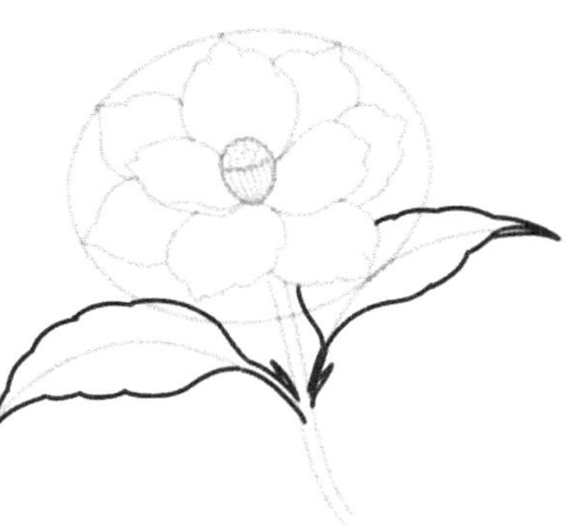

10

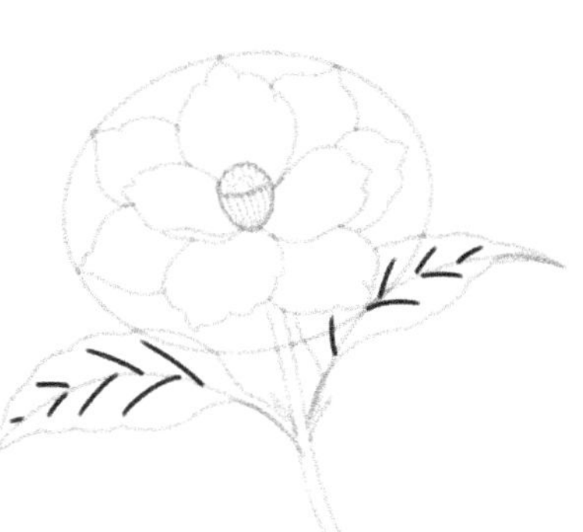

11

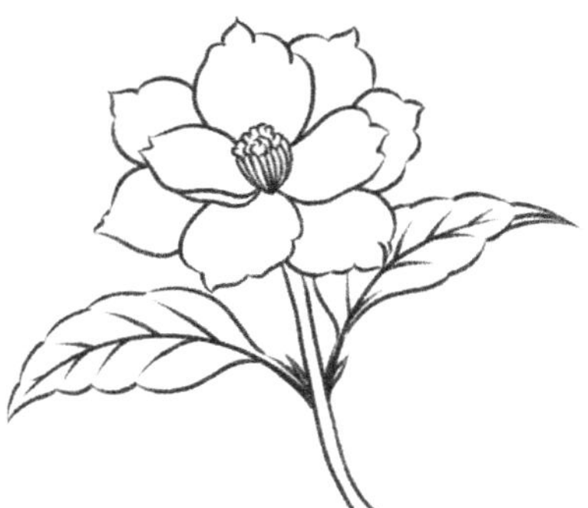

12

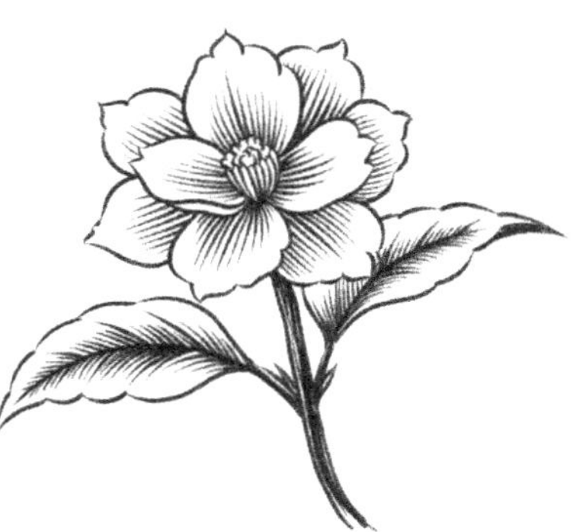

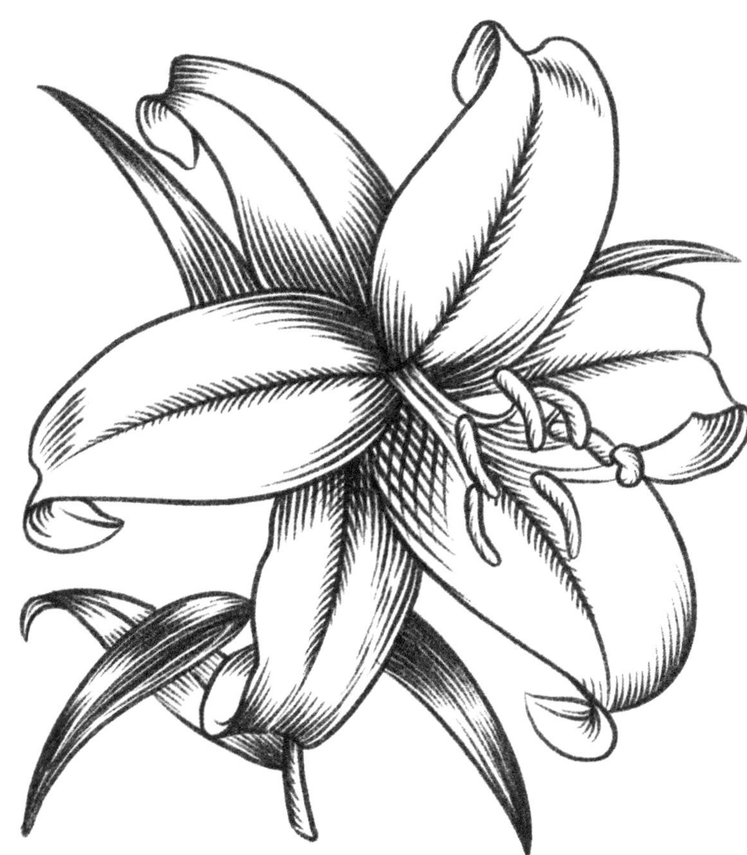

LILY

Lilies symbolise purity, renewal, and transience, often associated with spiritual devotion, rebirth, and the serene beauty of life's delicate and ephemeral nature.

01   02   03

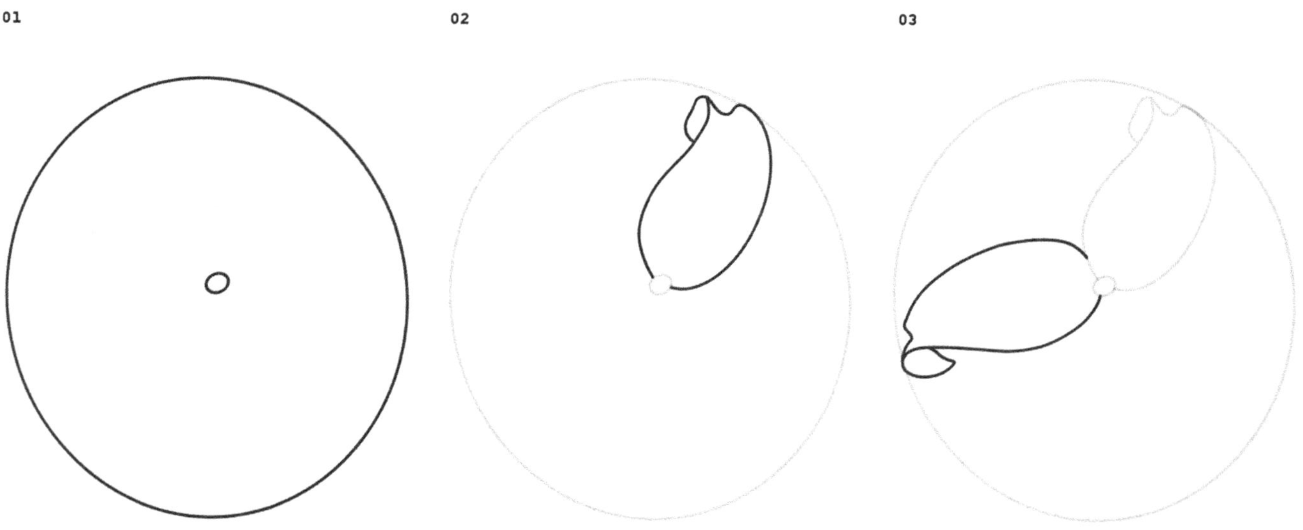

04

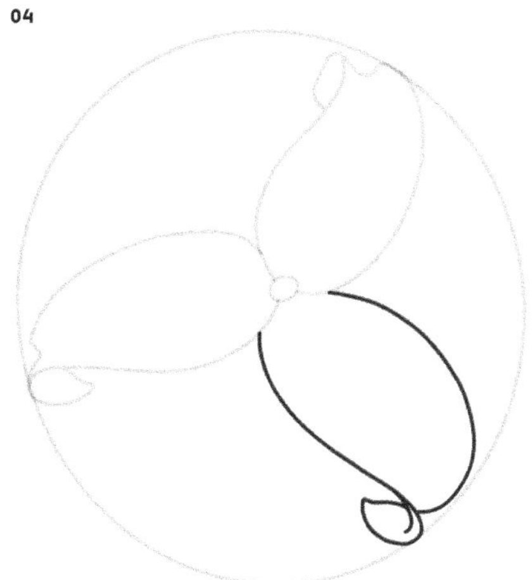

05

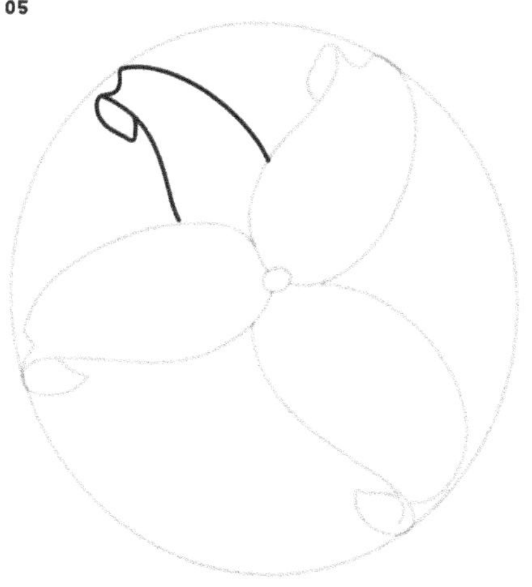

06

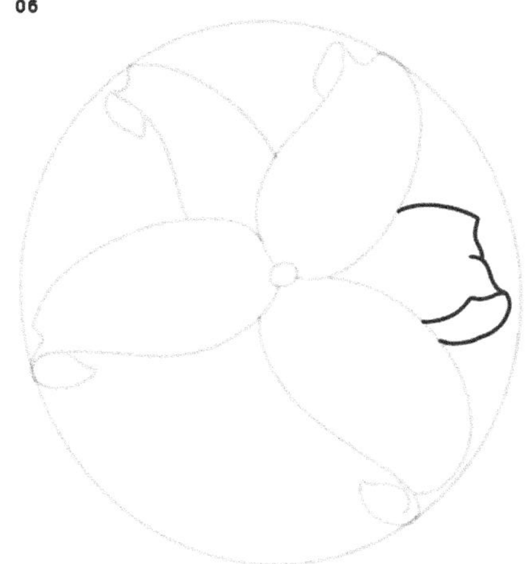

07

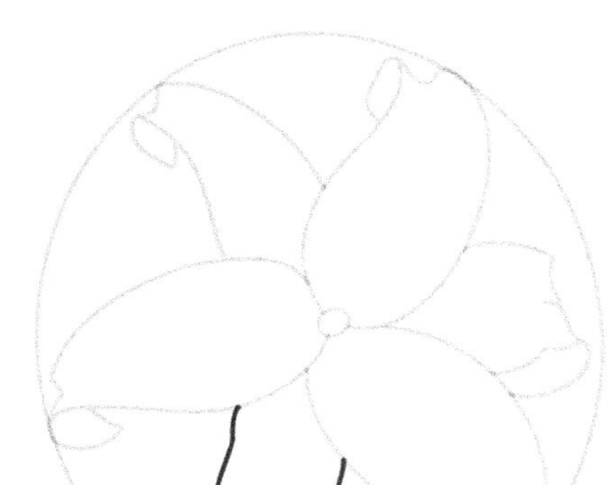

08

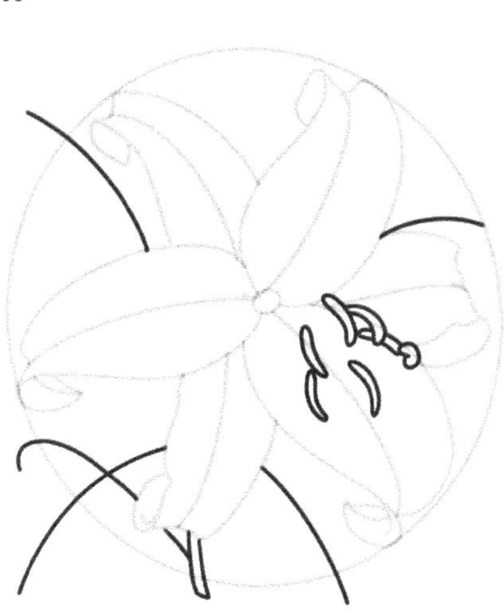

09

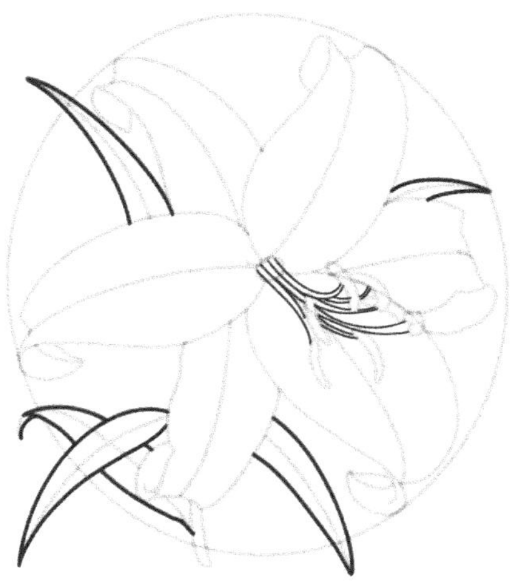

10

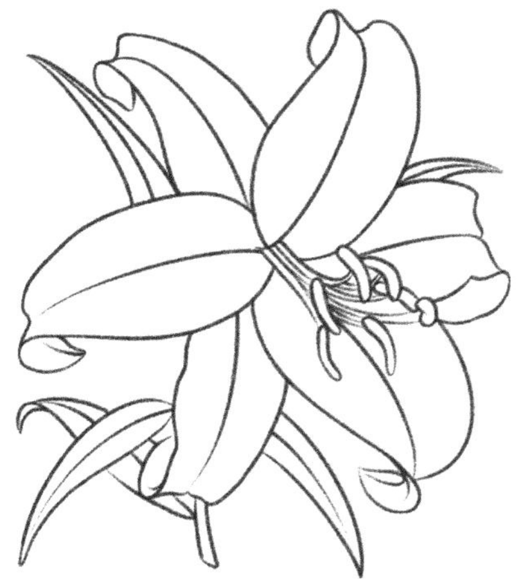

11

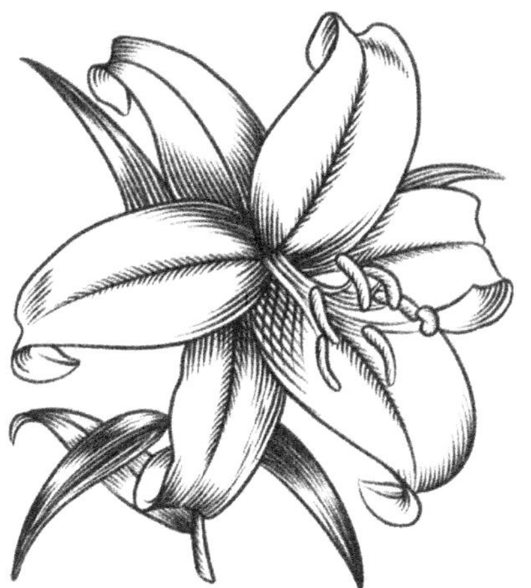

MAGNOLIA

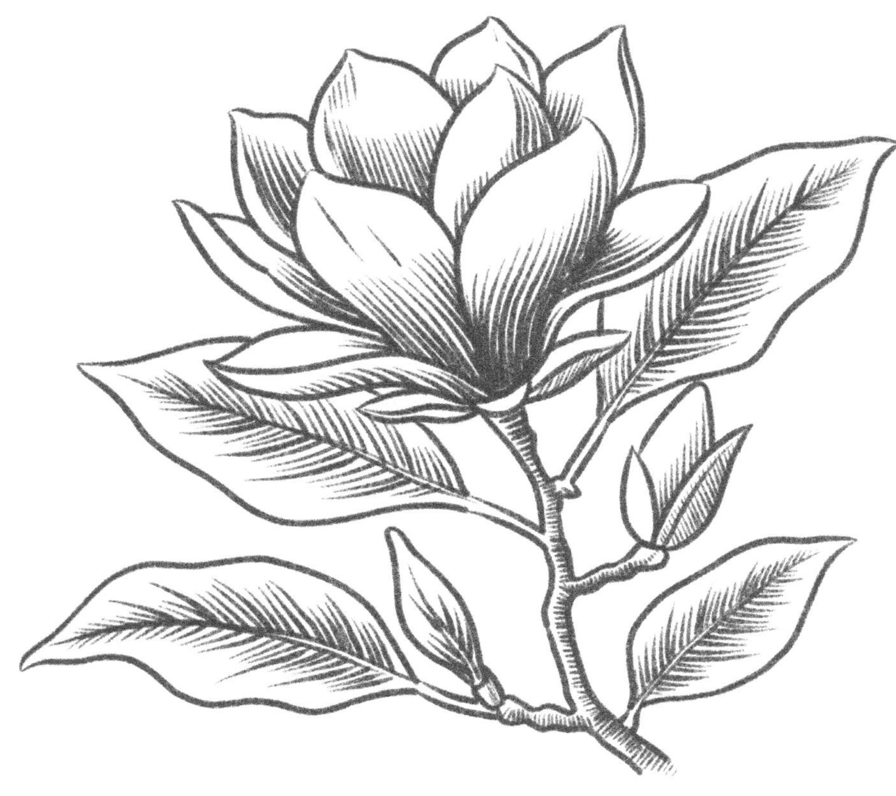

Magnolias symbolise dignity, perseverance, and beauty, often associated with strength, resilience, and the majestic grace that comes from enduring life's challenges with poise.

01

02

03

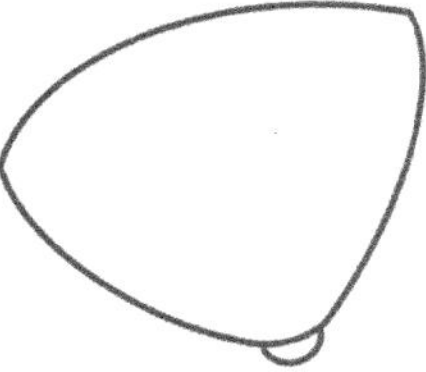

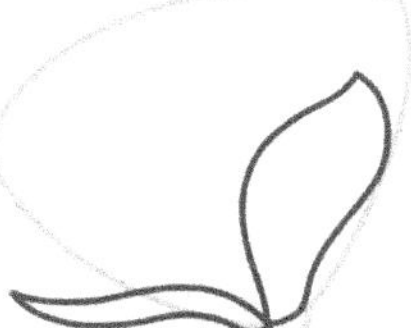

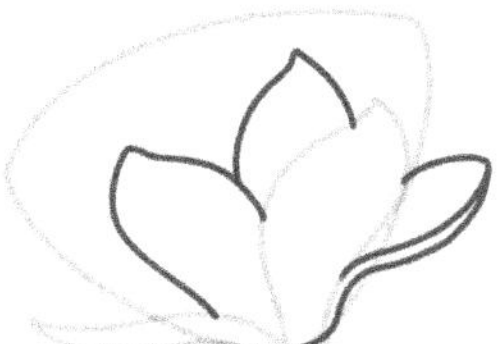

04

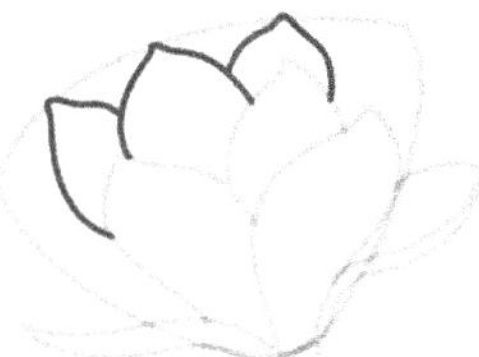

05

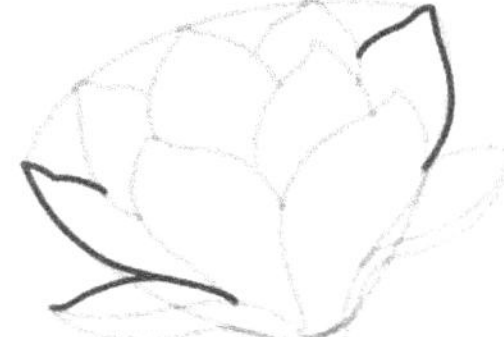

06

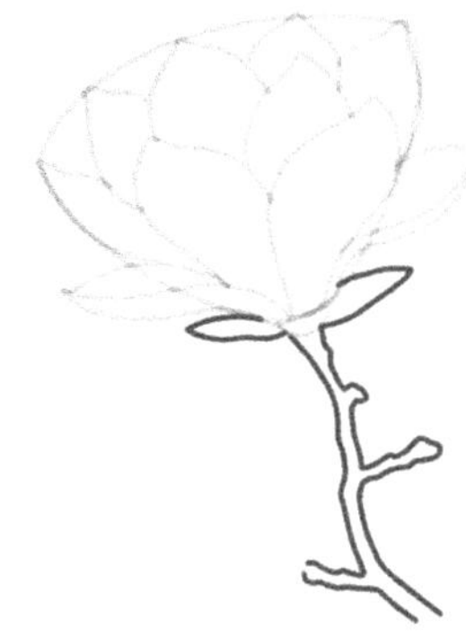

07

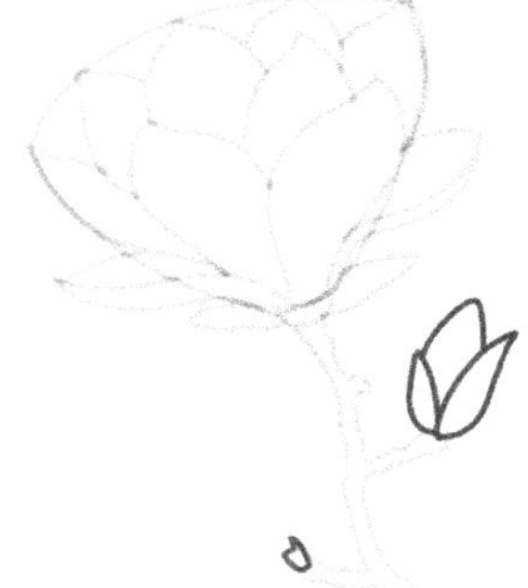

08

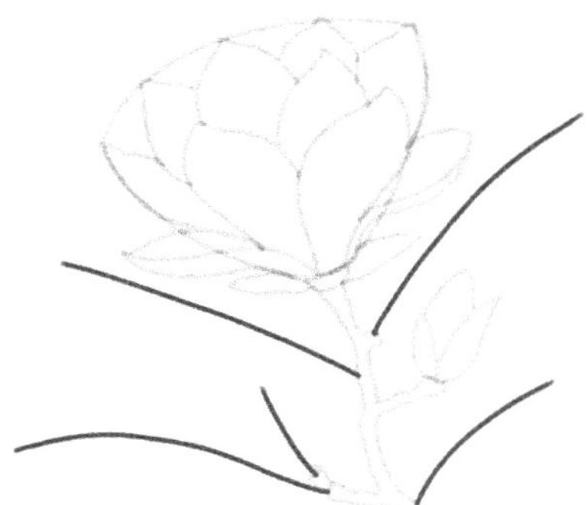

09

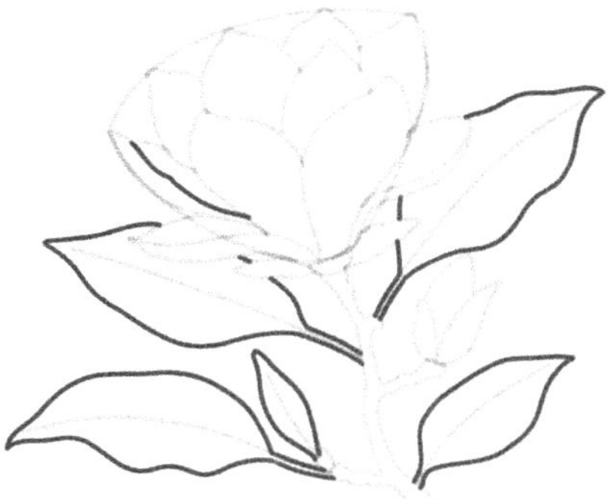

HOW TO DRAW FLOWERS

10

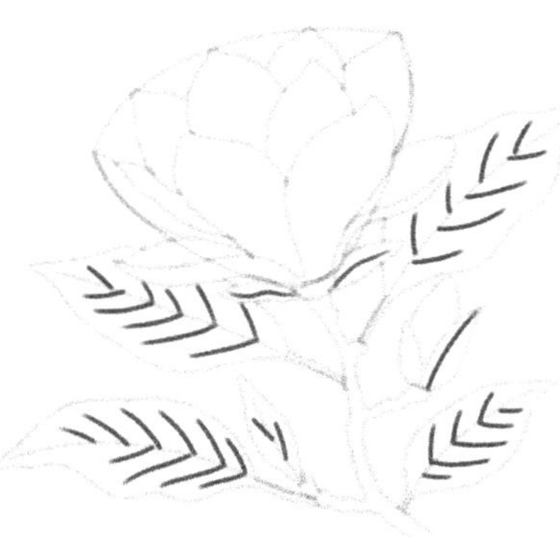

11

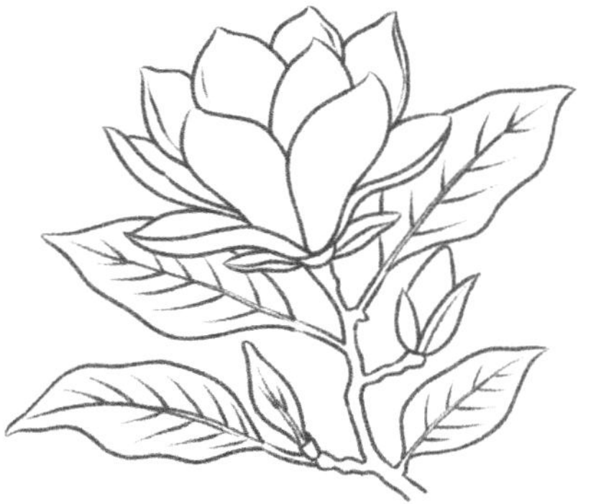

12

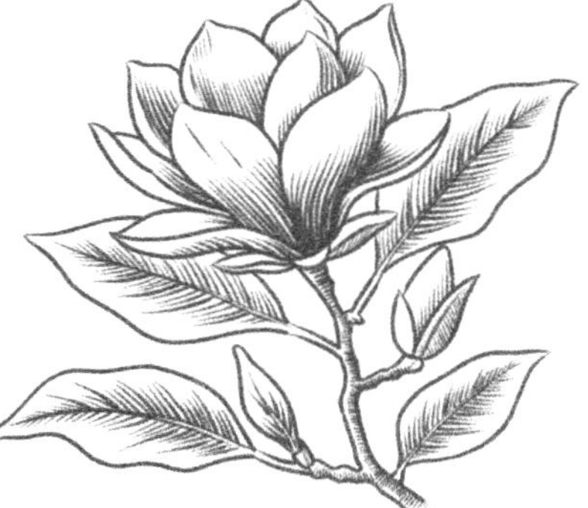

MEXICAN FLEABANE

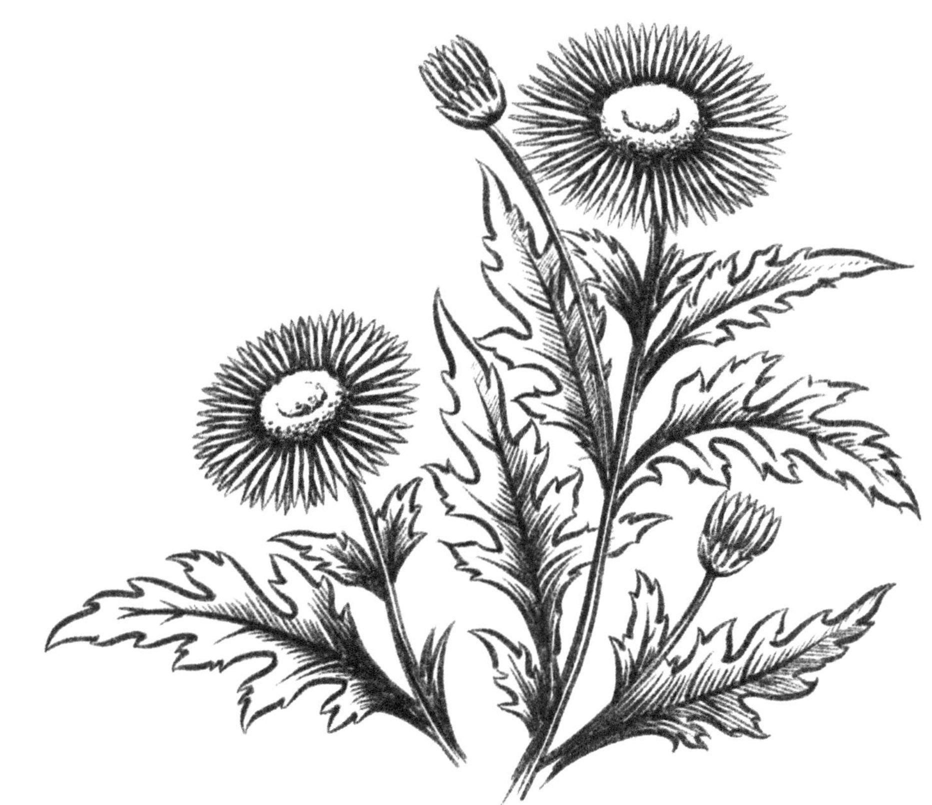

Mexican Fleabane symbolises resilience and adaptability, often associated with cheerful persistence, thriving in unexpected places, and bringing simple beauty to overlooked spaces.

01

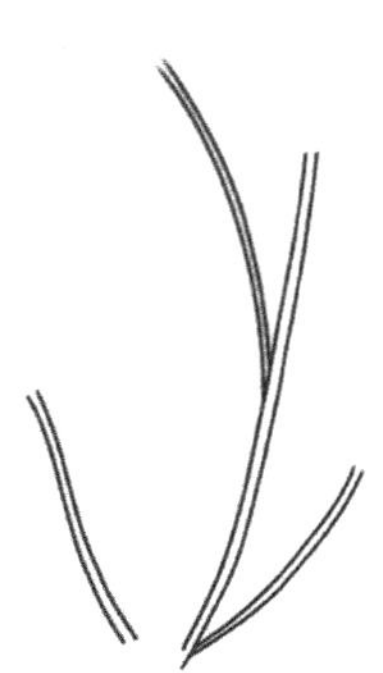

02

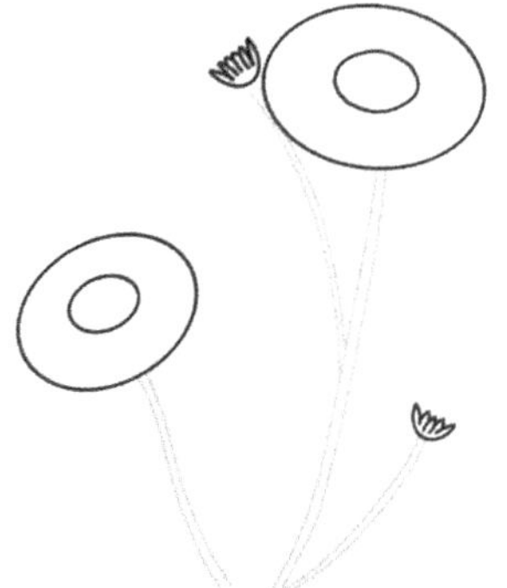

03

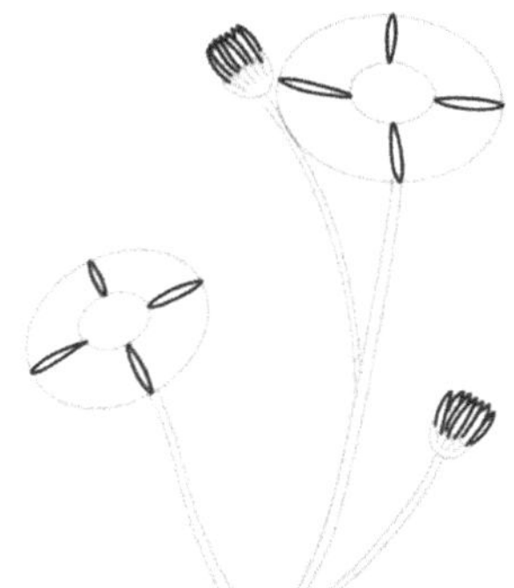

04

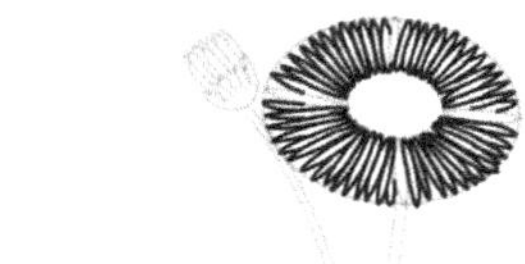

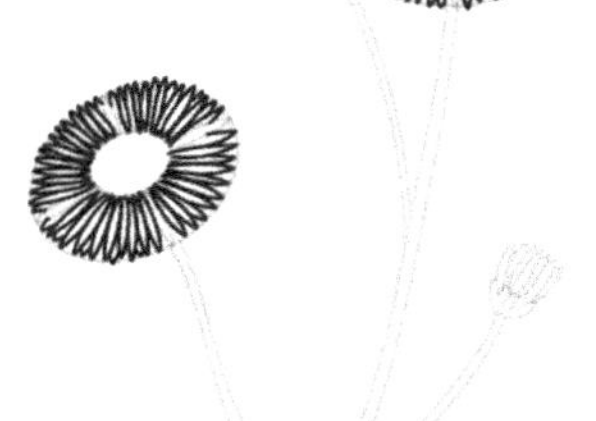

05

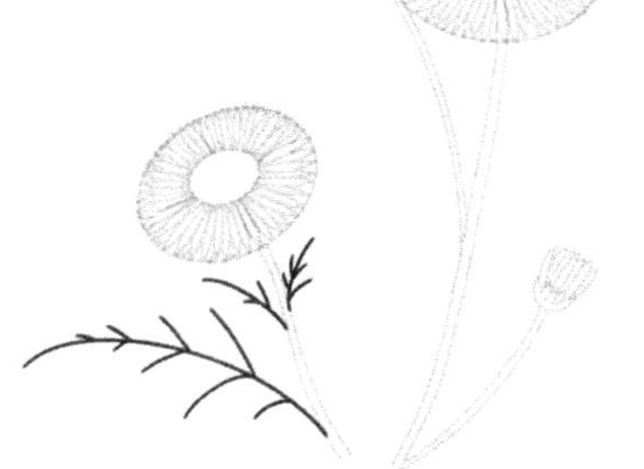

06

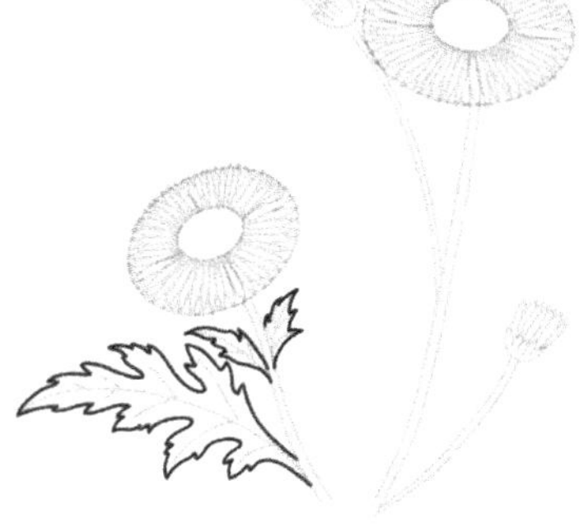

07

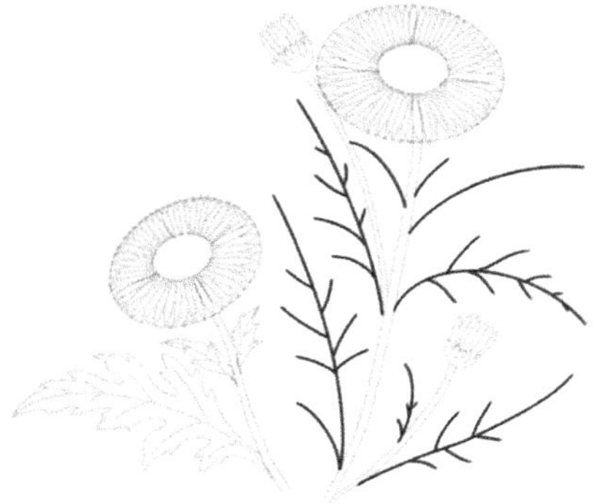

08

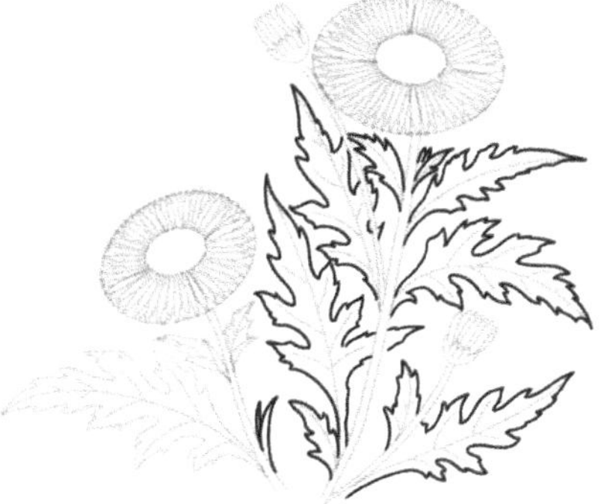

09

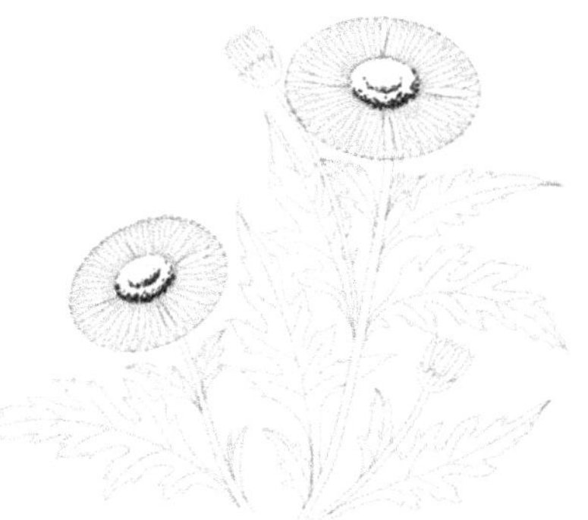

10

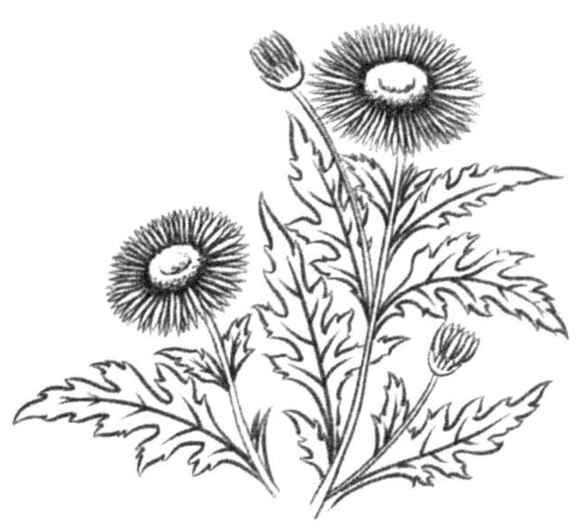

11

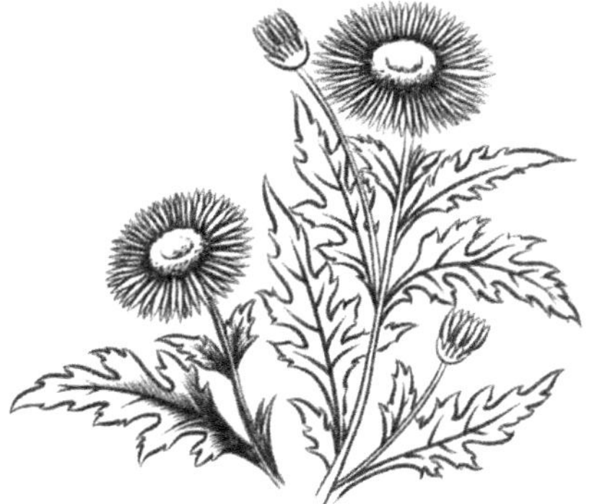

12

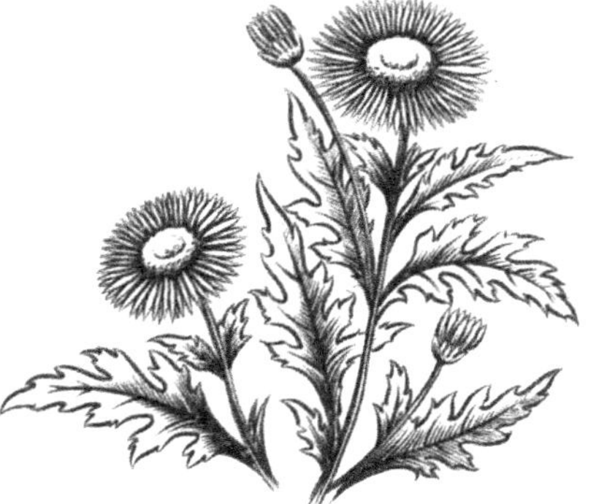

MORNING GLORY

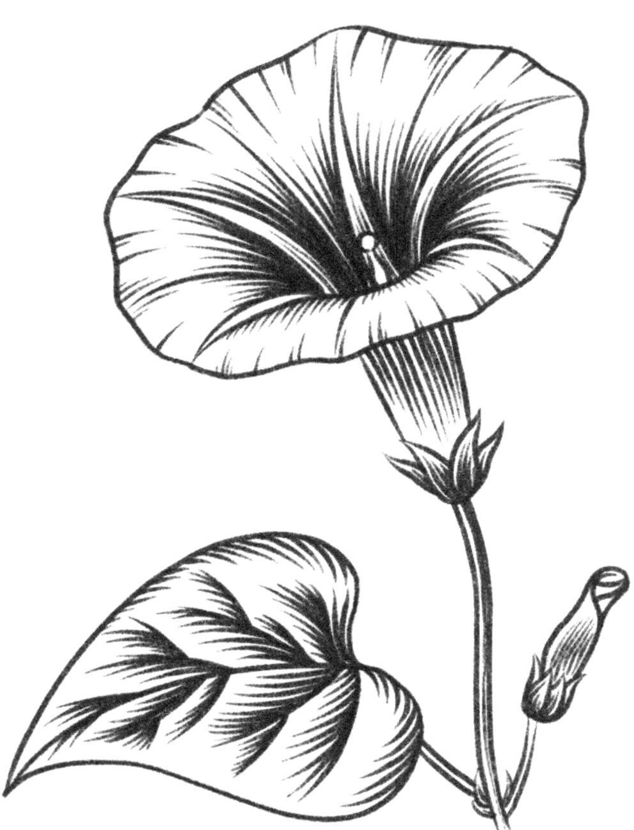

Morning Glories symbolise love, affection, and the fleeting nature of time, often associated with renewal, the beauty of dawn, and the reminder to embrace life's precious moments.

01

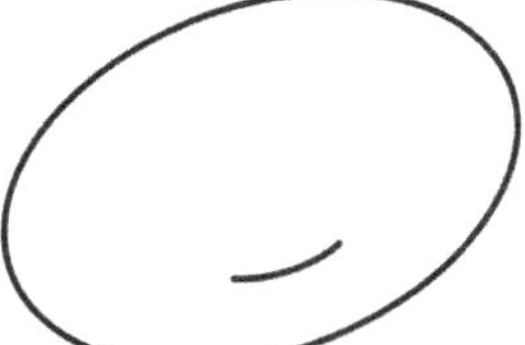

02

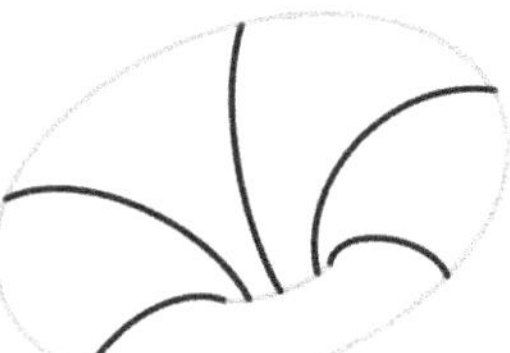

03

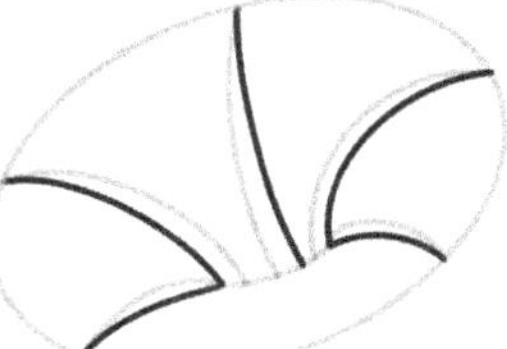

04

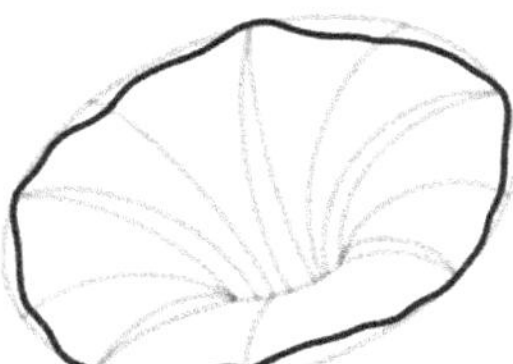

05

06

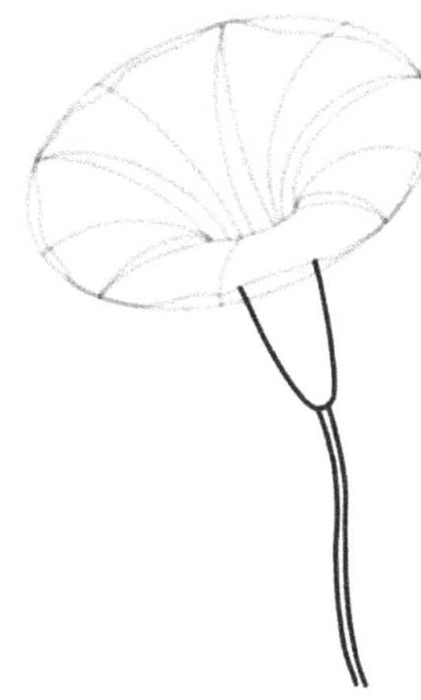

07

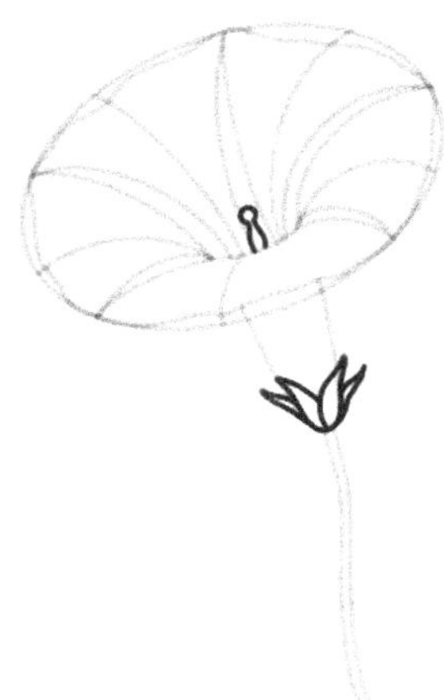

08

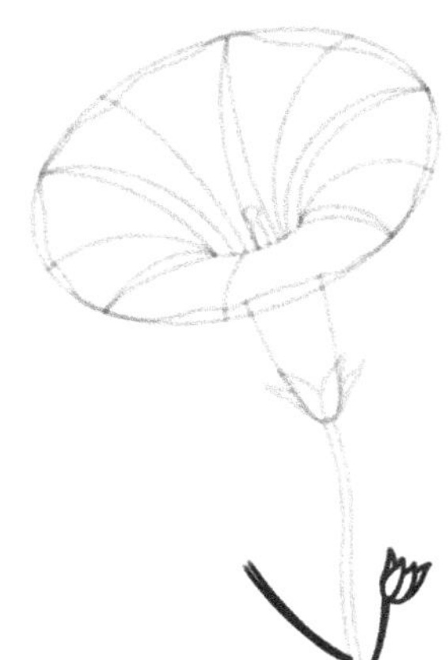

09

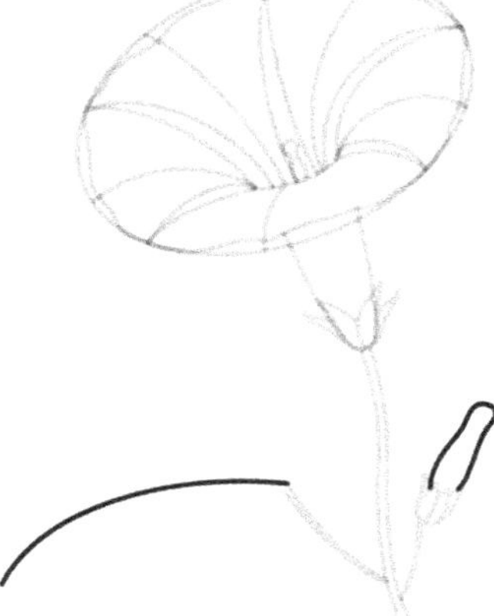

10

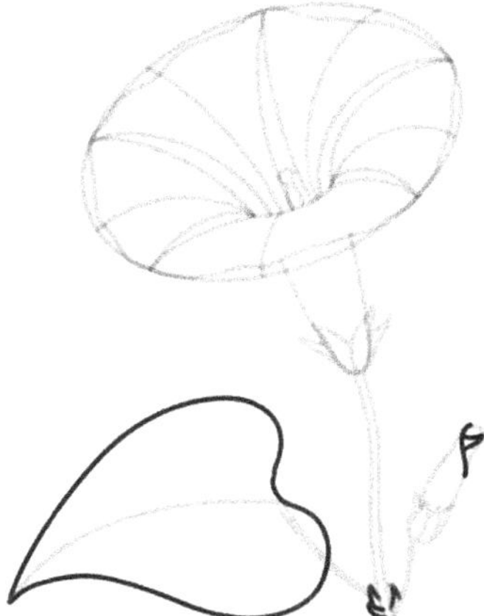

11

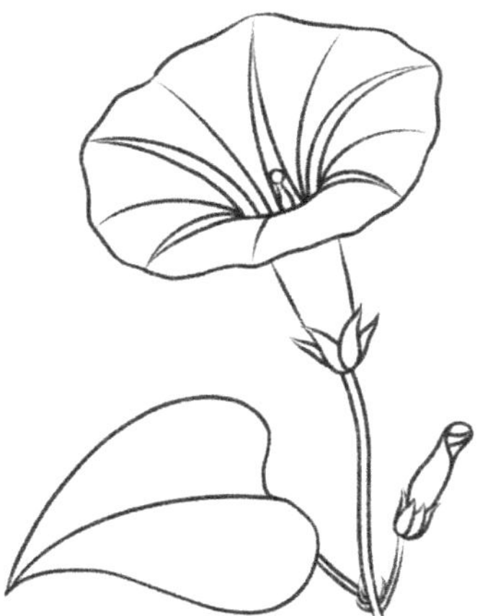

12

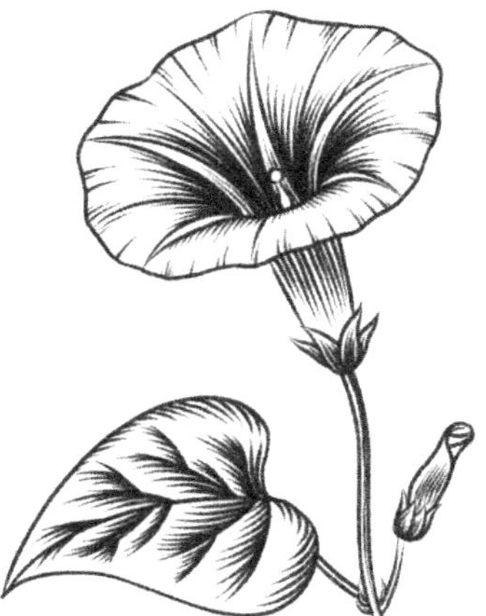

PANSY

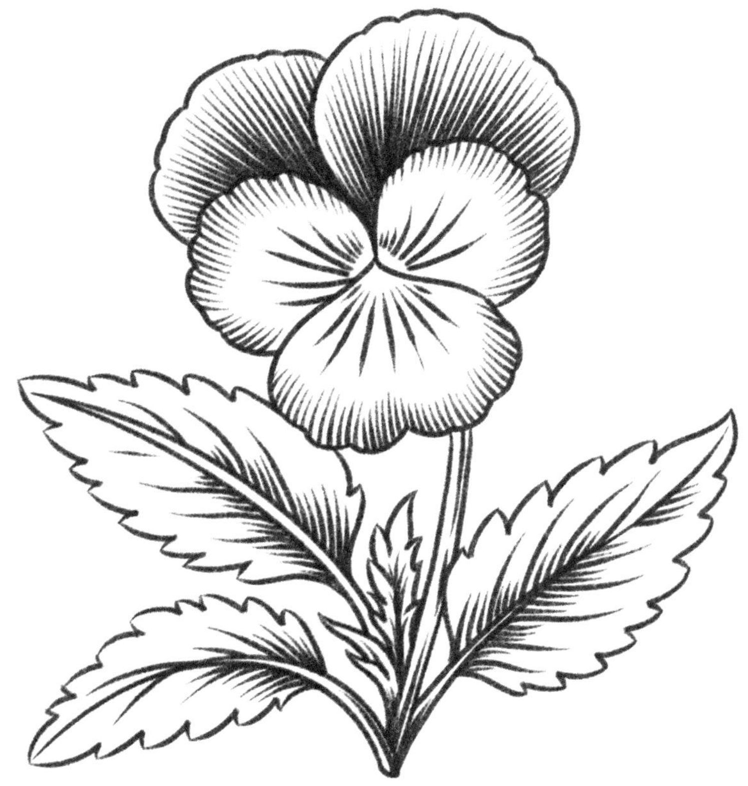

Pansies symbolise remembrance,
thoughtfulness, and free-spirited joy,
often associated with tender memories,
loving thoughts, and the enduring
beauty of heartfelt connections.

01

02

03

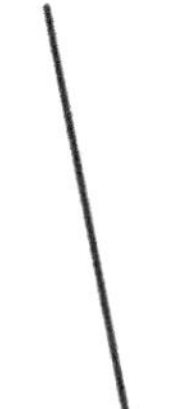

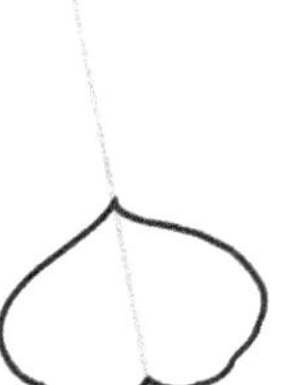

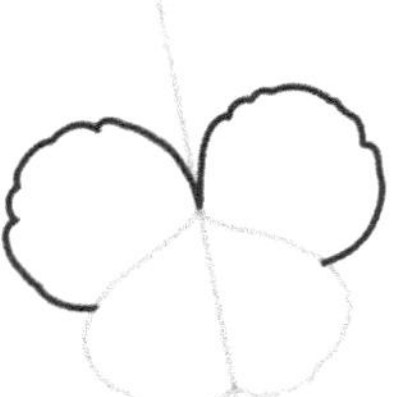

04

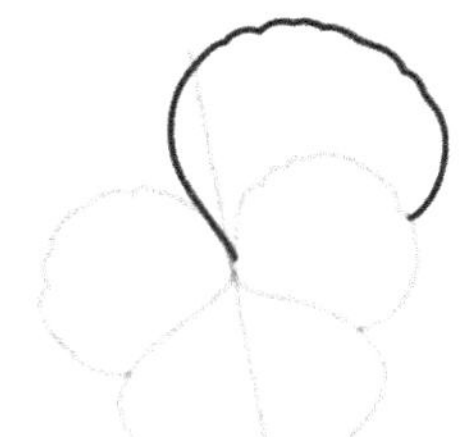

05

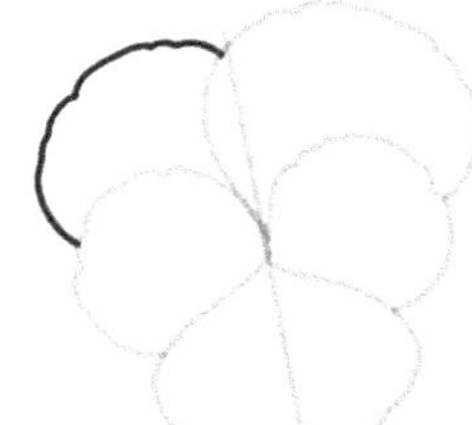

06

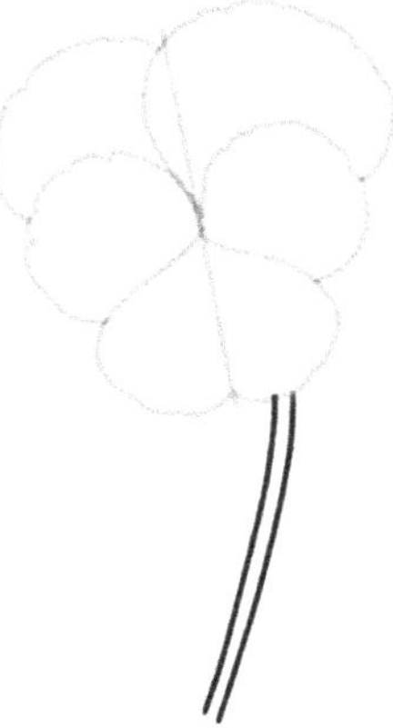

07

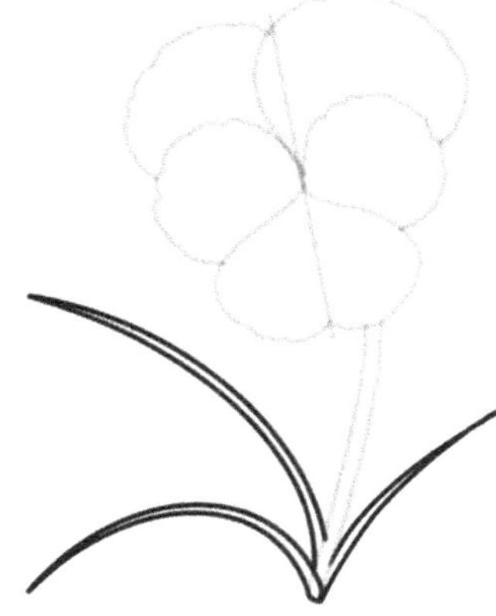

08

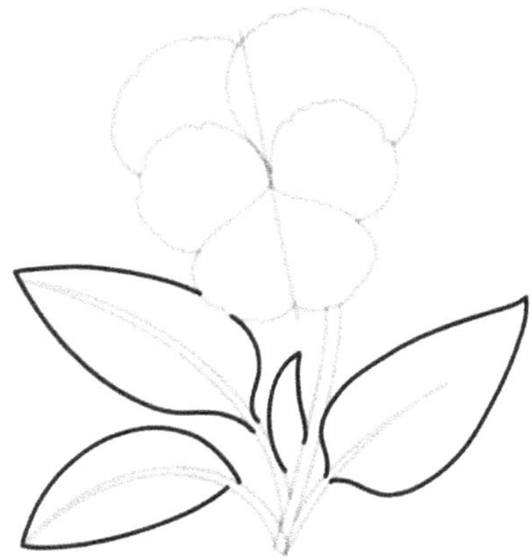

09

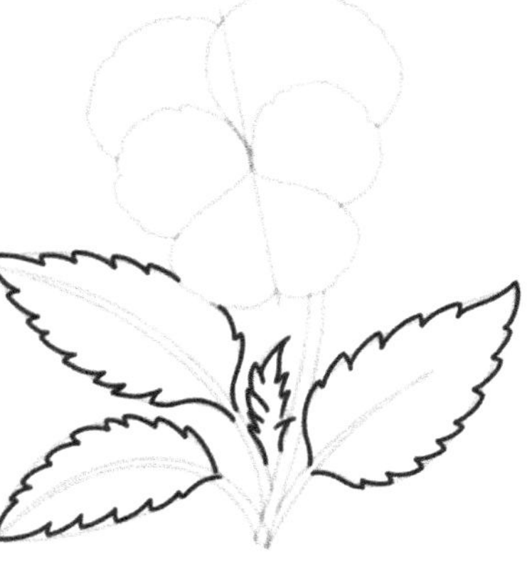

10

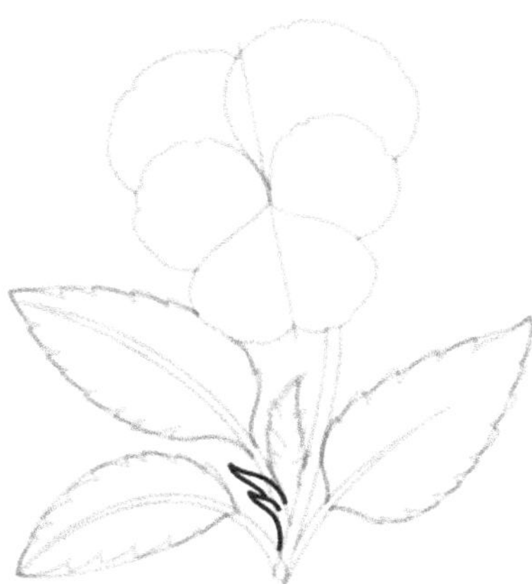

11

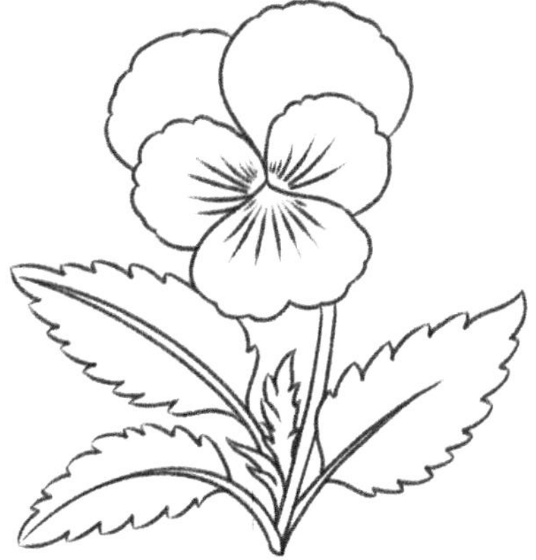

12

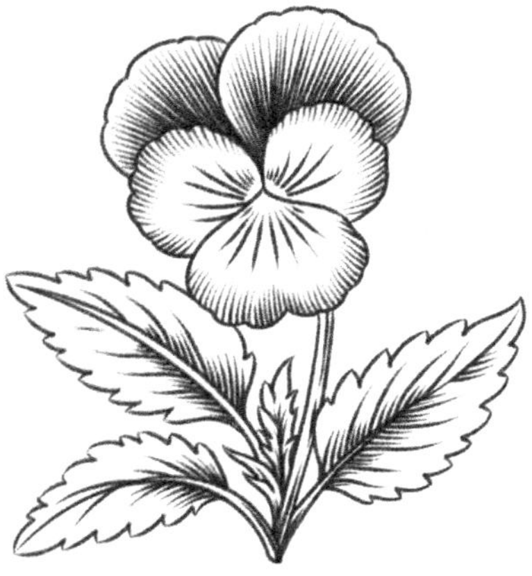

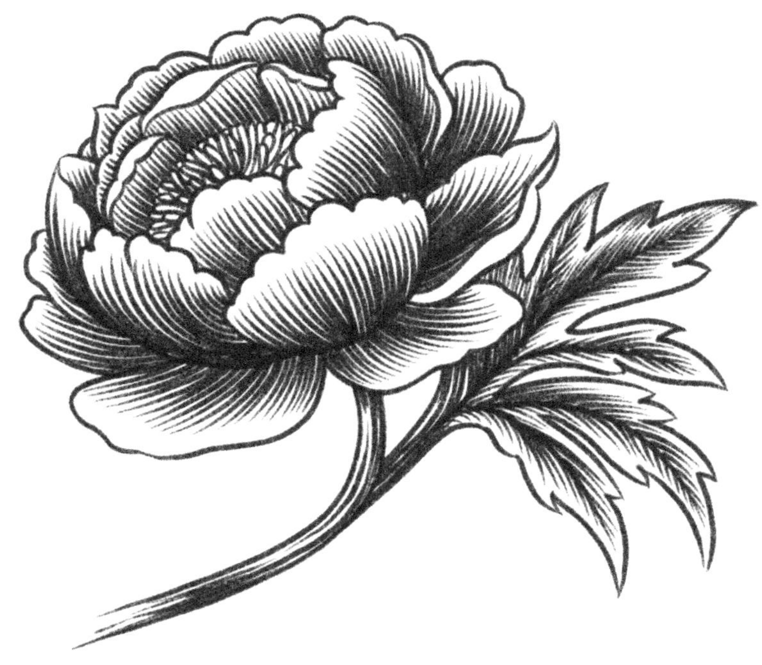

PEONY

Peonies symbolise prosperity, romance, and honour, often associated with happy marriage, compassion, and the lush beauty of abundance, good fortune, and a fulfilling, harmonious life.

01

02

03

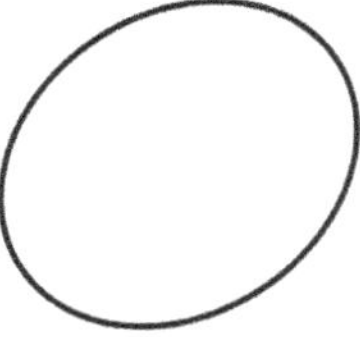

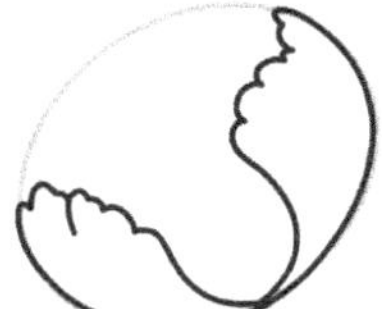

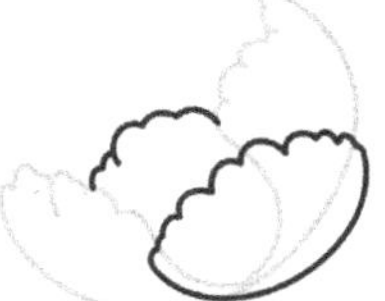

04

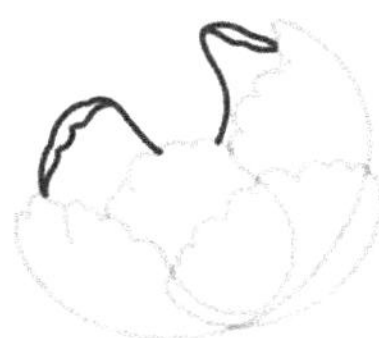

05

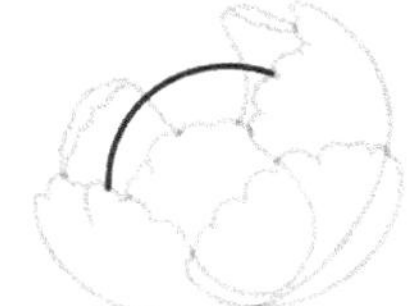

06

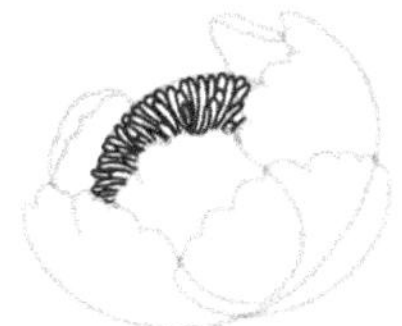

07

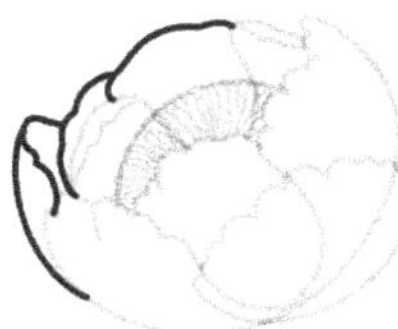

08

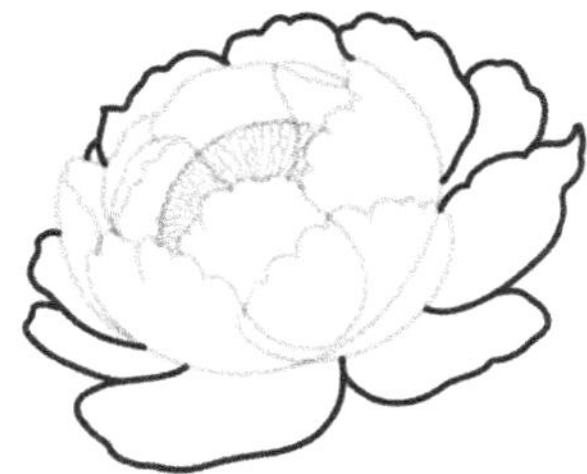

09

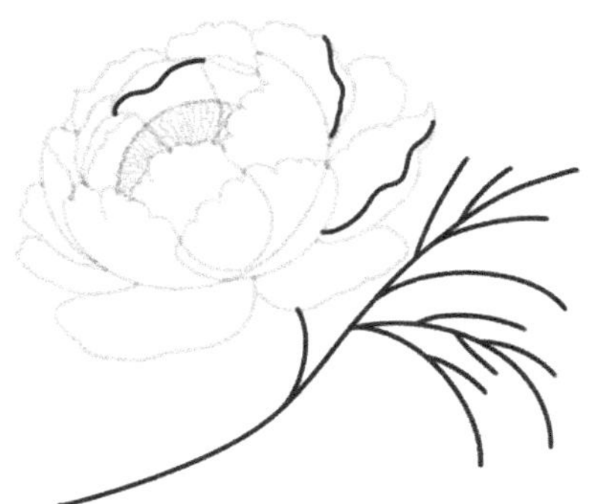

HOW TO DRAW FLOWERS

10

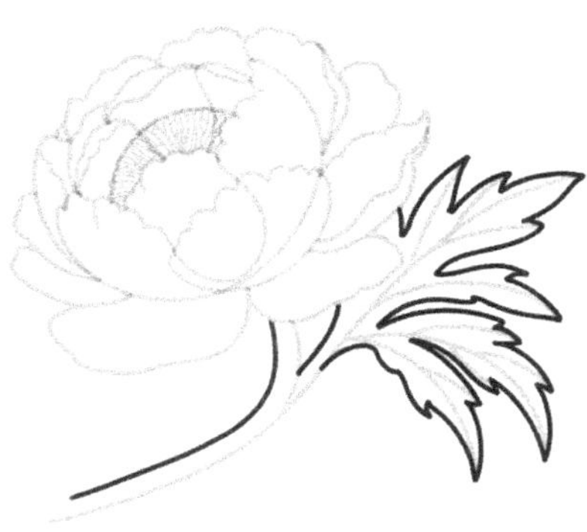

11

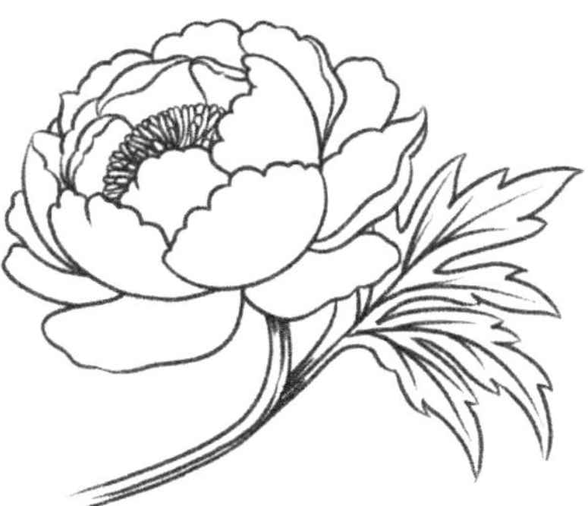

12

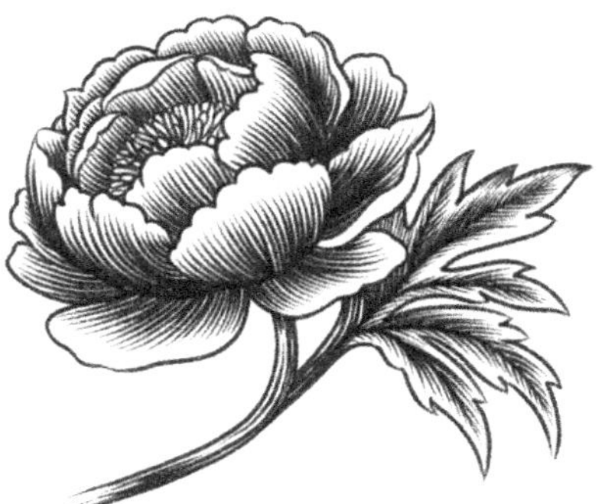

PERIWINKLE

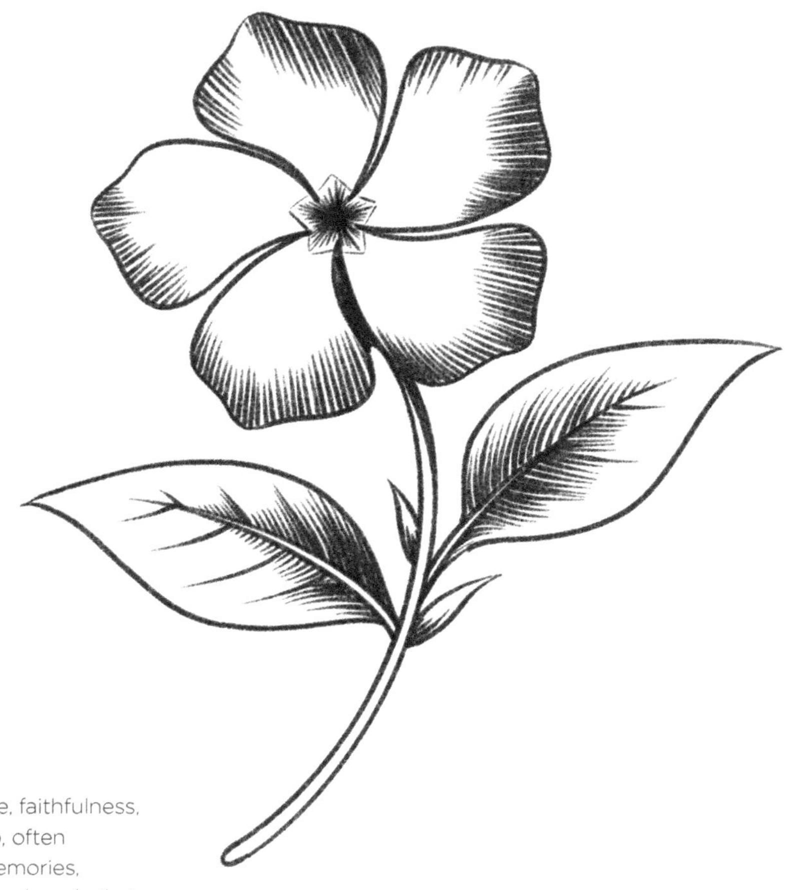

Periwinkles symbolise love, faithfulness, and everlasting friendship, often associated with gentle memories, resilience, and the enduring bonds that withstand the tests of time.

01

02

03

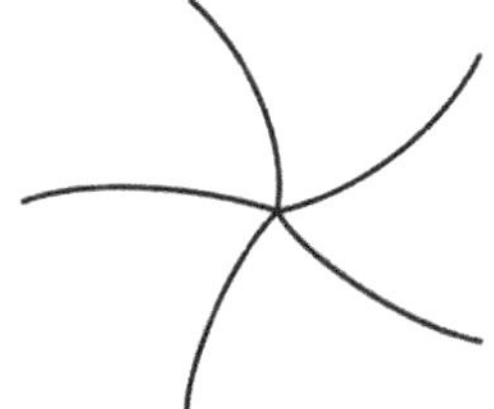

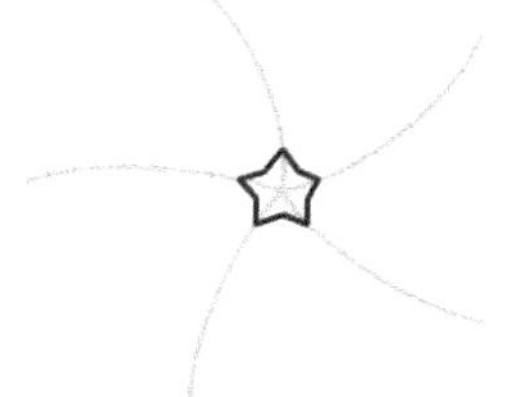

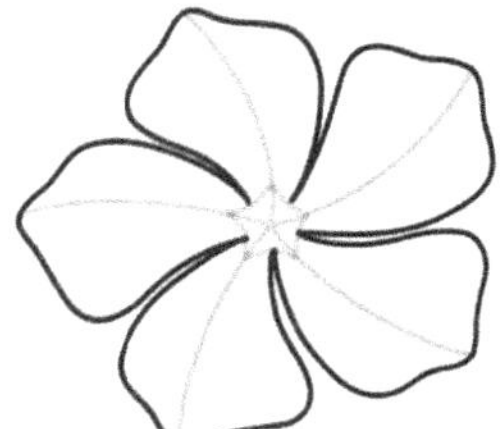

04

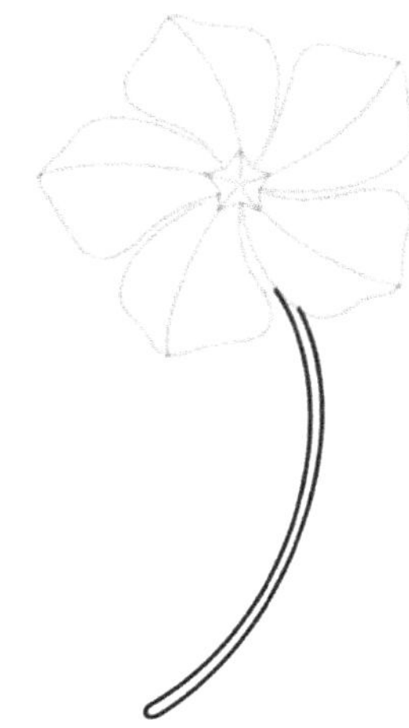

05

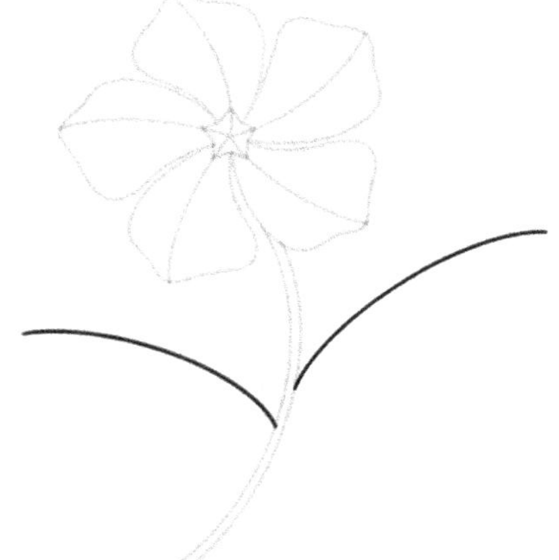

06

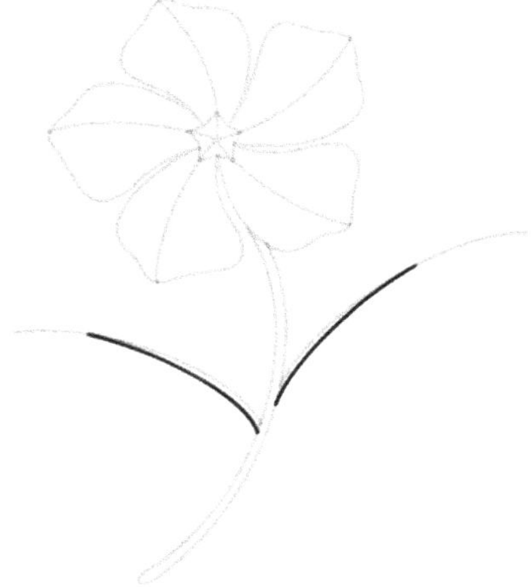

07

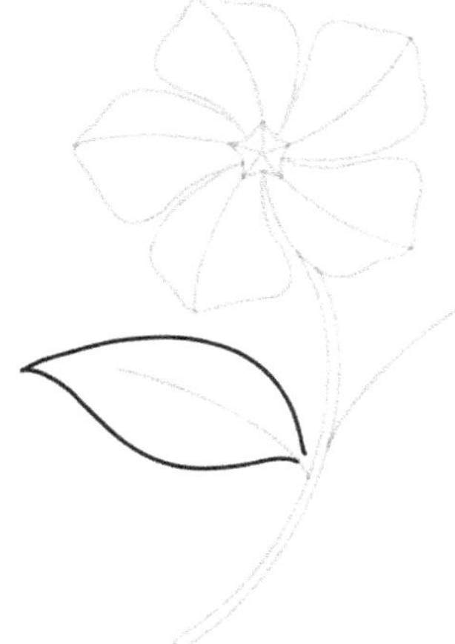

08

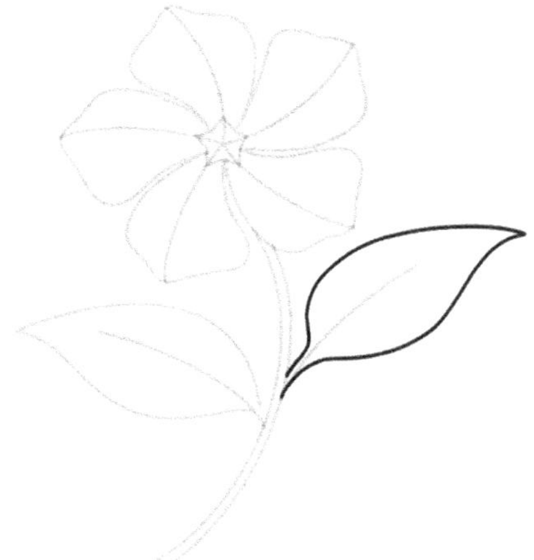

09

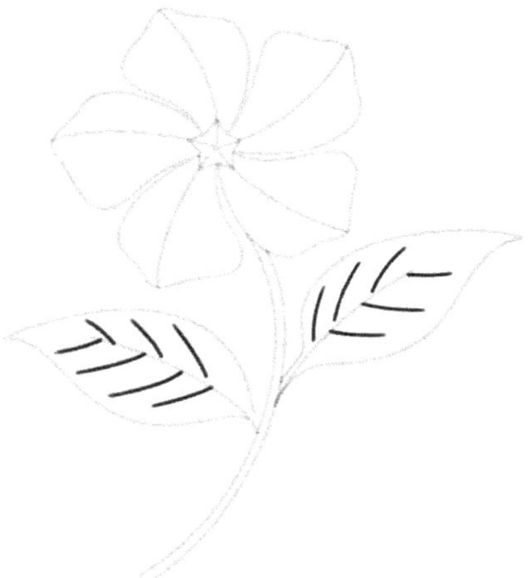

10

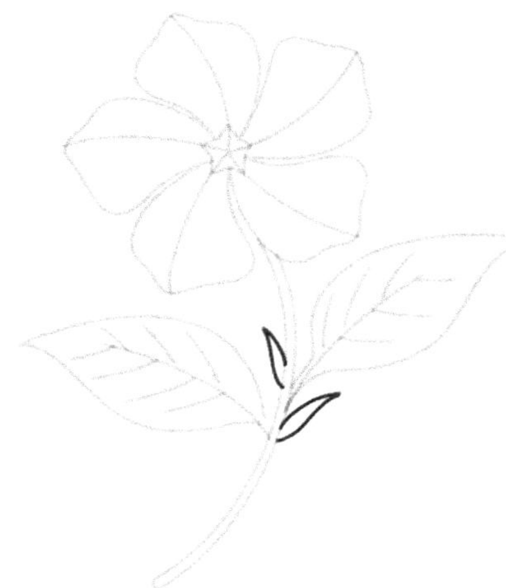

11

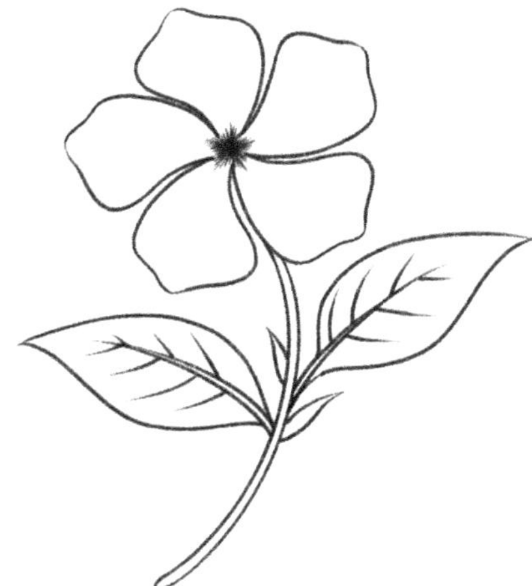

12

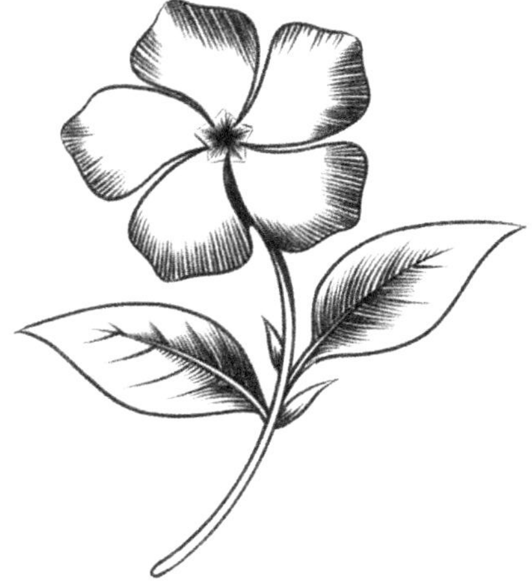

PETUNIA

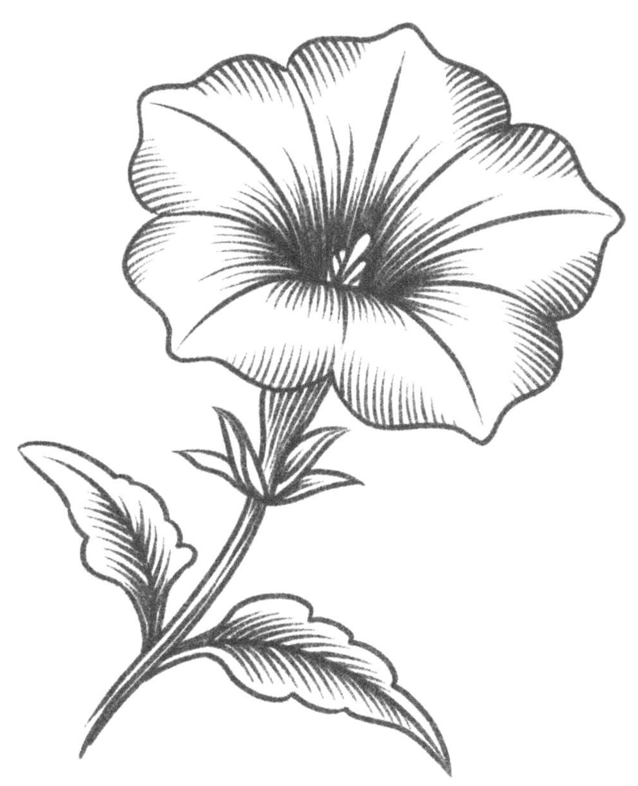

Petunias symbolise resilience, anger, and longing, often associated with deep emotions, the complexities of relationships, and the vibrant beauty that arises from overcoming life's personal challenges and hardships.

01

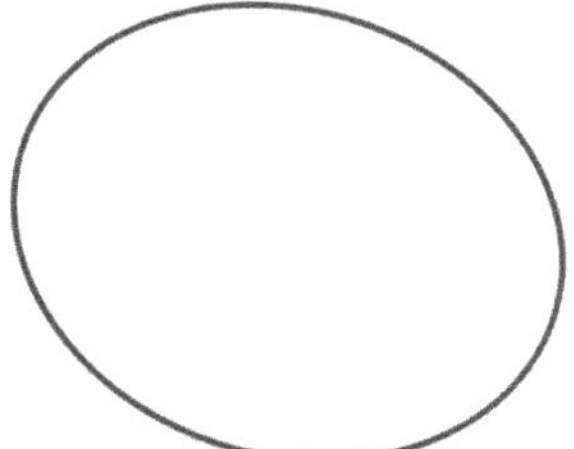

02

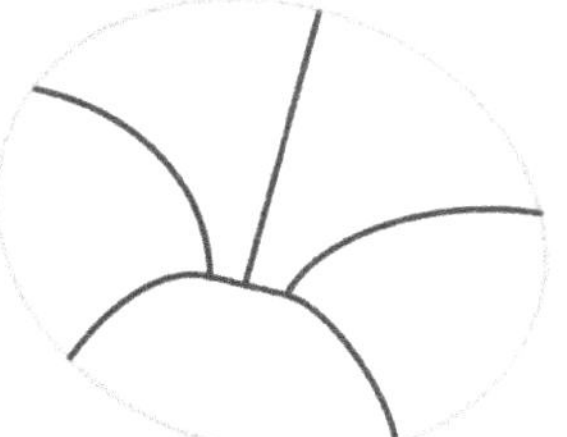

03

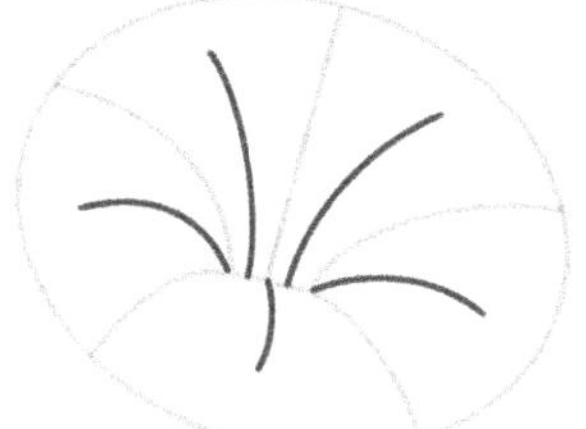

04

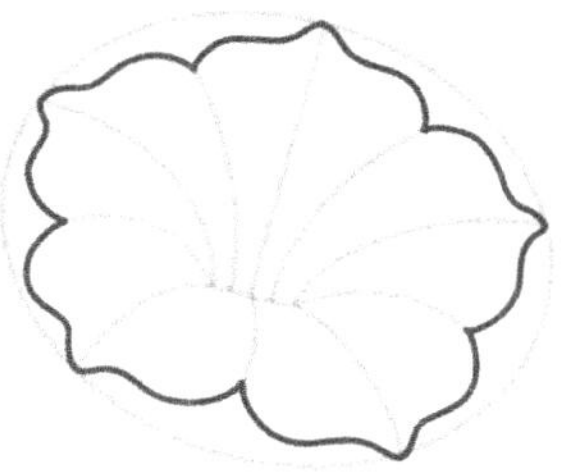

05

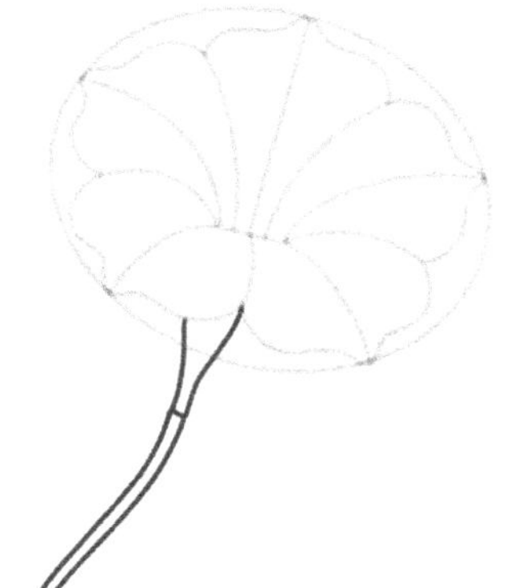

06

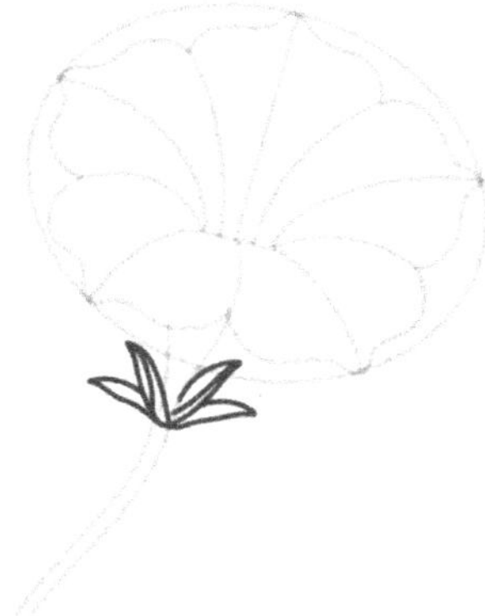

07

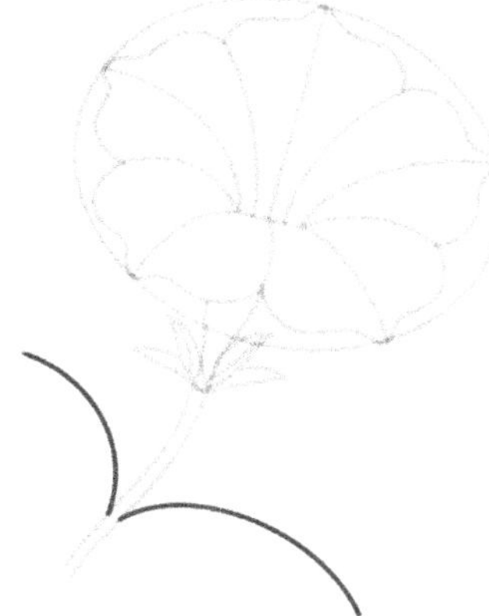

08

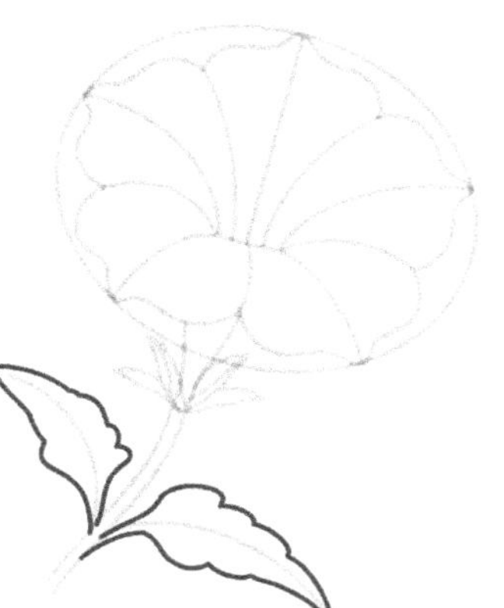

09

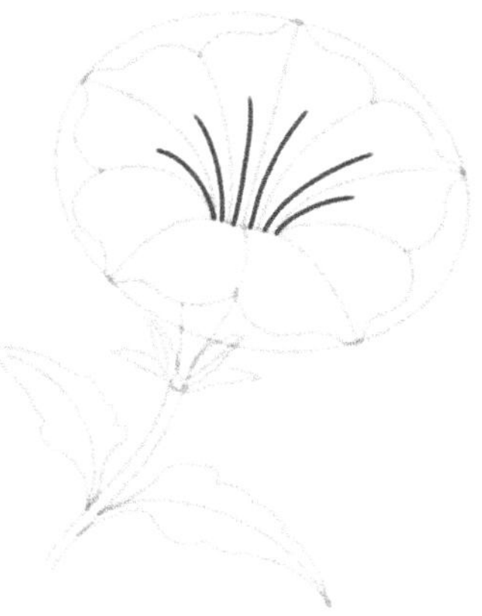

10

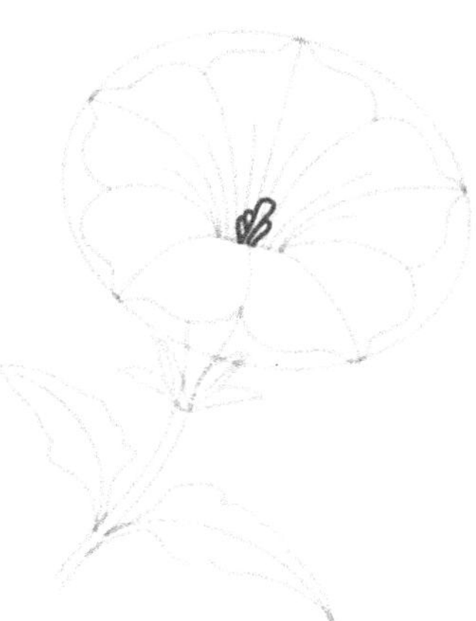

11

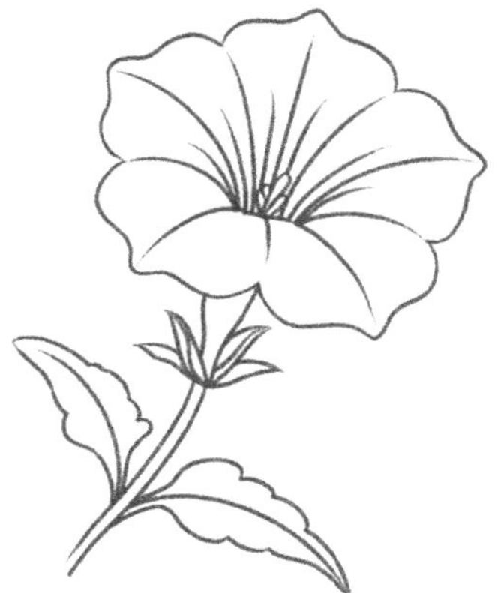

12

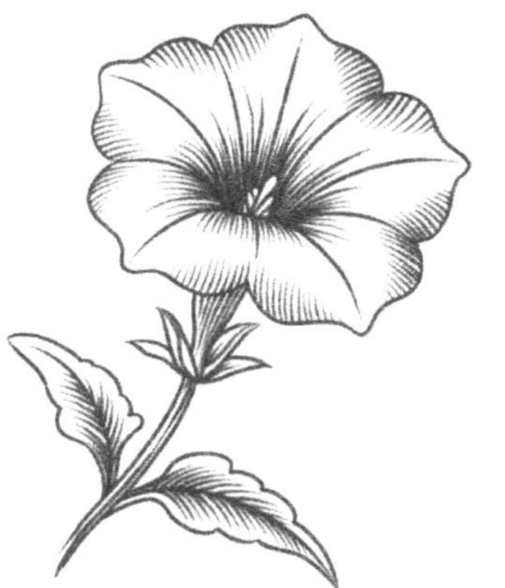

HOW TO DRAW FLOWERS

POPPY

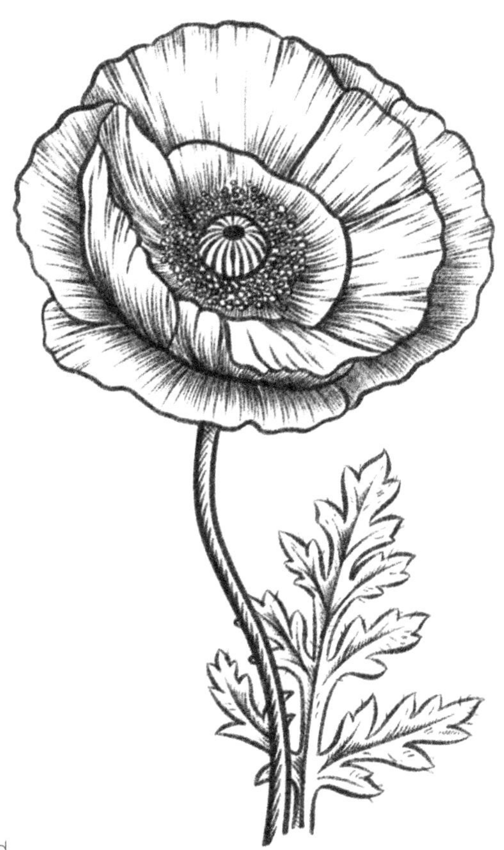

Poppies symbolise remembrance, peace, and consolation, often associated with sleep, eternal rest, and the delicate beauty that honours life, loss, and the hope for renewal.

01

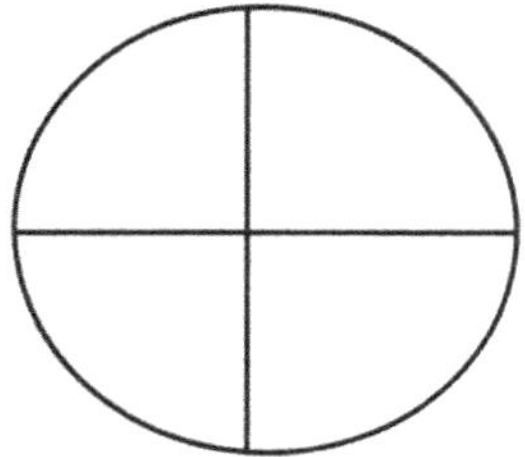

02

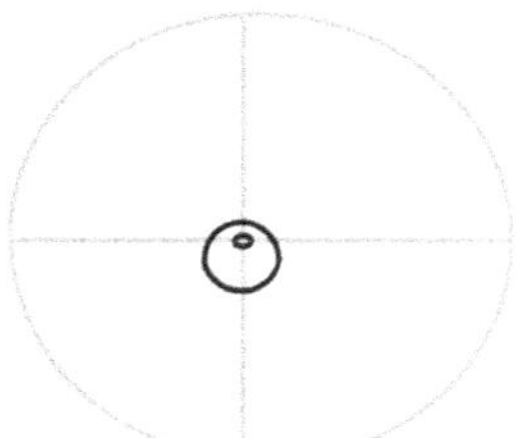

03

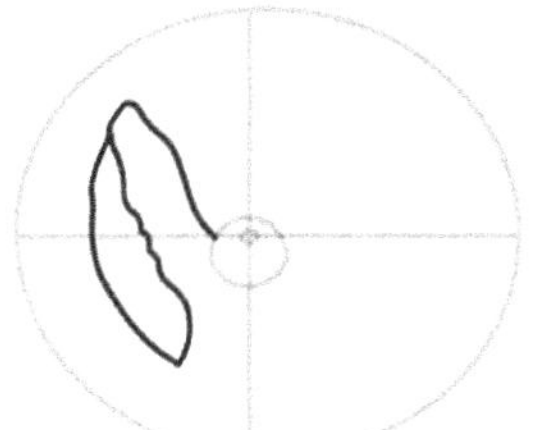

04

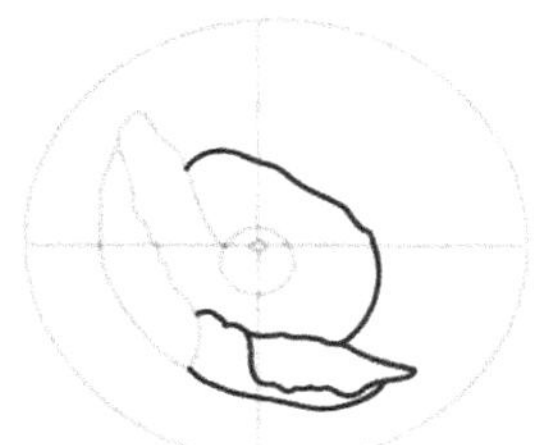

05

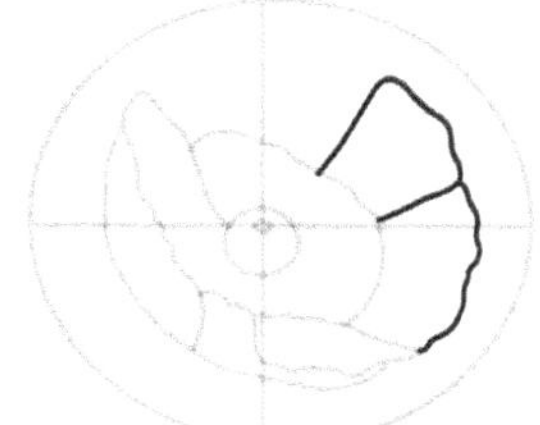

06

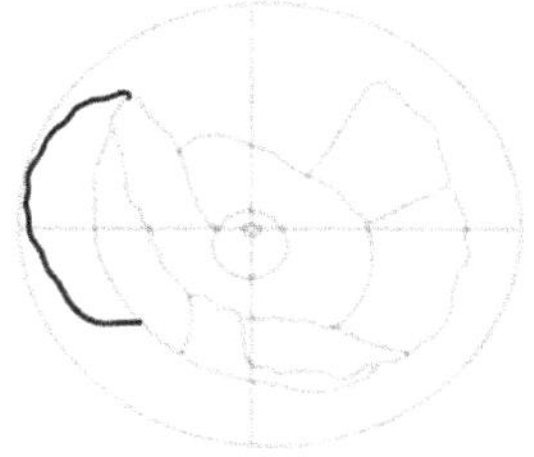

07

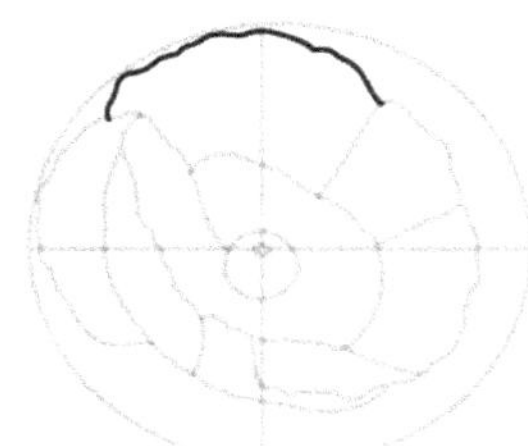

08

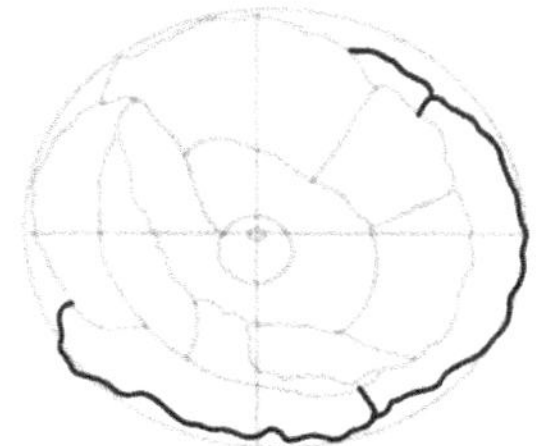

09

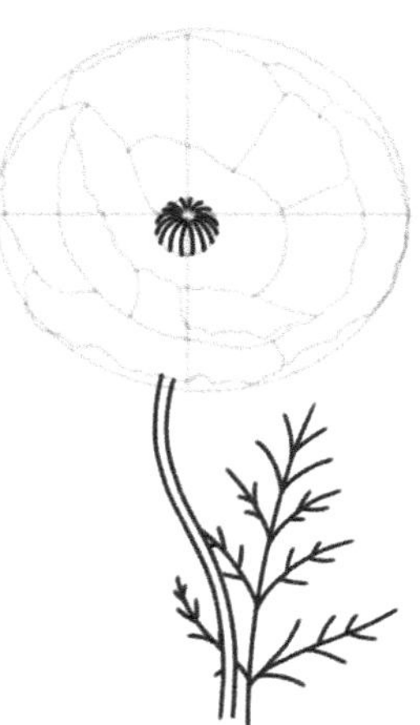

10

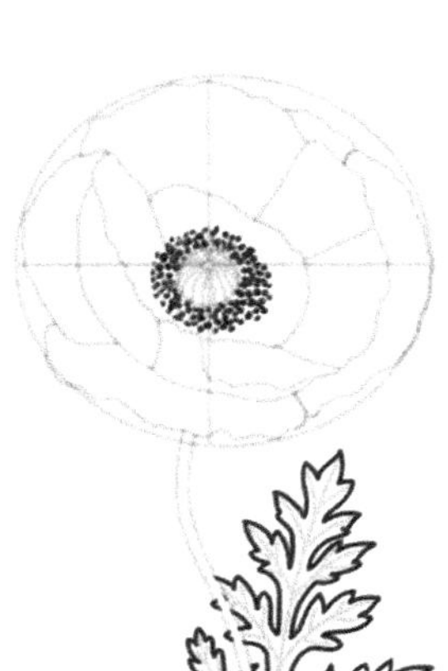

11

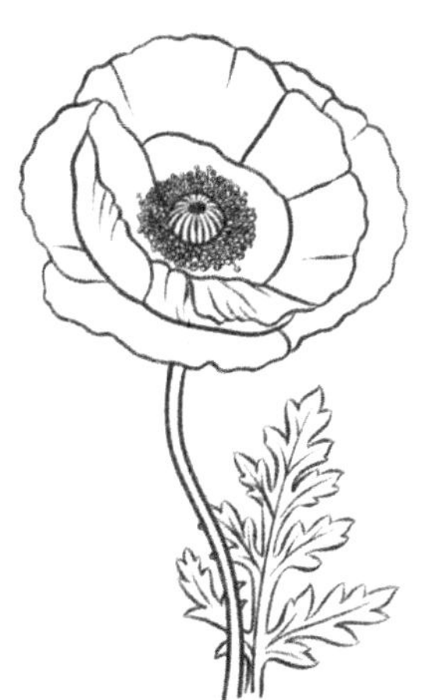

12

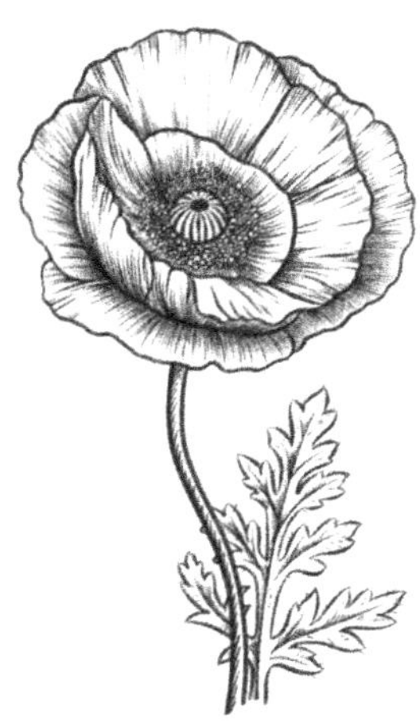

PRIMROSE

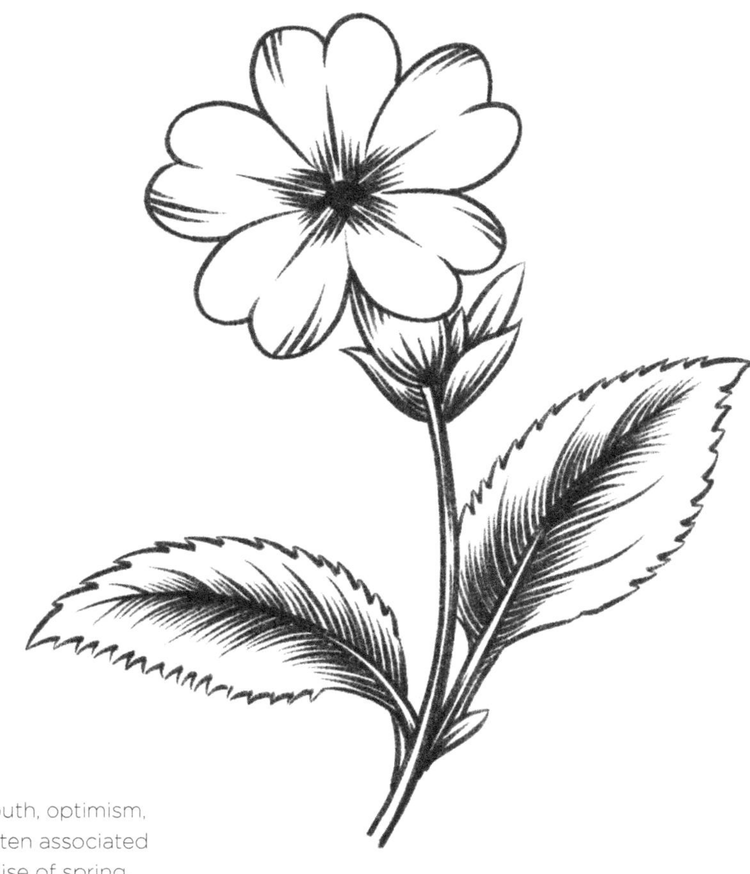

Primroses symbolise youth, optimism, and new beginnings, often associated with first love, the promise of spring, and the gentle beauty of life's earliest, most hopeful moments.

01

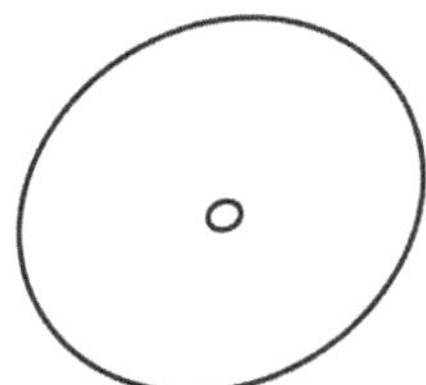

02

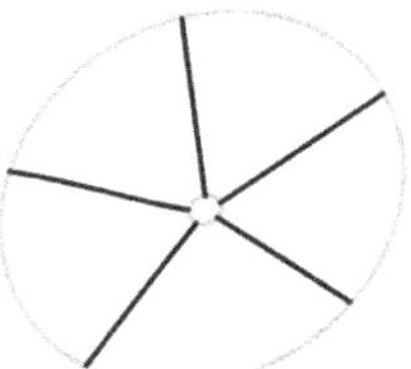

03

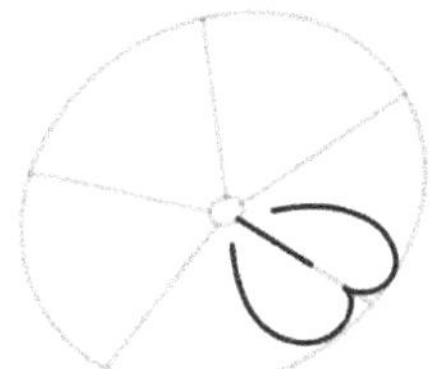

04

05

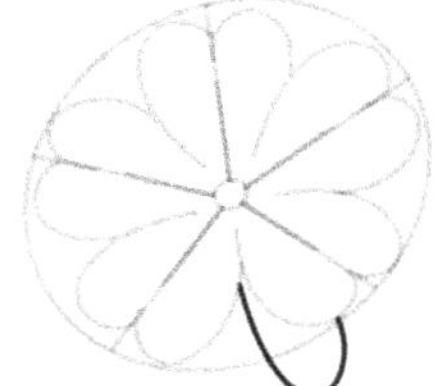

06

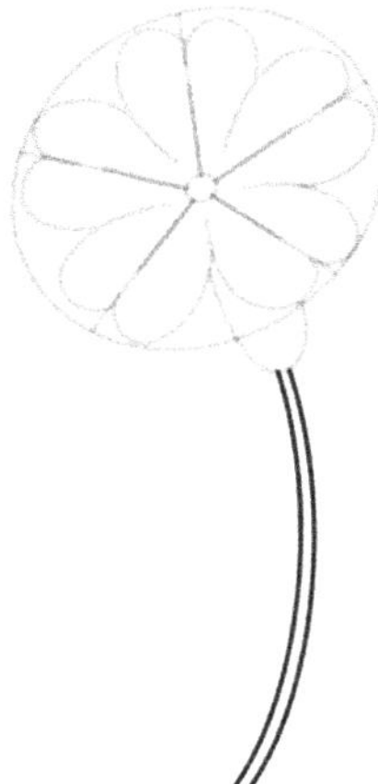

07

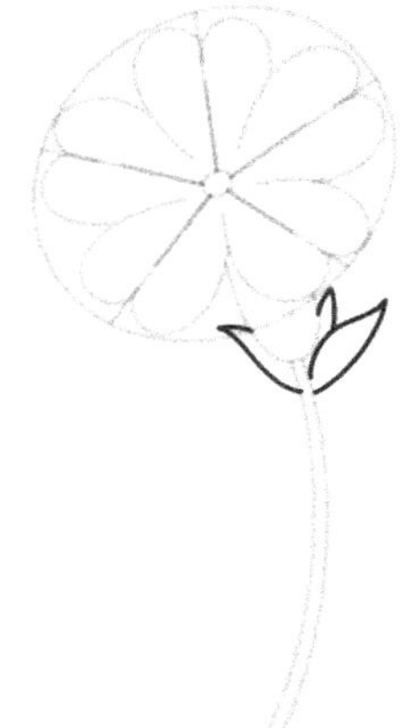

08

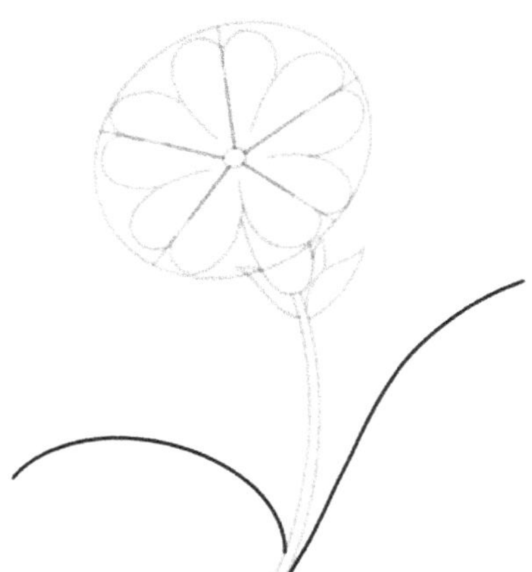

09

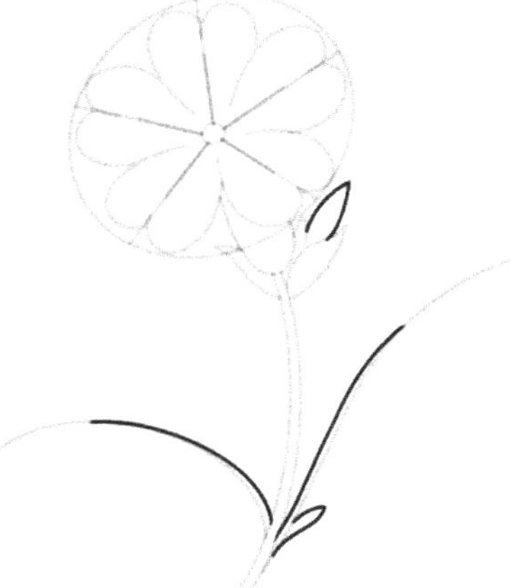

10

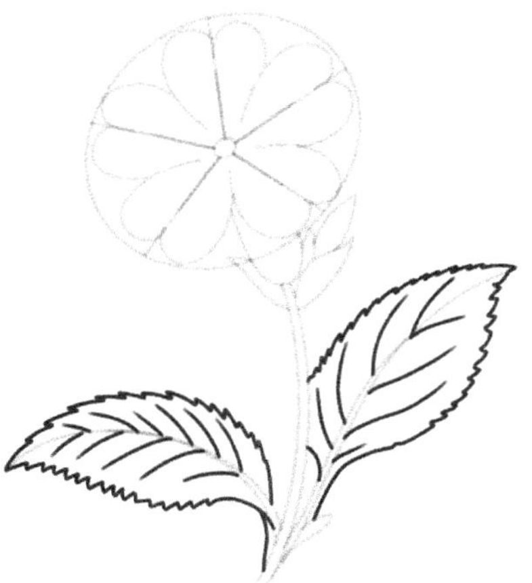

11

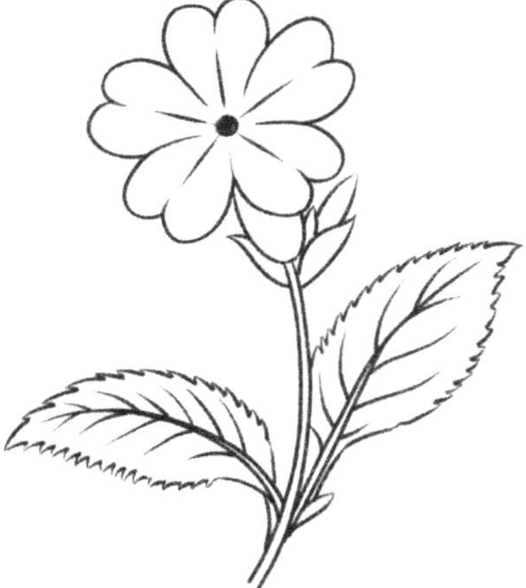

12

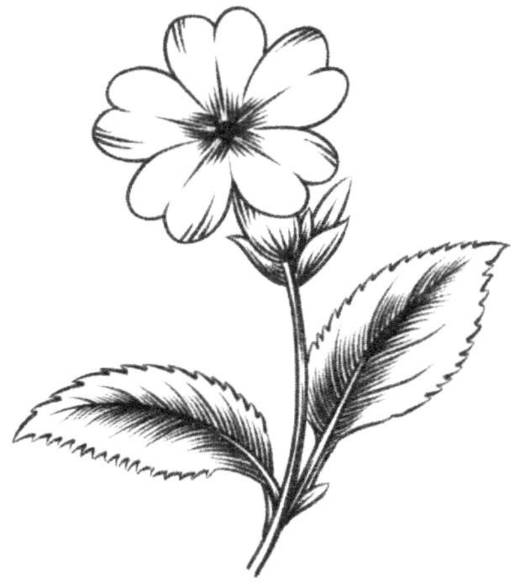

RANUNCULUS

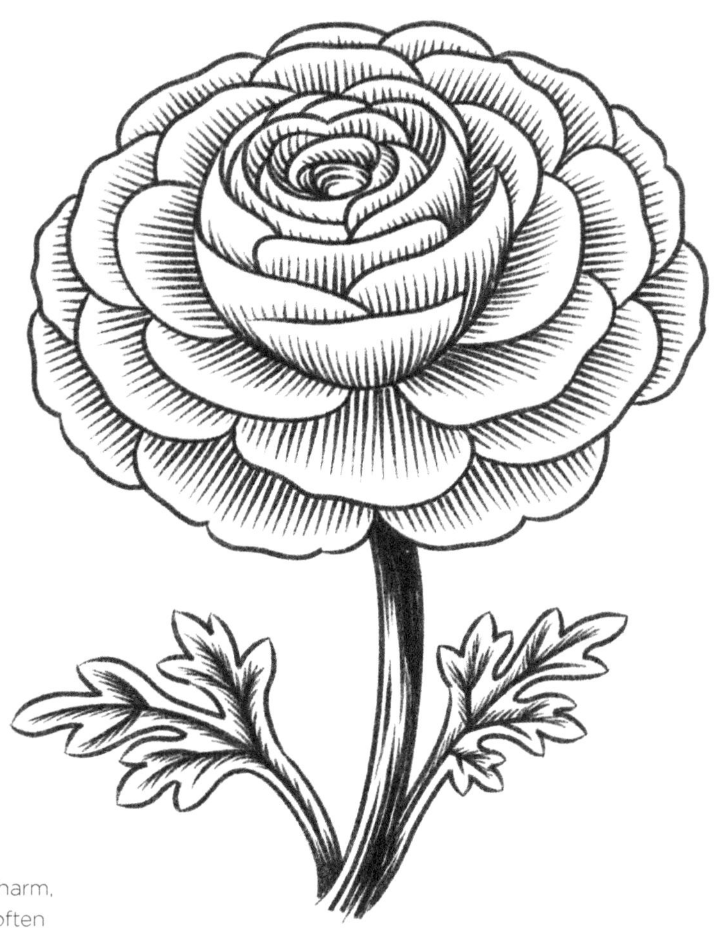

Ranunculus symbolises charm, attraction, and radiance, often associated with dazzling beauty, magnetic personality, and the joyful warmth that lights up any environment.

01

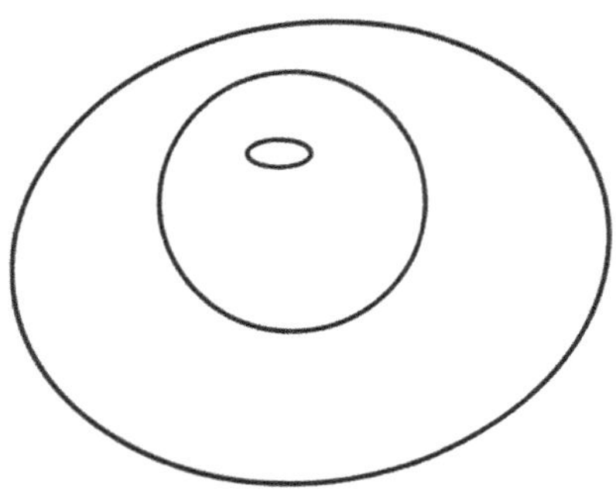

02

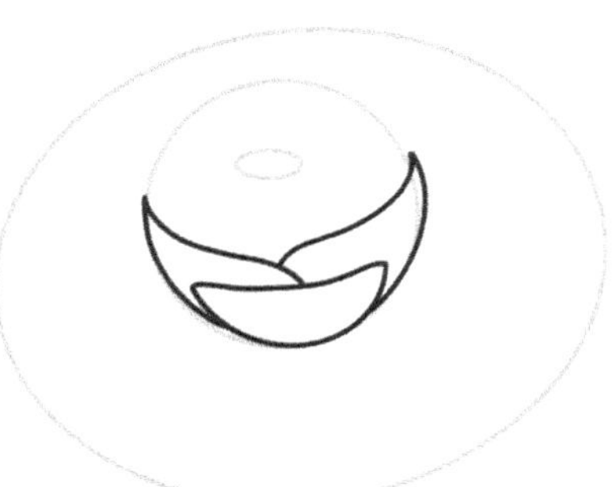

03

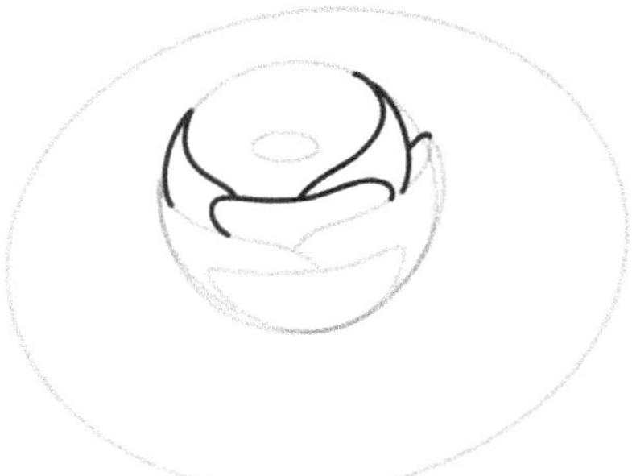

04

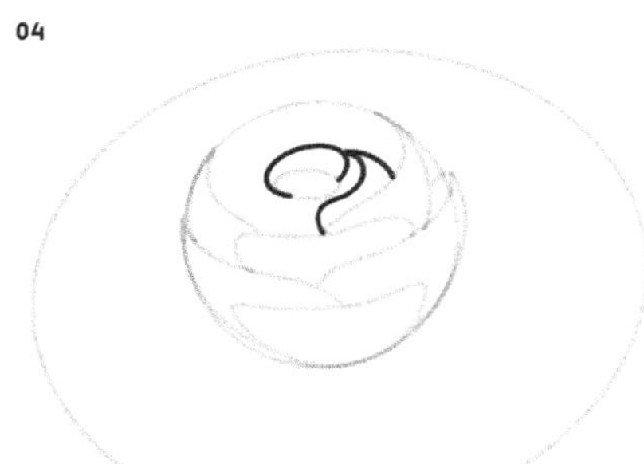

05

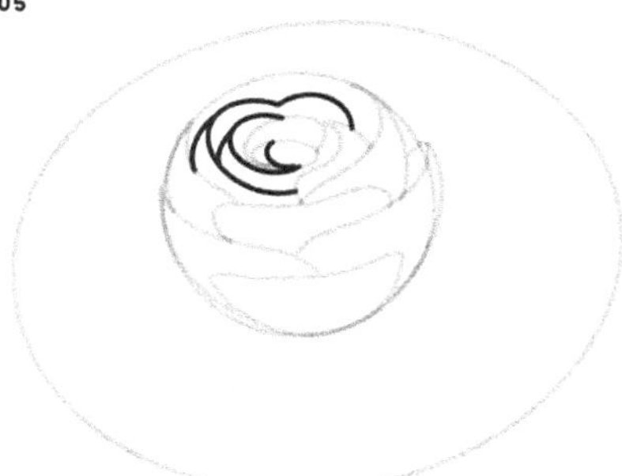

06

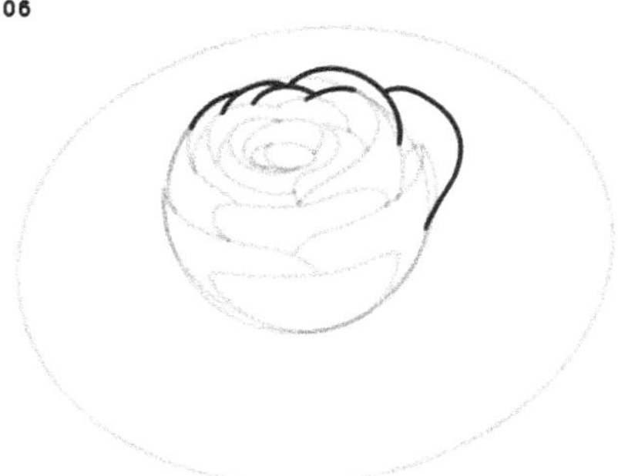

07

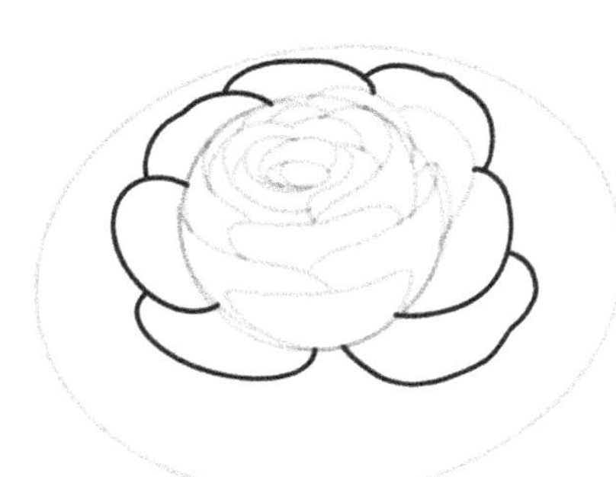

08

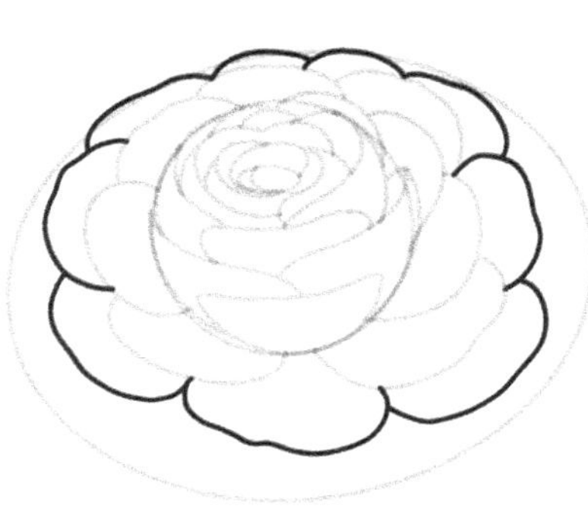

09

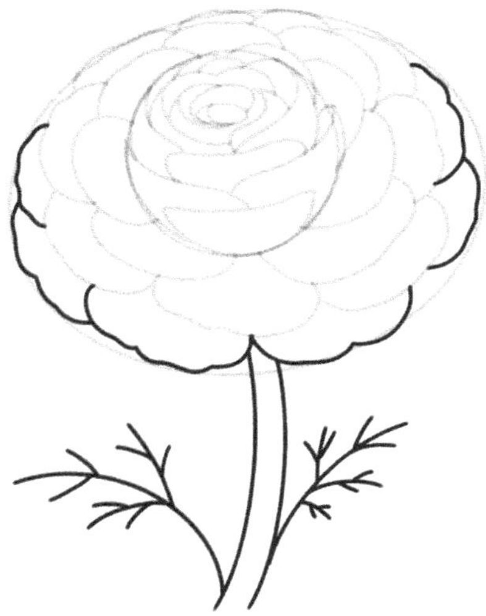

10

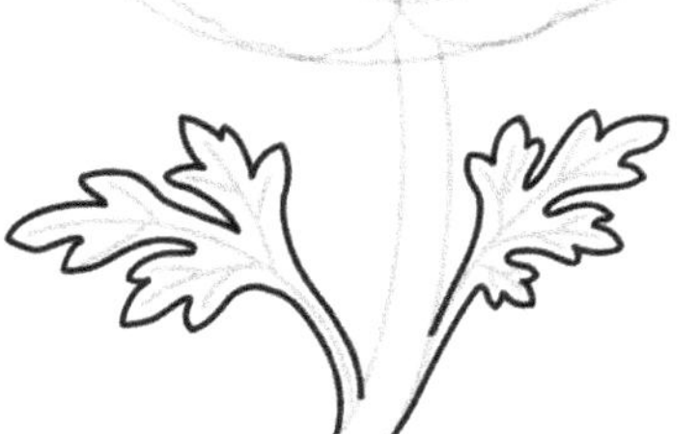

11

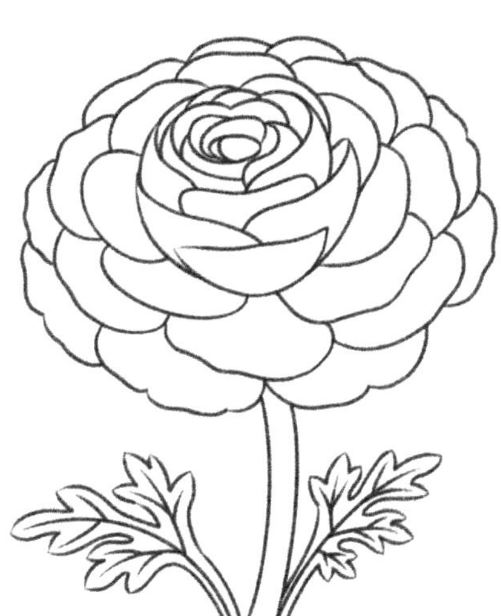

12

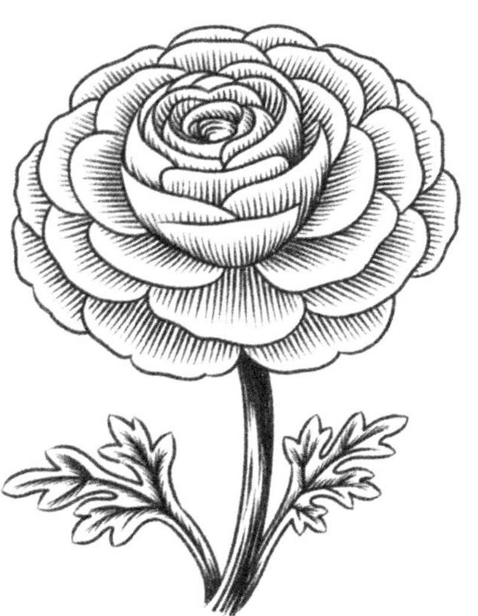

HOW TO DRAW FLOWERS

ROSE

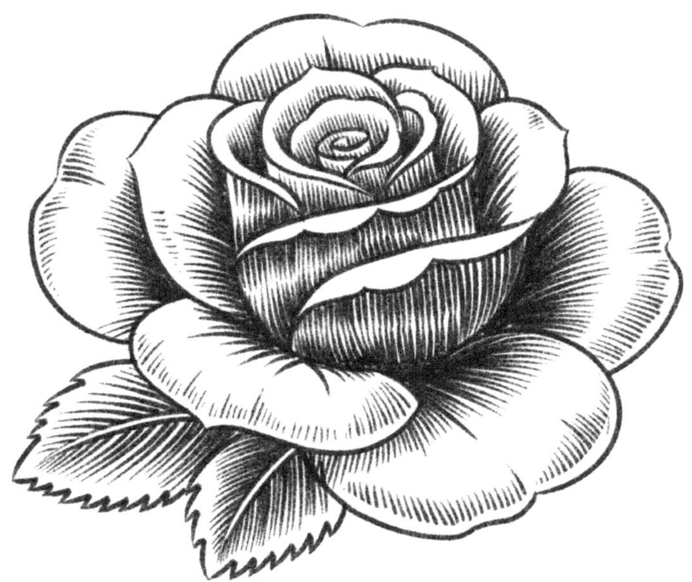

Roses symbolise love, passion, and
beauty, often associated with romance,
mystery, and the delicate balance
between desire and vulnerability,
as shown through their petals and
protective thorns.

01   **02**   **03**

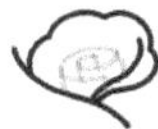

04

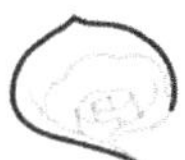

05

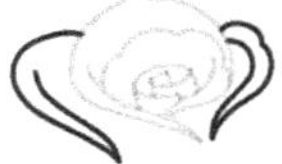

06

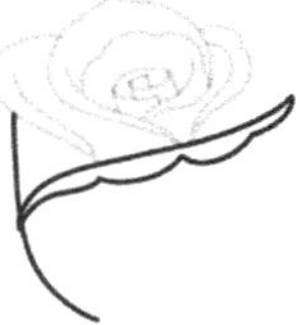

07

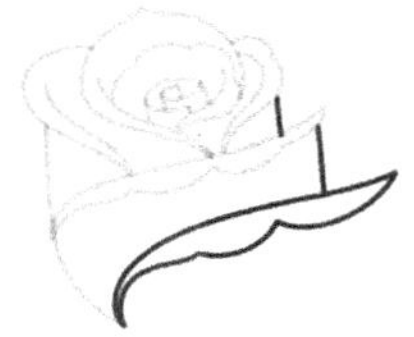

08

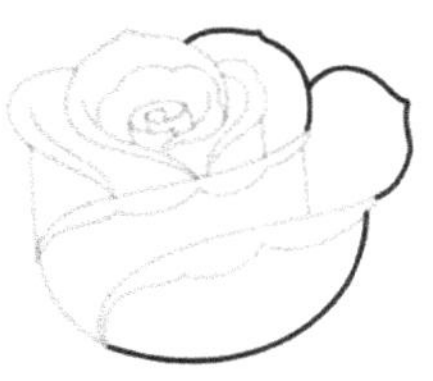

09

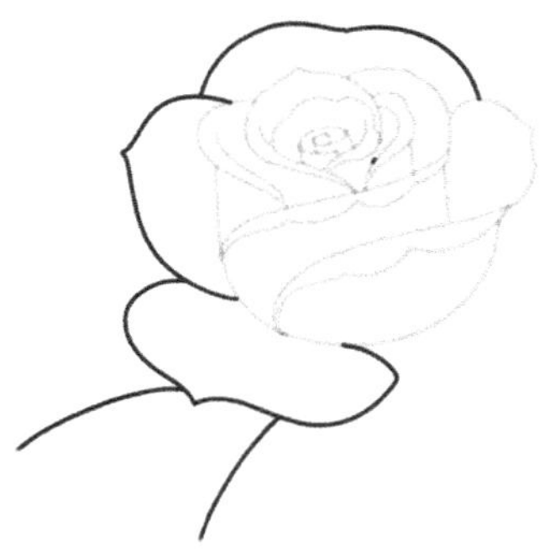

10

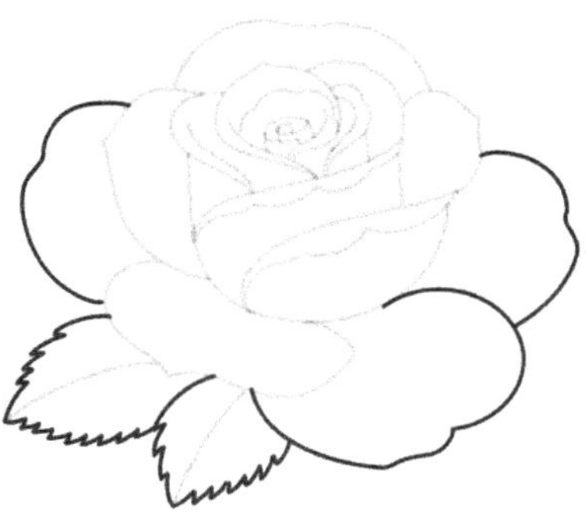

11

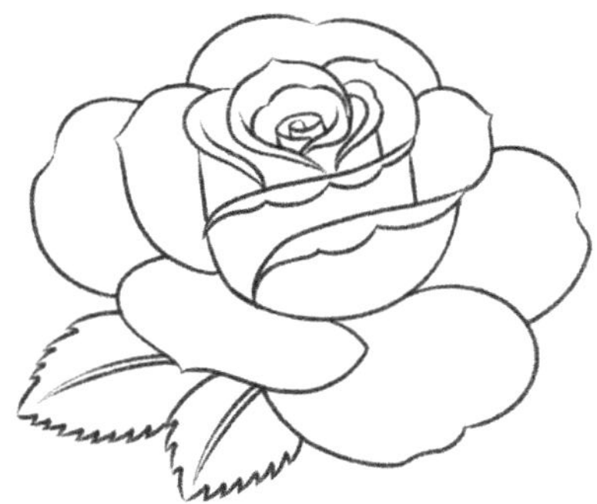

12

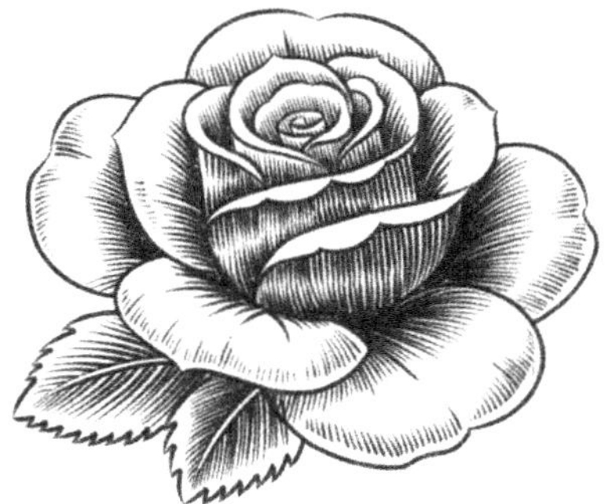

HOW TO DRAW FLOWERS

SUNFLOWER

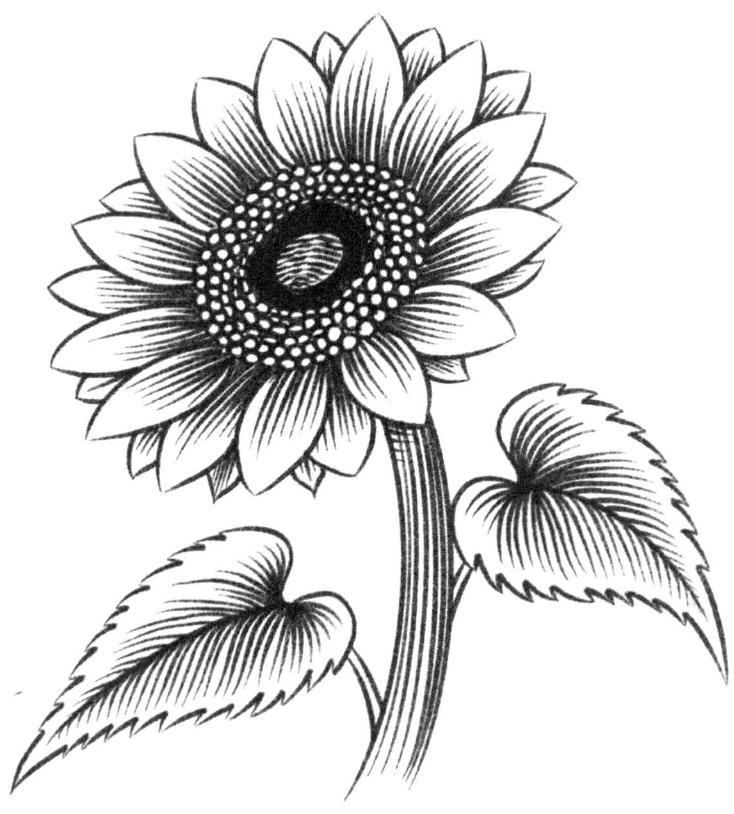

Sunflowers symbolise loyalty, adoration, and positivity, often associated with warmth, vitality, and the uplifting energy that follows light, reflecting unwavering devotion and optimism.

01

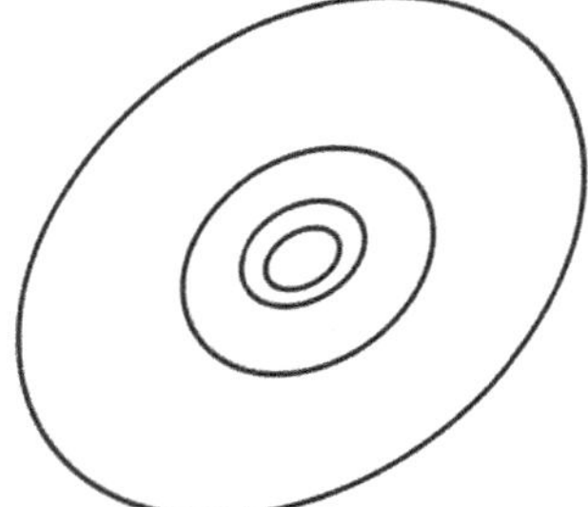

02

03

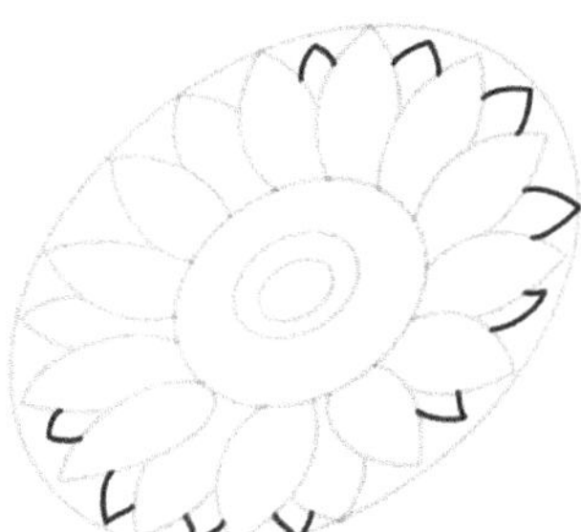

04
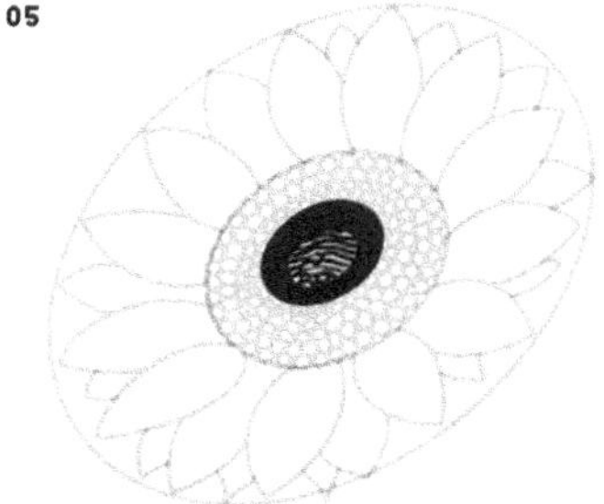

05
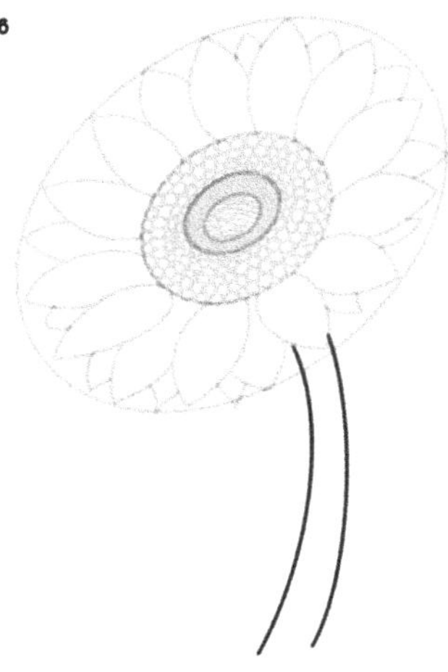

06

07
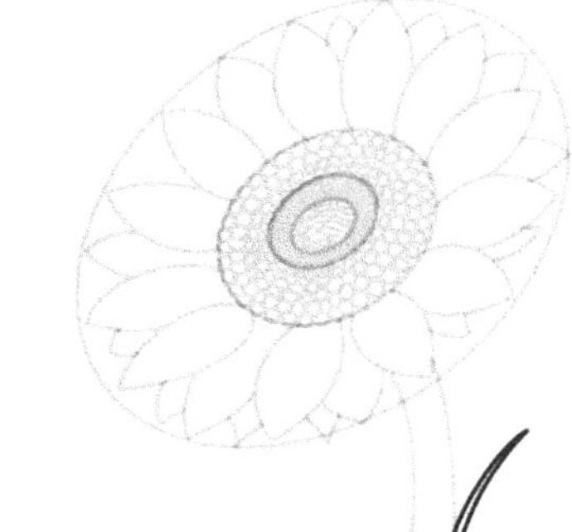

08
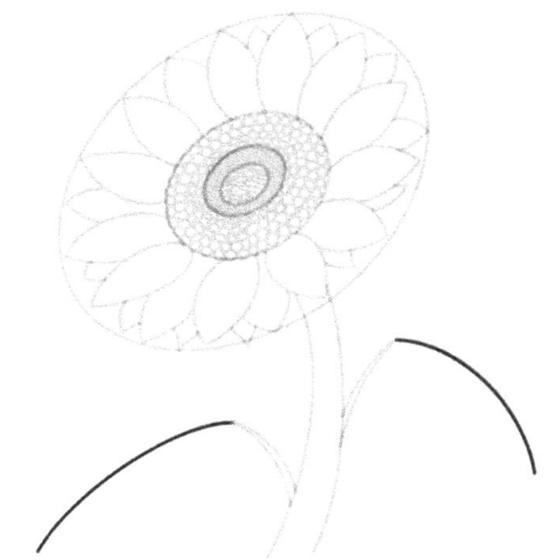

09
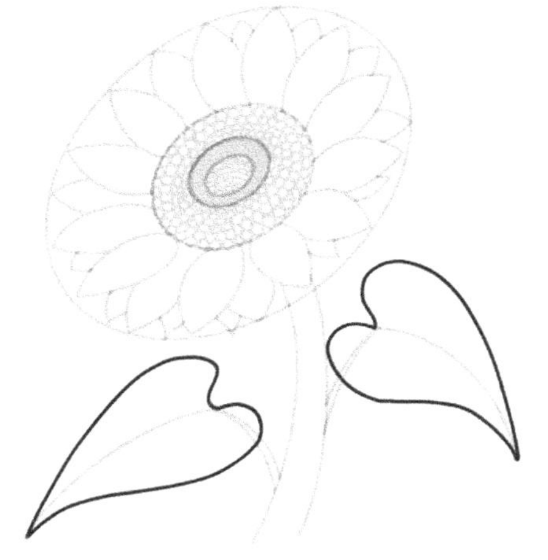

10
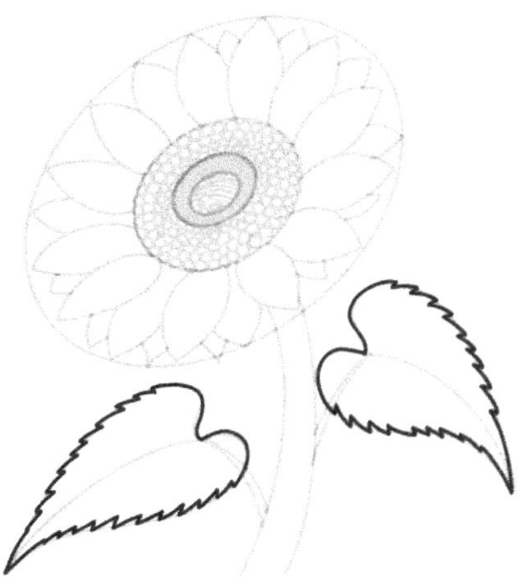

11
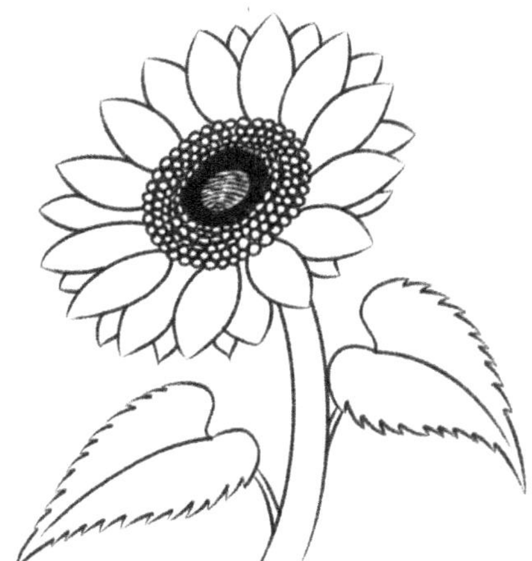

12
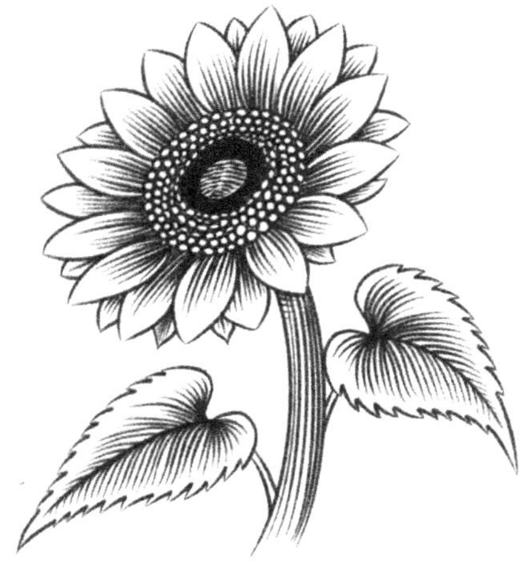

TROLLIUS

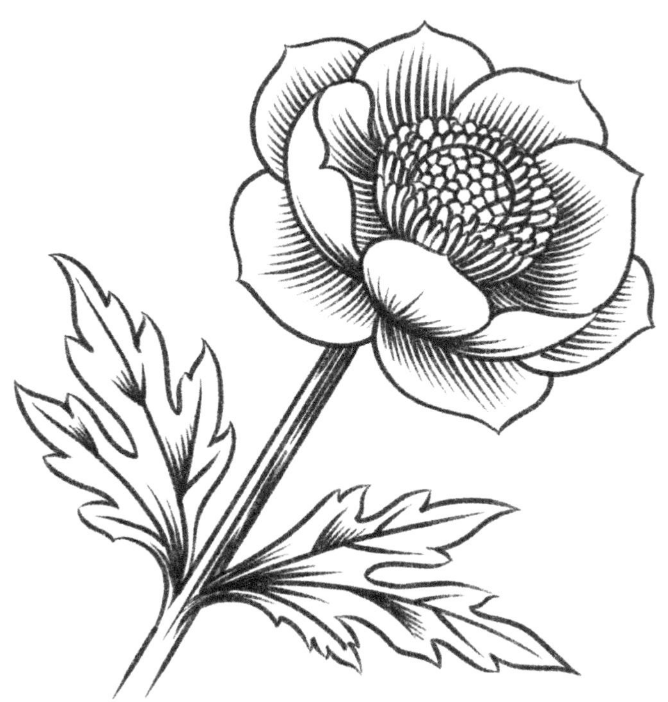

Trollius symbolises gratitude, harmony, and inner peace, often associated with quiet beauty, resilience, and the balance found in embracing life's gentle, enduring moments.

01

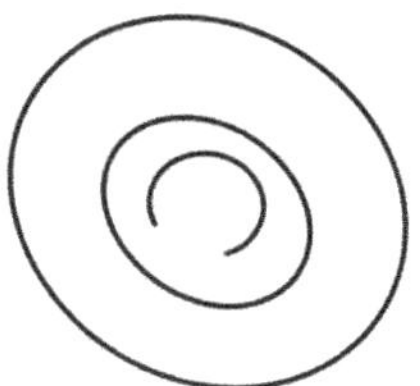

02

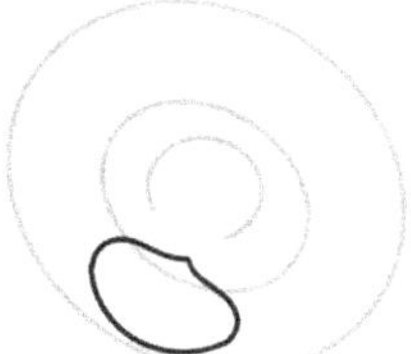

03

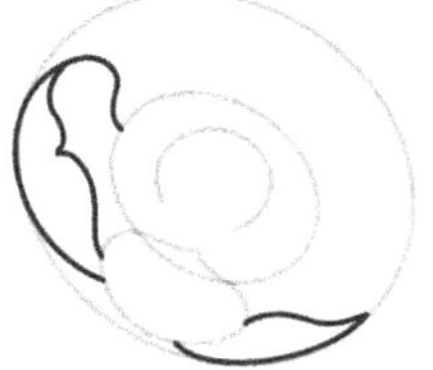

04

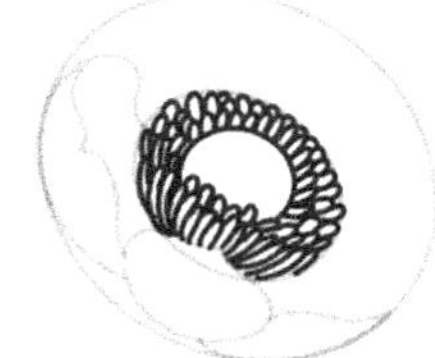

05

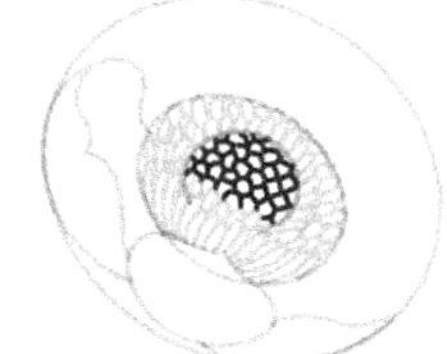

06

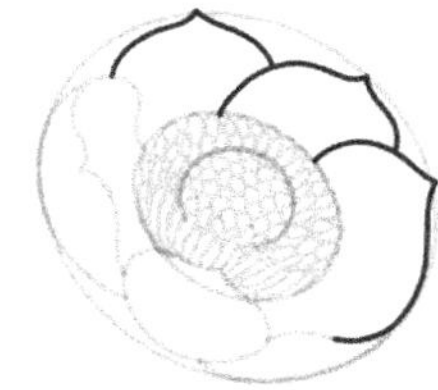

07

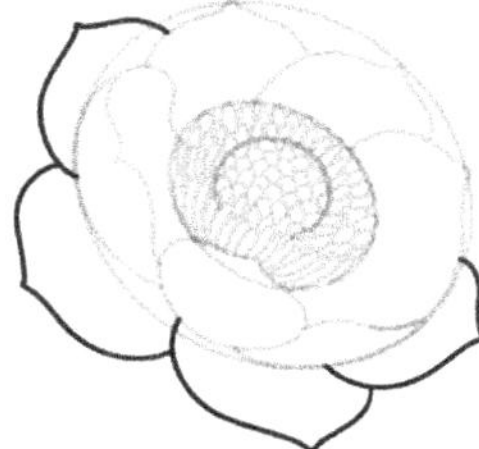

08

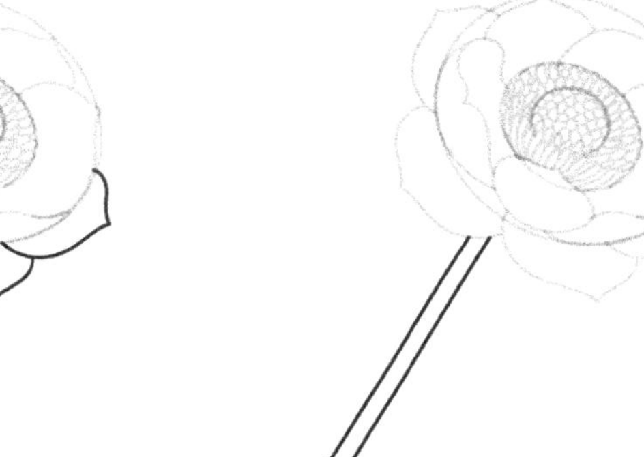

09

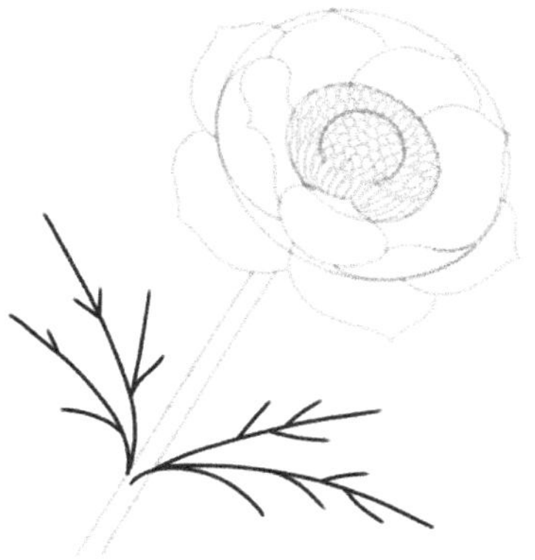

10

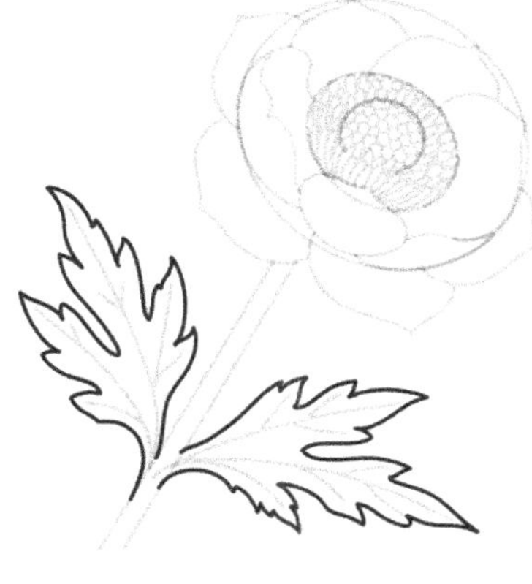

11

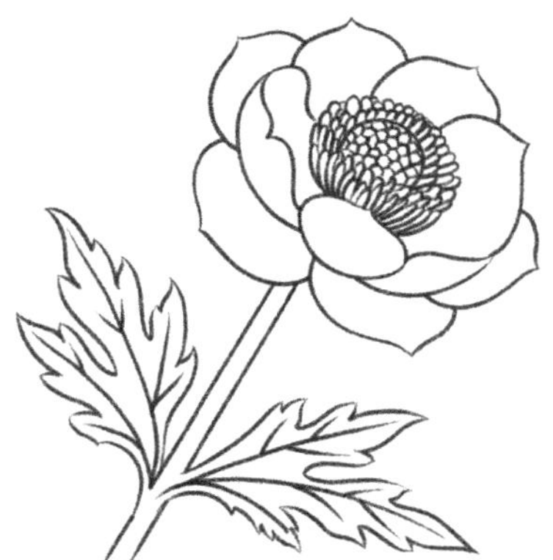

12

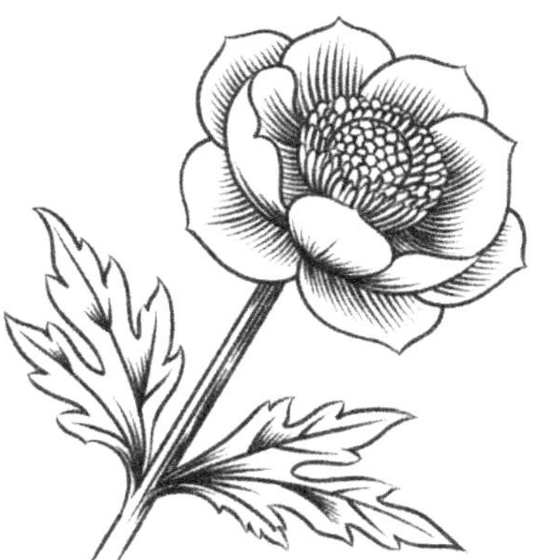

HOW TO DRAW FLOWERS

TULIP

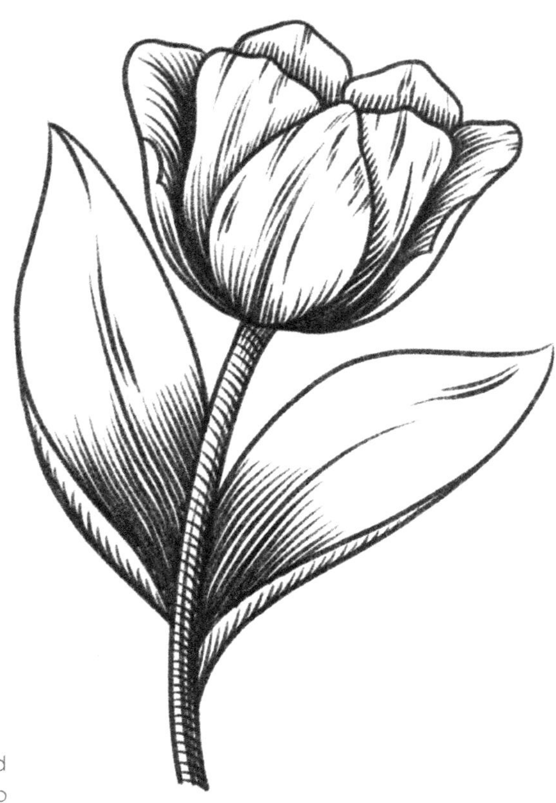

Tulips symbolise love, elegance, and renewal, often associated with deep emotions, grace, and the vibrant beauty of spring's hopeful return.

01

02

03

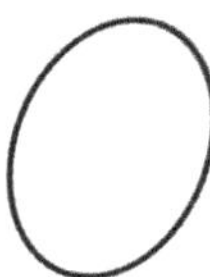

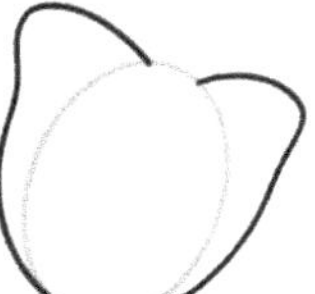

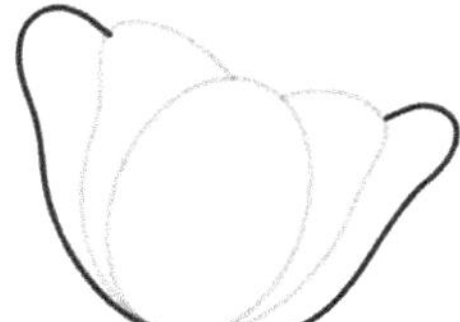

04

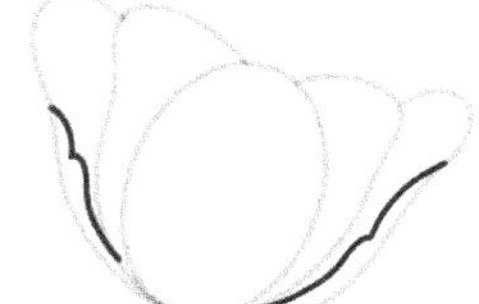

05

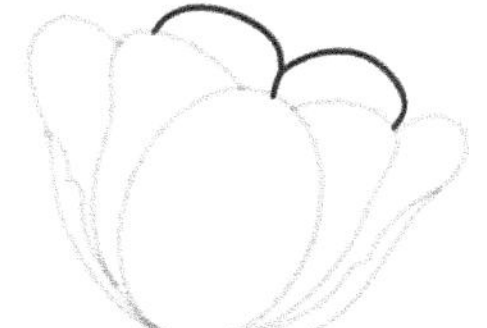

06

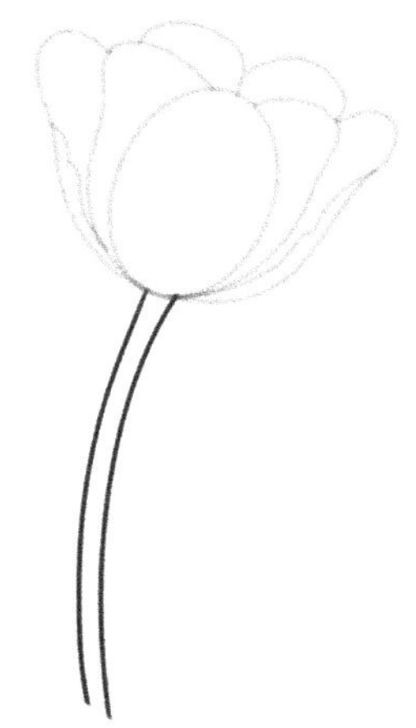

07

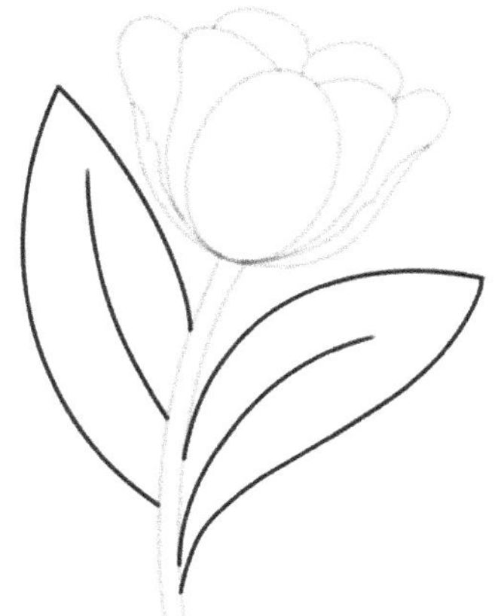

08

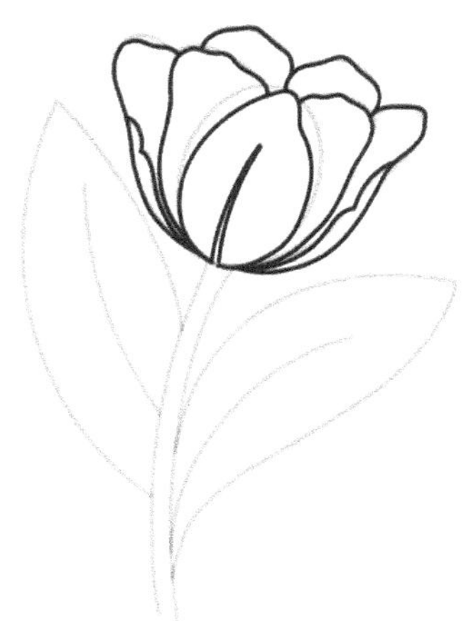

09

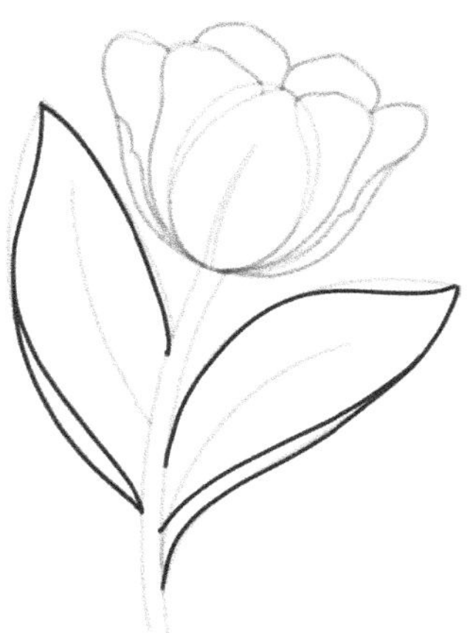

10

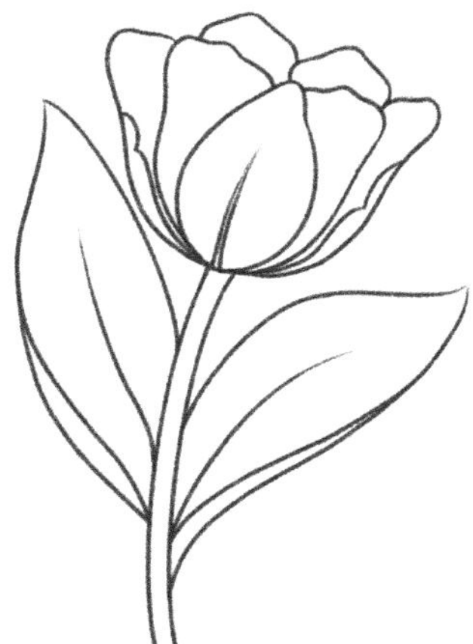

11

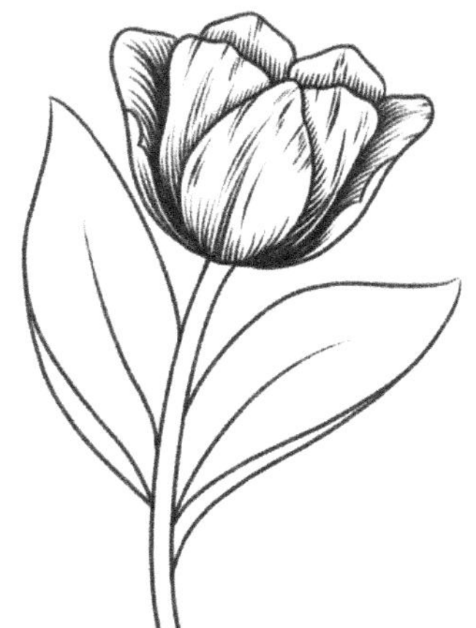

12

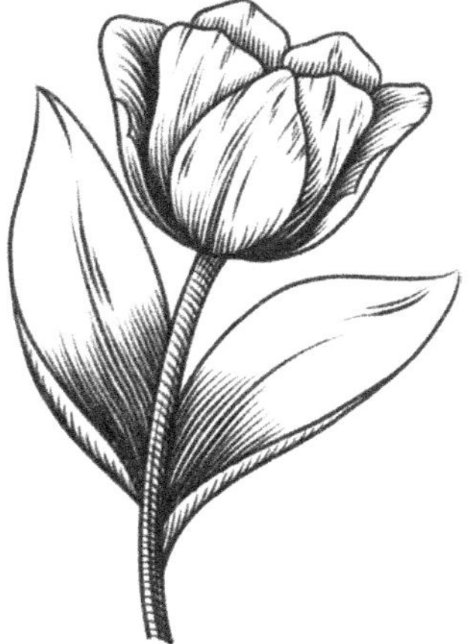

HOW TO DRAW FLOWERS

WATER LILY

HOW TO DRAW FLOWERS

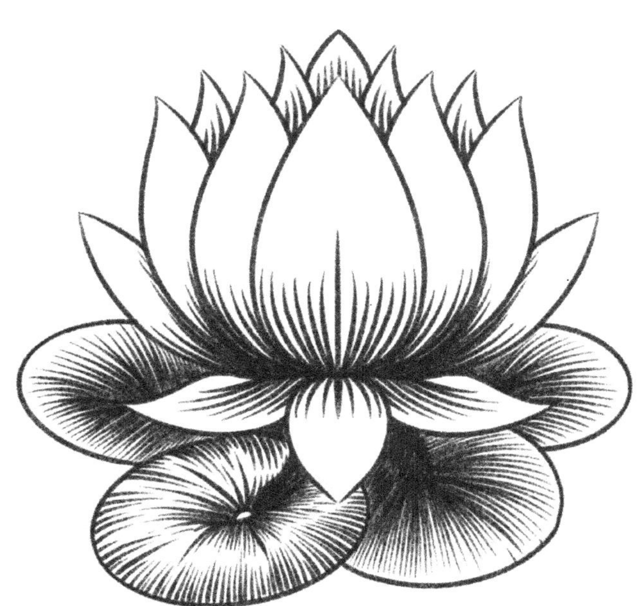

Water Lilies symbolise purity, enlightenment, and rebirth, often associated with serenity, spiritual depth, and the tranquil beauty that rises from calm, reflective waters.

01

02

03

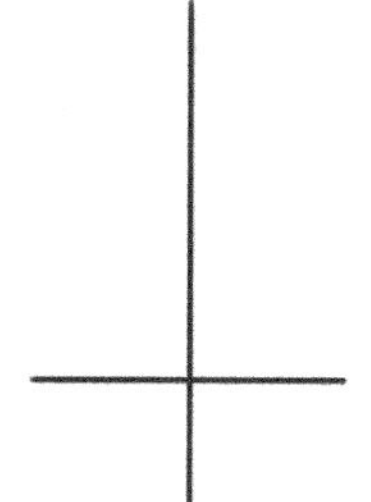
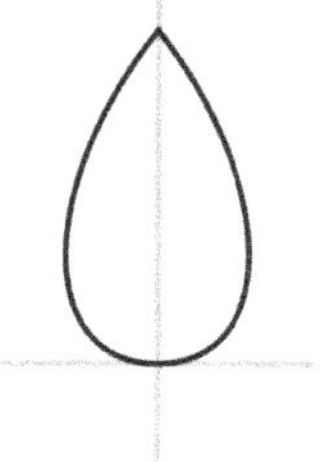
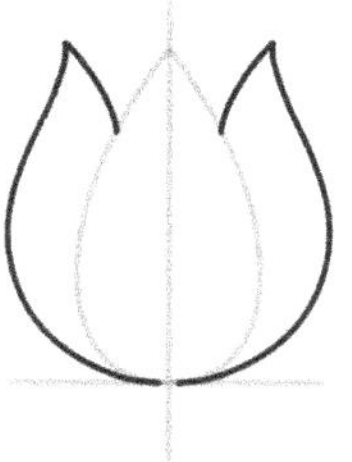

04

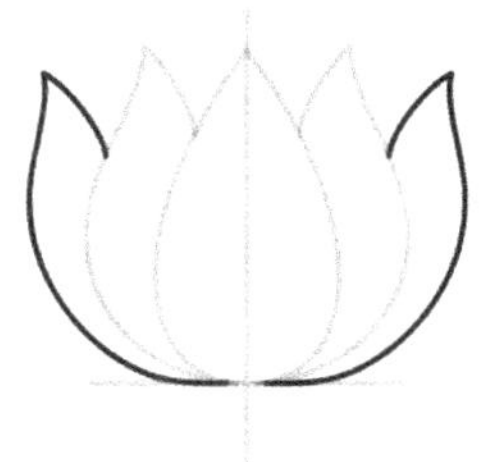

05

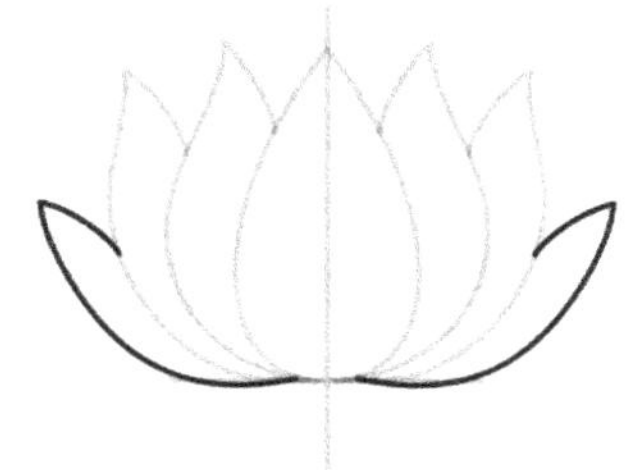

06

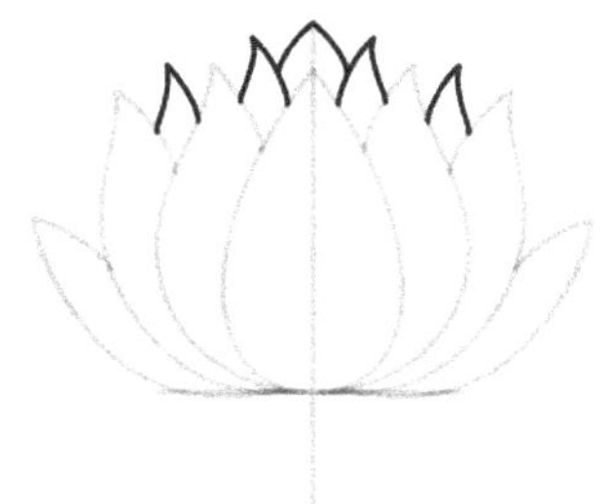

07

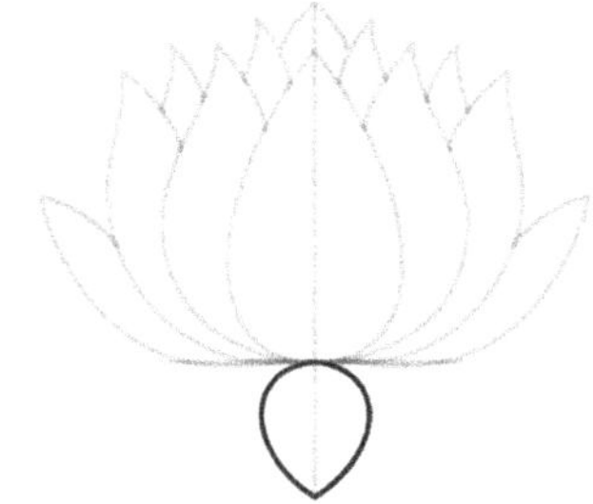

08

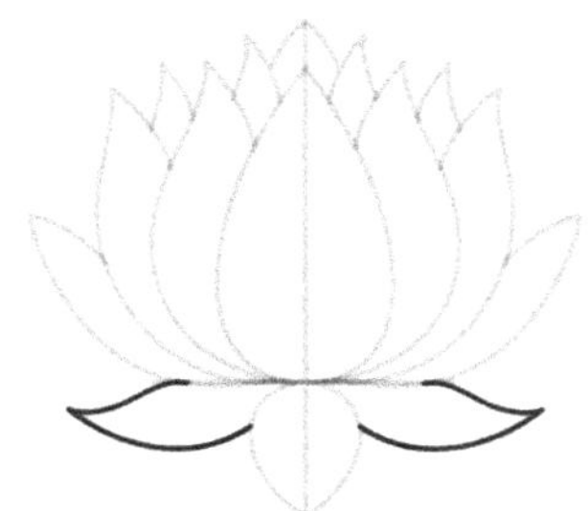

09

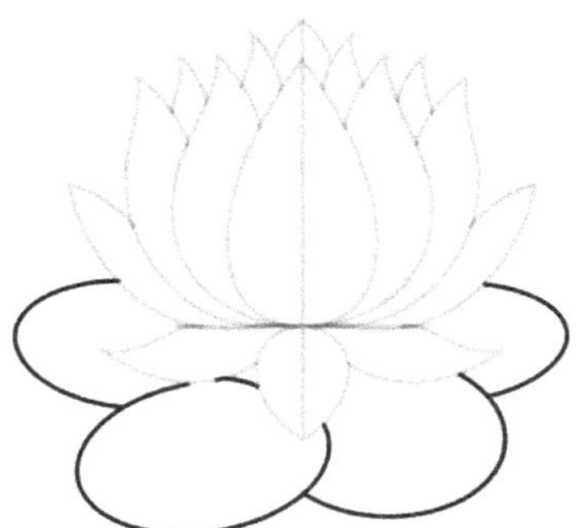

10

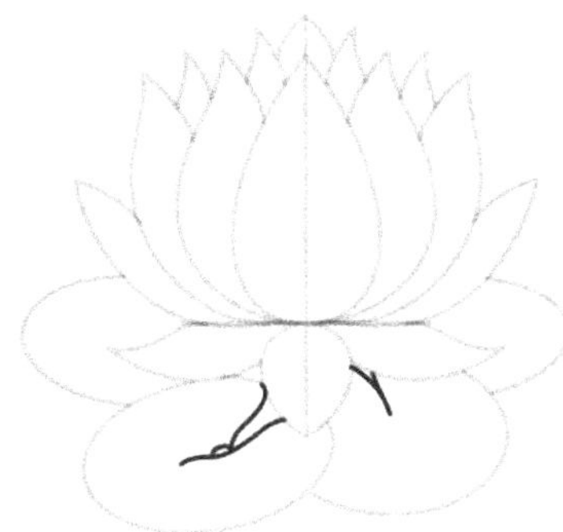

11

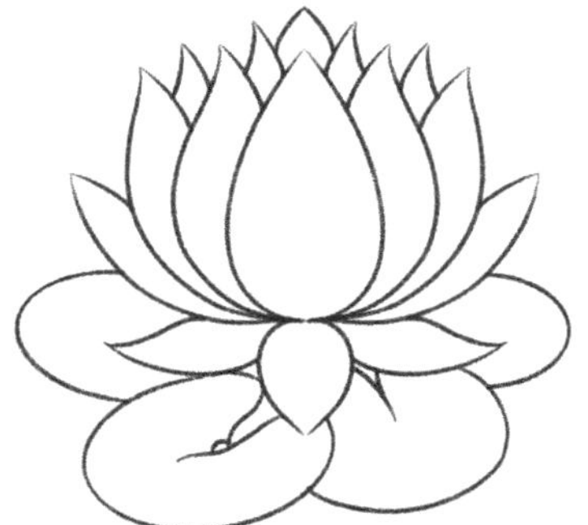

12

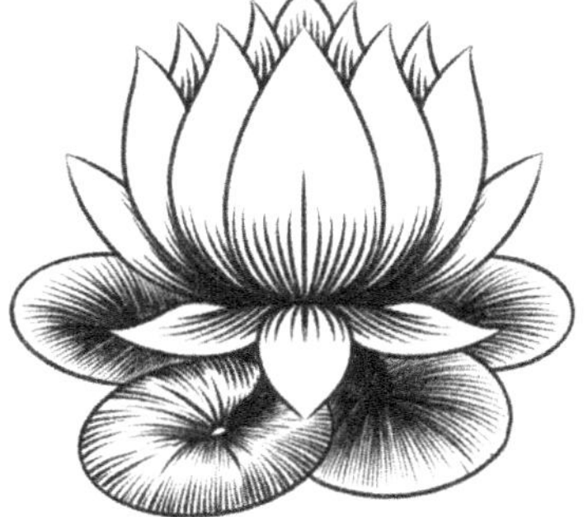

HOW TO DRAW FLOWERS

PRACTICE MAKES PERFECT
T R D   M R K

HOW TO DRAW FLOWERS

PRACTICE MAKES PERFECT
T R D   M R K

Vault Editions Ltd

CURATION AND RESTORATION SERVICES

LEARN MORE

VAULTEDITIONS.COM

T R D PRACTICE MAKES PERFECT M R K

HOW TO DRAW
FLOWERS

T R D PRACTICE MAKES PERFECT M R K

HOW TO DRAW FLOWERS

Vault Editions Ltd

CURATION AND RESTORATION SERVICES

LEARN MORE

VAULTEDITIONS.COM

PRACTICE MAKES PERFECT
T R D
M R K

HOW TO DRAW
FLOWERS

PRACTICE MAKES PERFECT
T R D
M R K

Vault Editions Ltd

CURATION AND RESTORATION SERVICES

LEARN MORE

VAULTEDITIONS.COM

PRACTICE MAKES PERFECT
T R D   M R K

HOW TO DRAW
FLOWERS

PRACTICE MAKES PERFECT
T R D   M R K

Vault Editions Ltd

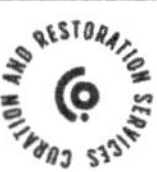

LEARN MORE

VAULTEDITIONS.COM

PRACTICE MAKES PERFECT

T R D · M R K

HOW TO DRAW FLOWERS

PRACTICE MAKES PERFECT

T R D · M R K

Vault Editions Ltd

CURATION AND RESTORATION SERVICES

LEARN MORE

VAULTEDITIONS.COM

PRACTICE MAKES PERFECT

T R D

M R K

HOW TO DRAW
FLOWERS

PRACTICE MAKES PERFECT

T R D

M R K

Vault Editions Ltd

CURATION AND RESTORATION SERVICES

LEARN MORE

VAULTEDITIONS.COM

PRACTICE MAKES PERFECT
T R D
M R K

HOW TO DRAW
FLOWERS

PRACTICE MAKES PERFECT
T R D
M R K

Vault Editions Ltd

CURATION AND RESTORATION SERVICES

LEARN MORE

VAULTEDITIONS.COM

PRACTICE MAKES PERFECT
T R D   M R K

HOW TO DRAW FLOWERS

PRACTICE MAKES PERFECT
T R D   M R K

HOW TO DRAW FLOWERS

Vault Editions Ltd

CURATION AND RESTORATION SERVICES

LEARN MORE

VAULTEDITIONS.COM

PRACTICE MAKES PERFECT

T R D   M R K

HOW TO DRAW
FLOWERS

PRACTICE MAKES PERFECT

T R D   M R K

Vault Editions Ltd

CURATION AND RESTORATION SERVICES

LEARN MORE

VAULTEDITIONS.COM

PRACTICE
MAKES
PERFECT
TRD
MRK

HOW TO DRAW
FLOWERS

PRACTICE
MAKES
PERFECT
TRD
MRK

Vault Editions Ltd

CURATION AND RESTORATION SERVICES

LEARN MORE

VAULTEDITIONS.COM

PRACTICE MAKES PERFECT
T R D
M R K

HOW TO DRAW
FLOWERS

PRACTICE MAKES PERFECT
T R D
M R K

Vault Editions Ltd

CURATION AND RESTORATION SERVICES

LEARN MORE

VAULTEDITIONS.COM

HOW TO DRAW FLOWERS

Vault Editions Ltd

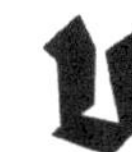
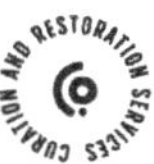

LEARN MORE

VAULTEDITIONS.COM

PRACTICE MAKES PERFECT
T R D
M R K

HOW TO DRAW FLOWERS

PRACTICE MAKES PERFECT
T R D
M R K

Vault Editions Ltd

CURATION AND RESTORATION SERVICES

LEARN MORE

VAULTEDITIONS.COM

PRACTICE
MAKES
PERFECT

T R D

M R K

HOW TO DRAW
FLOWERS

PRACTICE
MAKES
PERFECT

T R D

M R K

Vault Editions Ltd

CURATION AND RESTORATION SERVICES

LEARN MORE

VAULTEDITIONS.COM

CONCLUSION

As you reach the end of *How to Draw Flowers: A Step-By-Step Guide to Drawing Botanical Art for Beginners*, you've honed your drawing skills and gained a deeper appreciation for each flower's timeless symbolism. By exploring these blooms' intricate forms and meanings, you've connected with a tradition of botanical artistry that celebrates nature's beauty and diversity.

Remember, each flower is a world in itself, offering endless inspiration and stories. Use the skills and insights you've gained here to continue creating, whether by drawing familiar flowers in new ways or experimenting with the undiscovered forms and symbols of flowers. Let this journey be the foundation of a lifelong exploration of botanical art, where every petal drawn invites a new perspective.

Thank you for joining us on this artistic journey. May your path in botanical illustration continue to blossom with creativity and meaning.

LEARN MORE

At Vault Editions, our mission is to provide the highest-quality reference materials for artists and designers, offering meticulously curated resources that inspire and empower creativity. If you've found value in this book, we invite you to explore more of our expertly crafted titles at vaulteditions. com, where you'll discover a world of visual inspiration and practical tools designed to elevate your creative work.

REVIEW THIS BOOK

As a family-owned and operated independent publisher, reviews are essential to the success of our business. Please leave an honest review of this book wherever you purchased it.

JOIN OUR COMMUNITY

Are you the creative and curious type? If so, you will love our community on Instagram. Every day, we share bizarre and beautiful artwork ranging from 17th and 18th-century natural history and scientific illustrations to mythical beasts, ornamental designs, anatomical drawings and more; join our community of 300K+ people today by searching @vault_editions on Instagram.

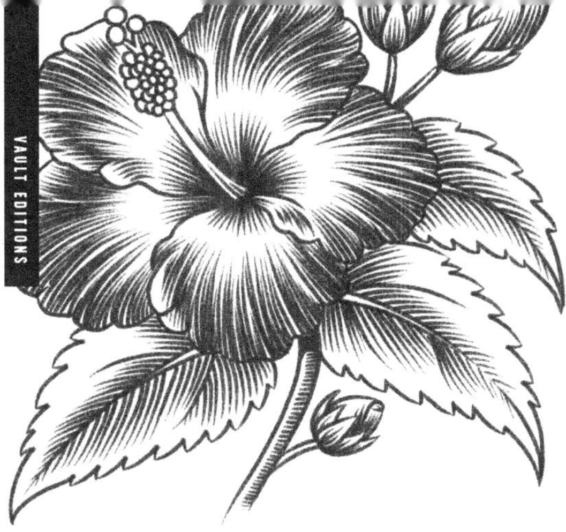

DOWNLOAD YOUR FILES

To enhance your creative journey, *How to Draw Tattoo Flowers* comes with a digital PDF version of the book and a specially designed set of Procreate brushes. These resources are tailored to help you refine your skills and streamline your workflow, whether you're working traditionally or digitally.

The digital PDF provides easy access to the book's contents on any device, so you can reference the designs anytime, anywhere. It's perfect for artists on the go, allowing you to study and practice whenever inspiration strikes.

The custom Procreate brushes are crafted to replicate the delicate textures and linework of botanical illustration, from fine details to soft shading. They make it easy for digital artists to capture floral beauty with precision and flexibility as they sketch, refine, and complete their work. Whether experimenting or perfecting final pieces, these brushes bring floral creations to life with the elegance that defines classic botanical art.

Download yours now and get creating!

STEP ONE

Enter the following web address on a desktop or laptop computer in your web browser.

vaulteditions.com/pages/hdf

STEP TWO

Enter the following password to access the download page:

hdf826287sxda

STEP THREE

Follow the prompts to access your high-resolution files.

CONTACT

For technical support, please email: info@vaulteditions.com

Copyright © 2024
Vault Editions Ltd

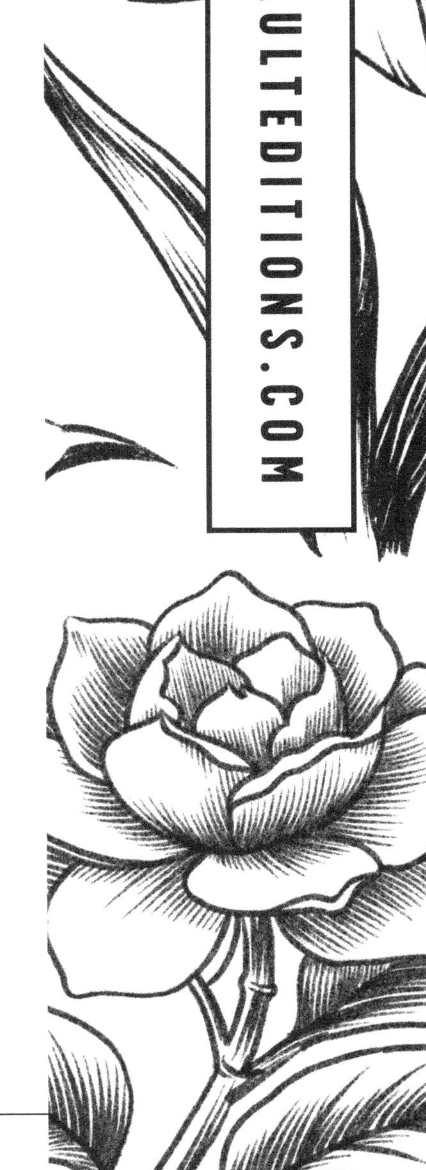

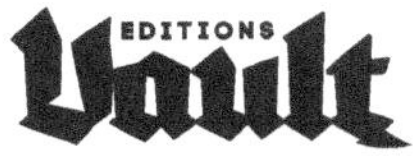

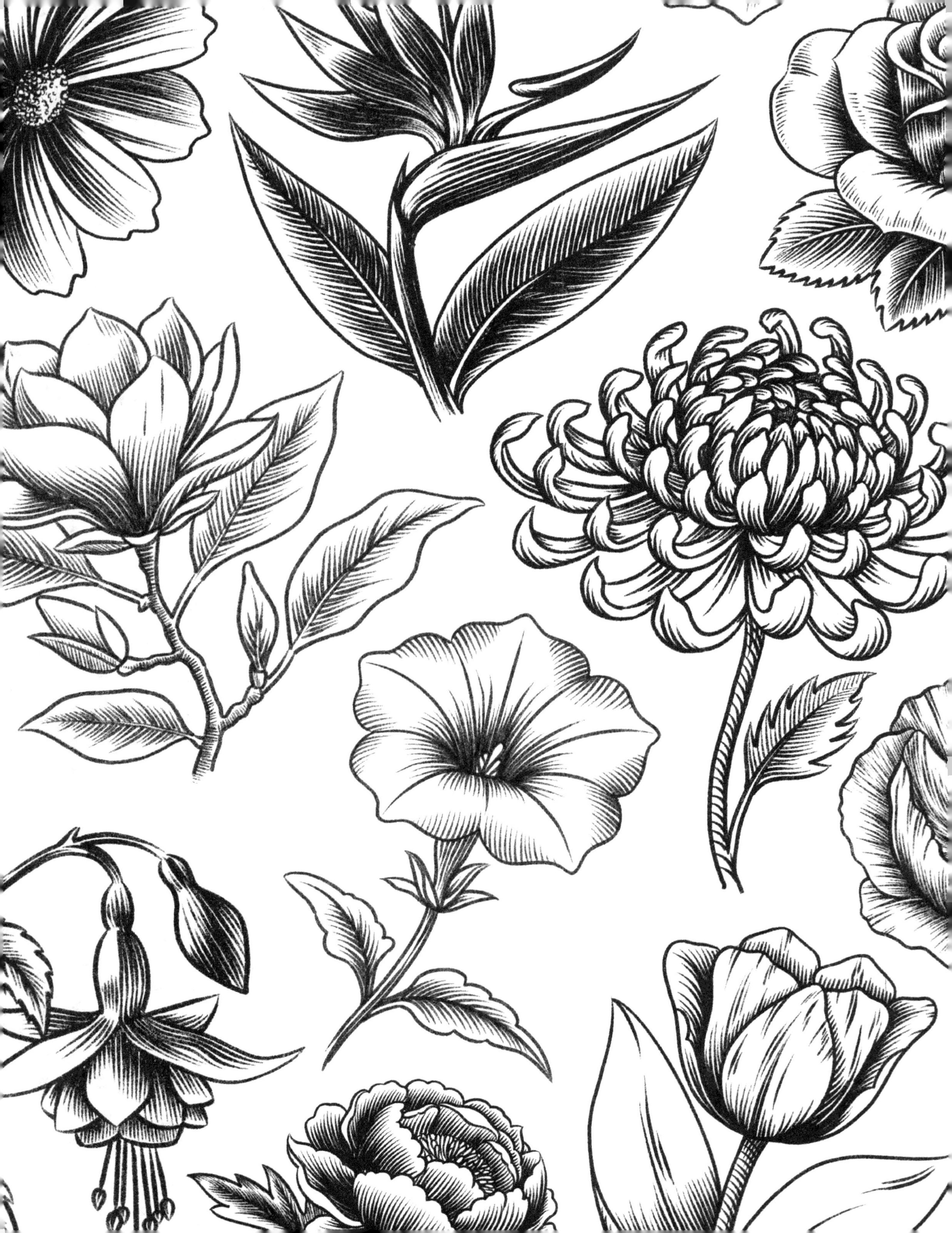